8-95

PIONEERS IN BRITISH PLANNING

D1612651

PIONEERS IN BRITISH PLANNING

Edited by
Gordon E. Cherry

The Architectural Press: London

Markland
914.202
CHE

First published in 1981 by The Architectural
Press Limited: London
9 Queen Anne's Gate, London SW1H 9BY

© Gordon Cherry 1981

ISBN: 0 85139 563 5

All rights reserved. No part of this publication
may be reproduced, stored in a retrieval system,
or transmitted, in any form or by any means,
electronic, mechanical, photocopying, recording
or otherwise, without the prior permission of the
publishers. Such permission, if granted, is subject
to a fee depending on the nature of the use.

LIVERPOOL INSTITUTE
OF HIGHER EDUCATION
THE MARKLAND LIBRARY
Accession No. 263424
86018
Class No.
914.202 CHE
Catal.
4.5.84 CE

Set in Baskerville
Printed in Great Britain
by Mackays of Chatham Ltd

CONTENTS

ACKNOWLEDGEMENTS

Out of the blue in 1979 I was asked by The Architectural Press whether I would consider editing a general history of town and country planning based on the lives of famous planners. My first word of thanks therefore must be to Jenny Towndrow who made the suggestion, and who has given support and guidance since. It so happened that I was already thinking on the lines of a collection of biographies, and therefore the venture has been able to proceed at speed. However, my thanks are due to my willing and energetic contributors who agreed to work to a tight time-scale in spite of other commitments.

I am particularly indebted to Professor H. Myles Wright and a delightful day I spent with him reminiscing about the 1940s; also to Professor Gordon Stephenson and his correspondence about Lord Holford and the team in the Ministry of Town and Country Planning during the war years and immediately after; and to Richard Gray, Lord Holford's partner from 1947 until his death, who is the custodian of the Holford papers.

My secretary, Sue Elias, has coped nobly with drafts and correspondence. My wife, Margaret, has relieved me of the tedium of the index.

To all, I am grateful for assistance in the real pleasure of being engaged on a work of planning history.

Gordon Cherry
Birmingham, April 1981

NOTES ON CONTRIBUTORS

Michael Bruton is Professor of Town Planning at the University of Wales Institute of Science and Technology. His publications include *Introduction to Transportation Planning* (1975). He has wide research interests including transport planning and policy, and planning practice. He is currently working on public participation and public inquiries in local planning.

Gordon Cherry is Professor of Urban and Regional Planning at the Centre for Urban and Regional Studies, University of Birmingham. He is a Past President of the Royal Town Planning Institute. His publications include *Town Planning in its Social Context* (1970), *Urban Change and Planning* (1972), *The Evolution of British Town Planning* (1974), *Environmental Planning, Vol. II, National Parks and Recreation in the Countryside* (1975) and *The Politics of Town Planning* (1981). He has research interests in the history of town planning thought and practice.

Gerald Dix is the Lever Professor of Civic Design at the University of Liverpool. He formerly held a chair at Nottingham. As Chief Architect-Planner in Addis Ababa he was senior assistant to Sir Patrick Abercrombie in the preparation of the Addis Ababa Master Plan of 1956.

Michael Hebbert lectures in Planning Studies at the London School of Economics. He was awarded a PhD at the University of Reading for his work on the history of the planning movement in Britain. His research interests include comparative planning issues as well as the historical development of the planning movement.

Helen Meller is a Senior Lecturer in the Department of Economic and Social History at the University of Nottingham. She was awarded a PhD at the University of Bristol for her work on 19th century Bristol; this found expression in *Leisure and the Changing City, 1870–1914* (1976). She has also published *The Ideal City* (1978). Her research interests include the life and work of Sir Patrick Geddes, concepts in planning ideology and practice, and women and work in contemporary society.

Mervyn Miller, an architect and town planner, is Principal Planning Officer for North Hertfordshire District Council. Following extensive research on Barry Parker and Raymond Unwin, he is preparing a book entitled *An Environment for Everyman*. He is working for a PhD at the University of Birmingham on the contribution of Raymond Unwin to British town planning. He has written and lectured extensively on the garden city movement.

Michael Simpson is a Lecturer in History and American Studies at the University College of Swansea. He is currently completing a full biography of Thomas Adams.

Kathy Stansfield works for The Architectural Press, writing for *The Architects' Journal*. She undertook research for a Master's degree at the University of Manchester on the life of Thomas Sharp. She has worked in private practice with landscape architects and has contributed to publications on landscape design and the environment.

1

BIOGRAPHIES AND PLANNING HISTORY

Gordon Cherry

When a discipline or a profession can show interest in its history, it is a demonstration of a growing institutional maturity. There develops a curiosity about origins; a determination to get the record right, to destroy myths and to bolster new impressions; and there is a sense of pride in reflecting on the roll call of honour to do homage to famous men.

Town planning has reached that stage. The term was used initially half way through the first decade of this century, and the concept of modern town planning extends over little more than the last hundred years. (Town building as a conscious form of urban design and layout, of course, dates from the earliest civilisations, but the contemporary practice known as town planning, with various derivative terms, is a product of the State's reaction to the economic, social and technical transformations referred to as the Industrial Revolution.) In Britain we can reasonably date the first recognisable signs of modern town planning within the decade 1895–1905, though the first town planning legislation dates from 1909 and the formation of the parent profession from as late as 1914. However, in those ten years there were a number of clear and growing pointers to something novel and emergent: innovation in the design movement with Raymond Unwin as an exponent of new ideas; public housing ventures in London; the writing of Ebenezer Howard and the success of the garden city movement; the creation of Bournville and New Earswick; and the founding of Letchworth and Hampstead Garden Suburb.

Since then town planning has made its mark on the 20th century. Today as both the academic and practitioner strive to make some sense of these years of achievement, and to explain how and why things have happened as they have, there will be a search for a theoretical framework of understanding complemented by empirical case studies of particular events. Intellectual speculation on

1

theoretical constructs has been tardy and weak, and case studies have lacked much penetration. The creation in 1974 of the Planning History Group, an international body of scholars and practitioners interested in this subject field, sparked off a vigorous growth in research, as evidenced in a spate of new writings and the holding of conferences and seminars.[1]

Biographical studies in context

So far, planning history successively has tended to be seen against three backgrounds. The first is a history of techniques and performance, and this has been the longest and most popular frame of reference. The second is a history of professional involvement. The third is a history of a social and institutional settings. A brief comment about these three phases is necessary before we argue that a fourth dimension, that of biographical histories, has been neglected too long and that we shall find it has much to offer.

The history of techniques and town planning performance has its essence in an art history approach. Traditionally, it has seen town planning as the logical unfolding of successive phases of townscape, civilisation by civilisation from earliest antiquity, and as a demonstration of man's creative capacities and building achievements. Art is seen as a continuous process, with man constantly responding 'to the tranquility and assurance of certain geometrical forms such as the square and the circle, although the manifestations of these in the landscape vary according to geography, society, economics, morals and philosophy, all of which are local and transitory'.[2] So town building has been seen as part of man's evolutionary control and shaping of landscape, embracing Babylon, Egypt, Greece, the Roman Empire, Islam, Ancient India, China and Japan, pre-Columbian America, and the Western Civilisations from the Middle Ages onwards.

This perceived linear progression of art achievement has greatly affected approaches to town planning history for much of this century. Hiorns,[3] for example, writing in 1956, thought town building 'the most comprehensive' of the major arts of civilisation. He went on to point out the 'remarkable consistency' in the fundamental qualities of the progressive development of towns. That progression was broken, it was argued, by the advent of the machine age when 'the resultant lack of direction brought about the monstrous pseudo-urban confusion that, in its major forms, surrounds us'. This is an important key, for it was held that town planning in the 20th century was essentially an enlightened restoration to order out of chaos, and quality out of squalor. In other words, 20th century town planning history was interpreted as a corrective against errant, 19th century philistinism. It had that perspective; town planning history took root in art history, and 20th century planning was described in terms of its developing techniques, the plans that were prepared, and the schemes that were implemented. Port Sunlight, Bournville, Letchworth, Welwyn Garden City, Patrick Abercrombie's *Greater London Plan*, the New Towns and a succession of urban design improvements became typical, cardinal points of reference. The 20th century was seen as the culmination of a long evolution: it was simply the last chapter in a long book.

The history of professional involvement viewed town planning rather as the product of specific groups of people: in Britain, these were the professional planners and like minded people engaged in what was vaguely known as the planning movement. This particular phase was never well articulated, and took shape, if at all, against a primacy willingly accorded to the art historians. Perhaps it was a defensive mechanism of an insecure profession and subject field, but certainly in planning education there developed a trend to see planning history as the history of what planners have done in the recent past, admittedly against the longer term backcloth of evolutionary civilisations. Hence an emphasis came to be placed on the contributions of particular individuals – including those who would not normally have been included in the art historians' brief, such as Patrick Geddes (the sociologist), Ebenezer Howard (*per se*, as well as his garden city movement), Alker Tripp (Police Commissioner and traffic expert), William Booth (social scientist) and Lord Reith (political zealot).

The third phase is the most recent and represents a noticeable break from the other two. It offers a more challenging dimension because it attempts to place contemporary town planning in a context from which certain theoretical explanations grounded in the social sciences, as well as in certain traditions in political economy, might be derived. It observes that 20th century town planning has a framework where the influences are social, political and institutional, rather than technical and professional. It is held that the key to understanding how and why town planning has developed in its inimitable way this century lies in changes in society as a whole: in societal structures and institutions, and in community attitudes and political values. Conversely, the theories, achievements, techniques and organisational arrangements of planners themselves occupy a secondary level of importance. This has the effect of grounding modern town planning history firmly in the social sciences, where sociology, political science and organisational theory are more important than the building and design traditions of engineering and architecture, and where the embrace of political economy is crucial. This approach is providing a healthy, creative tension amongst the devotees of planning history. It seems to provide an appealing new dimension and offers real opportunities for theoretical speculation together with limitless empirical research. It may have the disadvantage of providing too wide a canvas, dispersing effort and permitting an important focus to escape: town planning history may run into the wider sands of social history, urban history and contemporary social studies. Academic scholarship in town planning history must of course follow truth where it is to be found, but the planning practitioner at least gains most from town planning history if it can be kept within definable bounds.

The three phases described above must not be taken too definitively. Many town planning histories have been written which far from neatly fit the categories that have been suggested. It is simply observed that the three phases have formed conceptual traditions within which planning history has been seen. It so happens that the phases have been successive and that, beginning with art history, the dominant influence has moved now to the one of social and institutional settings.

All of which brings us to biographies. This volume collects eight essays, each the careful description and evaluation of the work of an esteemed 20th century planner, a pioneer in his field. We would not suggest that this should be regarded as a fourth phase; rather that it offers a further dimension helpful to all three. We should not dismiss the claims of art history, for example, in preferring to stress the claims of other aspects of planning history; we offer case studies of the lives and contributions of particular individuals in the belief that they will provide a more rounded understanding and explanation of events. Neither are we simply replicating the history of the profession phase. Instead, we are selecting particular people to see both how the course of planning history has been affected by their work, and how a set of influences has acted on them. In this way we pay full acknowledgement to the context of social and institutional settings, while respecting the traditions of art and professional histories for those who wish to observe them.

Biographical studies as correctives

It has become fashionable to see 20th century planning not so much as a contemporary set of adjustments in a long pedigree of town building through the ages, but rather as an element of land and environmental management in the context of State intervention through public policy. Town building there may be, and the common threads of conscious design and community welfare may be in evidence as they have been in earlier civilisations and cultures, but what we recognise and study today is conceptually different. We see British town planning grounded in the socio-political framework of the 19th and 20th centuries. During this period State enterprise has extended to tackle an increasing variety of problems thrown up in the economic, social and technological transformations of the last 150 years and more; the purpose has been to provide order and stability, and amenities and community rewards, for an increasingly prosperous society, which the capitalist order could not deliver. Planning, used in a generic sense, covers any activity which implies a sequence of purposive actions designed to achieve a particular set of events over time; town planning, used more specifically, has come to refer to purposeful control over land and the shaping of physical environments. Town planning, as this specialist field of activity, emerged relatively late, but it was clearly rooted in developing forms of Victorian urban management. First of all effective local administration was established. A new apparatus of government replaced the loose collection of local *ad hoc* bodies which existed prior to 1830. Municipal reform transferred power gradually to new local authority bodies, their new power soon to be reflected in the great Victorian town halls of the second half of the century. In London the Metropolitan Board of Works (1855), responsible for great improvement projects, was replaced in 1888 by the London County Council (with its 28 constituent metropolitan boroughs in 1899). Counties were established also in 1888, with Urban District and Rural District Councils in 1894.

Advances in local administration were paralleled by extensions of State power both at local and central levels. The innovation of police for London in 1829 spread to all Counties and Boroughs by 1856. Factory Acts dealt with hours of work and child labour; factory inspectors for conditions of work were established and codes of statutory regulations drawn up. Local authorities began to provide playgrounds, baths and wash-houses and public libraries; they attended to burial grounds; and 1870 saw the creation of Board Schools and universal primary education. The municipalisation of public utilities and transport was adopted vigorously by the larger cities. The problems of public health were progressively tackled through the great Acts of 1845 and 1875; Victorian Britain was paved, lit and sewered. Housing action was both late and slow in the face of preference for philanthropic support and private, rather than State initiative, but from limited powers over insanitary housing (1868 and 1875) there was some progression to the building of dwellings for the working classes (1890), especially in London.

The intellectual burst of energy which marked the years at the end of the century pointed to the limitations and indeed deficiencies in what had so far been accomplished. The recognition of a Victorian urban crisis succeeded in highlighting the arguments of various reform movements: sanitary improvements, housing and land reform and enlightened social provision. An enhanced role for the State appeared more and more likely as the 20th century unfolded, not only in policies relating to housing and the relief of overcrowding and conditions of squalor, but also in aspects of social welfare, although at first, to use George Dangerfield's term, the high promise of Liberal England had a 'strange death'.[4]

The enlargement of the State sector grew with World War I and developed with the intentions of the immediate reconstruction years. New, high standards were set for working class accommodation (Tudor Walters' Report, 1918) and 1919 saw the advent of the council house built under subsidy. During the inter-war period 4 million dwellings were built in Britain, one quarter by the State. A change of policy in the 1930s introduced an important slum clearance programme to housing policy. Control over the use of land was regulated through town planning legislation (1919, 1932). The idea of State aid for National Parks was raised. Intervention in economic affairs, at first uncertain and halting, became necessary in the face of the plight of the disadvantaged regions. J. M. Keynes' *The General Theory of Employment Interest and Money* (1936) provided the new economic gospel.

The 1930s ended in a welter of dissatisfaction on social, economic and environmental fronts. There was urban (and rural) poverty; a backlog of depressing housing conditions; unemployment ravaged the older industrial areas; British towns and cities were held by influential opinion to be ugly and unworthy; and our countryside was being despoiled by unplanned development. World War II and its aftermath provided a new opportunity for the State advance of regulation, support and control over our economic and social life, as well as its environmental base. Provisions for national insurance, education, health and the nationalisation of public utilities, transport and key industries were followed by enlarged State policies for agriculture, the distribution of industry, new towns, land planning, national parks, all in the 1940s.

The post-war period has continued the tentacular expansion of public sector responsibilities. The history of town planning after 1945 has this as its overriding context, just as it provides, indeed, an essential frame of reference throughout the century. This is not the occasion to speculate whether the inexorable rise of the State has reached its apogee (for the moment) in Britain and the western world. Certainly there are those who argue that unnecessary State control is wrong in principle and only serves to limit individual freedom. They argue that the State is not more efficient than the private sector, and that loosely fettered, self-regulation by private interests produces better results. Further, they would argue that the actual fruits of State control have been unpalatable; the operation of land planning has been insensitive to local needs and the results have not always been in the interests of those most affected.

But we must not pursue those arguments here. The preceding paragraphs have sought to establish the position that modern town planning occupies in the context of our economic and social affairs and our institutions of government as they have developed over the last century. With this sort of over-view the history of town planning practice in Britain this century may be thought to have a rather 'inevitable' flavour: town planning 'naturally' develops in the context set for it by the changing functions of the State. All is decreed; there is little room for unexpected manoeuvre. For historians, the context becomes the object of study, not town planning itself.

Certainly we see the importance of the State and its influence over town planning. It has recently become fashionable to be highly critical of the State in its manipulatory function, in that town planning has become branded as simply a tool of State repression. The State in capitalist society is seen as an instrument of class domination, and the characteristic function of the State is repression. Cockburn[5] for example, in her study of Lambeth, argues that the State's 'main role is to keep the working class in its place and to set things up, with forceful sanctions, in such a way that capital itself, business interests as a whole, normally survive and prosper'. More specifically, with town planning, the French urban sociologist Castells[6] argues in respect of a study of Dunkerque that 'Plans stamp all individual schemes with a double character: on the one hand, they come to be seen as "reasonable", rational, technical solutions to the problems posed and, on the other, they appear to bring about a convergence of the various social groups and urban functions. Town planning comes to embody social neutrality, by expressing the general interests of the community, in addition to its advantage of technical neutrality. It is for this reason that planning is a privileged instrument for the ideological embodiment of the interests of classes, factions and groups . . .'.

The 'pluralist-democratic' view of society, which holds that the State is a multitude of conflicting pressures from organised groups and interests, showing no marked bias towards some and not others, has lost favour in recent years (Miliband[7] for example, regards it as 'in all essentials wrong'). But nonetheless policy making in the public sector involves a long series of related activities. There is therefore a sense of continuous adjustment in a lengthy process, as the history of any line of policy shows. My study of National Park policy[8] is a case in point which illustrates the interplay of sectional interests, promotional lobbies, politicians, civil servants and sectors of government at local and central levels.

What actually happens, therefore, in a particular episode of town planning will be remarkably complex. To see town planning as simply the tool of the State, as an unqualified reflection of those who wield power, and with its parameters defined solely by the rise of the public sector over the last 150 years, is too simplistic. Town planning biographies allow us to see again the room for unexpected manoeuvre that may occur. Throughout town planning history, we should hold at arm's length any over-arching set of external relationships. Predetermined structures to our thinking, that will seem to explain the course of events in broad outline, will benefit from attention to the detail of actors' contributions on particular matters, as these will be likely to offer important correctives to particular stories.

One can understand the revolt against history as a 'history of events'; the influence of the social sciences led to a demand to penetrate the surface of history. Town planning history is no exception to this. A turning away from the chronological events in art history to a desire to reveal the structures of political behaviour and economic controls as perhaps the real factors that determine historical movements is understandable enough. But economic and social organisations do not totally supersede the capacity of the individual to break into historical events. History is a question of providing explanations. I would not wish to argue that history is simply made by Great Men, but neither would I wish to deny that they can have unforeseen and unpredictable effects. The town planner is interested in events as well as non-events: the history of the 20th century will be full of turning points – new openings and departures, and dead ends and unfulfilled hopes. New explanations will come from a study of the interplay of personalities, conflicts of interests, decisions both rational and irrational, and the element of sheer chance. The historian will be confronted with an unstructured world of relationships, which he cannot afford to neglect in favour of a comfortable order of theoretical abstractions. There is always a web of circumstances in which men contribute to making their own history. It is this contribution that biographical studies, and detailed empirical work in general, can offer to planning history. Lord Bullock has argued that the 20th century is particularly suited to revealing the weight of personal actions on history, exemplifying how ' a creature like Hitler can burst through the web of probability, turn the world upside down and leave behind him an incalculable legacy of disruption and suffering'.[9] Town planning has no such creatures but the point is relevant to its subject field.

Twentieth century figures

This volume briefly reviews the life and work of eight people, adjudged to have made a unique contribution to British town planning this century: Thomas Adams, Patrick Geddes, Raymond Unwin, Patrick Abercrombie, George Pepler, Thomas Sharp, Frederic Osborn and Colin Buchanan.

Thomas Adams became a leading planner in Britain, Canada and the United States. He was the first secretary of the Garden City Association, he became the first Town Planning Adviser to the Local Government Board, and was the first President of the Town Planning Institute. After a few successful years in Canada, he then spent most of the 1920s in the USA where he became the General Director of Plans and Surveys of the Regional Plan of New York and its Environs. Returning to Britain in the 1930s he assumed the mantle of 'elder statesman', and we are left to reflect on his drive and energy in three countries, in which his influence can readily be seen not only in planning techniques and methods but also institutional arrangements.

Patrick Geddes was a very different person. Trained as a natural scientist, he thought of himself as a sociologist, but is now disregarded as such. He associated himself with the town planning movement because of his interest in lines of future social development and because of his synoptic grasp of mass urbanisation and geographical scales of development. A prodigious writer, he was a veritable fount of ideas on social reconstruction and regional survey. He became a cult figure, made somewhat flamboyant perhaps with years spent in Palestine and India, although his Edinburgh and Dublin work was idiosyncratic enough. His genius lay in stimulating ideas, and as a generalist in a century of specialists he made a special contribution to the intellectualism of town planning.

By comparison Raymond Unwin is a relatively simple figure to describe and evaluate. The direction of his life's work had already been chartered in the first decade of the 20th century when he emerged as possibly the pivotal figure in British town planning. His achievements were a qualitative break from the past in terms of housing layout and environmental design, with Letchworth and Hampstead the key indicators. His contribution to housing reform proved of long standing and while in the 1920s he became an administrator rather than an innovator, nonetheless his work for the Greater London Regional Planning Committee was important and influential. His life bridged Arts and Crafts socialism and the anonymity of urban and regional planning, and he must be regarded as a seminal figure.

Patrick Abercrombie married a successful academic career to a vigorous consultancy. His literary work is refreshing and somehow timeless; he was a brilliant draughtsman; he was a warmly regarded entrepreneur who effortlessly produced a stream of Plans of various kinds. As a winner of the Dublin Town Planning Competition in 1914 his career unfolded through regional plans, city surveys and a deep concern for the protection of the countryside, expressed in the Council for the Preservation of Rural England (CPRE). After World War II his *Greater London Plan* (1944), followed by his work for Clydeside, the West Midlands and for various cities such as Hull and Plymouth, firmly established his reputation. His conceptual models for the dispersed, decentralised city became the orthodox wisdom of the day and permeated post-war planning ideology.

George Pepler is to be remembered as a civil servant and as a dedicated professional. The tender plant of planning was dependent on him on both counts. Town planning legislation largely succeeded between the wars because of the careful nurturing of local authority goodwill towards Scheme preparation, and Pepler was the key agent in the complex network of central-local relationships. His professional commitment made him an unrivalled ambassador to his Town Planning Institute, of which he was President twice and the first recipient of its Gold Medal. In other countries, his work for the International Federation of Housing and Town Planning served to promote the world wide town planning movement.

A more difficult figure to evaluate is Thomas Sharp, though there is no doubting the quality of his skills or the fact that he was, and remains, able to strike sympathetic chords for his principles with many planners. He had no benefits of a privileged social or educational background but he found a love for beauty and order in the environment which he was able to express both in a fine literary style and in design terms. A somewhat difficult man, rejected by many in his day, and ending his career in some isolation, he was nevertheless able to communicate fundamental planning principles with a force and direction that still command respect in professional circles. His concept of 'townscape' and the planning principles outlined in plans for Durham, Oxford and Exeter have been influential.

Pioneers tend to be well qualified people. Frederic Osborn had no qualifications, academically or professionally; he was a layman totally dedicated to his particular views on planning and the ways cities should be shaped, and through his Garden Cities and Town Planning Association (later the TCPA), enormously influential. With experience of Letchworth, but particularly of Welwyn, so vigorously prosylized, the whole of the New Towns movement was given that much greater strength. His vigorous advocacy of the planned decentralisation of large cities and low density residential development was a valuable foil for the technical experts who proclaimed varieties of the same message. As an 'old fashioned' social reformer and propagandist, he made his mark.

Colin Buchanan trained first as an engineer and it is in the technical construction side of town planning that he has contributed most. He gained the reputation of a household name when working in the early 1960s on the 'Traffic in Towns' project for the Ministry of Transport. The 'Buchanan Report' became a best seller, illustrative not only of the community's growing concern over urban traffic congestion, but also of the imaginative proposals put forward. More recently his stand over the location of the third London airport established him as a protector of human and environmental values in an age of science and technology. As a civil servant, consultant, professional and academic, the Buchanan imprint on British planning will be firmly established.

These eight brief biographies are offered as interesting case studies in themselves, reminders of the life and work of some key figures in British planning. However, as we have argued in this chapter, there are other lessons to be derived. Collectively they build up almost to the story of British 20th century planning: the pioneers weave their way through the very fabric of our time. The biographies reveal the strength of personal contributions and the circumstances in which those contributions were made. We can begin to ask how much of what we take for granted now stemmed from foresight, how much from opportunism; how much was almost preordained, how much was chance? We can see the interplay of personalities and forces of influence; we can acknowledge the transfer of ideas from man to man; group to group; country to country. We learn why certain events occurred and perhaps why some did not. In all, the biographies serve to 'get the record right' and to correct impressions; also to suggest again that in a very real sense men do make their own history.

An incomplete picture

The choice of the eight pioneers selected should not be seen as an exercise in according a priority accolade to those chosen as against others who are not. The eight are included not because of any conclusion that they have necessarily contributed more than others (although they may have); rather they appear in order that the variety of contribution might give some overall balance to the volume as a whole, and because (editor's prerogative) I knew of work ready for publication. Selectivity there is, therefore, but it is not based on qualitative judgement, either absolute or relative.

Hence it is proper to pay a wider respect to additional figures in British planning history, if only to affirm the importance of individual views, postures and contributions throughout the whole course of planning events. It is not only in the future that we see uncertainty; we see it in the past too. The history of planning was not ordained; it could have been different. The detailed careers and involvements of many people who have figured in the planning movement are therefore important to the overall story. The course of planning history is made up of a whole sequence of decisions, prods and responses by individuals in positions of influence or power, which collectively over time contribute to a recognisable movement or process. The rare individual will stand out as of supreme importance, but we should not neglect the others.

We can see this exemplified with regard to politicians and their influence over planning, though very often we can only ask questions rather than give explanations. What do we make, for example, of John Burns,[10] the first working man to enter a Cabinet, President of the Local Government Board at the time of the first Town Planning Act of 1909? Born in Lambeth, brought up in very humble conditions, organiser of the great dock strike of 1889, he was finally Liberal MP for Battersea, a man whose radical ideas faded and who broke with Keir Hardie. Dismissing Hyndman in that he 'could not run a whelk stall on Southend Pier on a Bank Holiday', he could remark (in 1931): 'I was born in a slum and this made me a town planner. Having slept in Windsor Castle and Pentonville I think I am an authority on housing'. How significant was this bombast and showman for the town planning movement?

In the early days much more directly influential perhaps were local authority councillors because of their ability to stimulate local events. Birmingham produced two: John S. Nettlefold[11] and his half cousin Neville Chamberlain.[12] In 1901 Nettlefold became chairman of a newly established Housing Committee in the city, visited Germany in 1905 where he was influenced by the idea of Town Expansion Plans, and proceeded to be an important figure urging town planning legislation on the Liberal Government. After 1909 Birmingham proved to be the outstanding local authority example in the preparation of Town Planning Schemes. Chamberlain was an enthusiastic chairman of the city's Town Planning Committee established in 1911. In later years as Minister of Health in the 1920s he proved to be a reformer in local government affairs.

Sir Ernest Simon was an active Manchester politician who played a key role in the development of Wythenshawe; he wrote and lectured widely on planning and housing matters. His confident articulation must have impressed his generation both on the need for planning and the capacity of a benevolent authority to undertake it. His message (in 1935) was simple and direct: 'conditions of life in a great city like Manchester can only be made pleasant, and even safe and tolerable, by an immense amount of conscious and expert planning and control, and that this can only be exerted through the City Council'.[13] What Simon achieved in Wythenshawe and Manchester, other authorities were moved to emulate.

In London, it fell to Herbert Morrison to enliven town planning, particularly when he was leader of the London County Council between 1934 and 1940.[14] Years of experience on Hackney Borough Council and in the London Labour Party led to a stream of oft-repeated policy statements covering such matters as housing, town planning and slum clearance, the establishment of new towns or garden cities in the home counties, public improvement schemes and the creation of public recreation grounds. His London programme in the 1930s instituted a town planning scheme over the whole of London, and saw the acquisition of land on the South Bank for its redevelopment, the building of the Waterloo Bridge, and the first steps in the creation of a London Green Belt.

To return to national government we see other figures who have clearly made personal impacts. In the 1940s there was Lord Reith, determined about post-war redevelopment but enthusiastic to the point of unreality; though helpful to the blitzed cities when receiving delegations for help. (To a party from Coventry: 'I told them that if I were in their position I would plan boldly and comprehensively, and that I would not at this stage worry about finance or local boundaries'.)[15] There was Lewis Silkin, chairman of the LCC Town Planning Committee, dedicated to the putting right of London's evils and to the improvement of the East End in particular. He became Minister of Town and Country Planning, and without any significant political power base and without a seat in the Cabinet he piloted through the House three major Bills which established the essential pattern of post-war planning (New Towns, 1946, Town and Country Planning, 1947, and National Parks, 1949). And there was Aneurin Bevan, a councillor in Tredegar in 1922 who applied his mind to housing, water, health and the beauty of the town. Housing conditions were then appalling: 'People were living in conditions not fit for criminals. No doubt horses, especially race horses, were housed much better than some of our citizens are being reared'.[16] This was the man who later, as Minister of Health, was to initiate the largest programme of Council building, backed by the largest subsidies, in British history.

The political examples could be continued, both at local and central government levels. Enough has been suggested to show the constant way in which personal influence can chart the course of planning history. The Crossman diaries tell us of the interplay between Minister and civil servant. Local authorities are the same. The Newcastle of the 1960s was irrevocably shaped by the combination of two men and the power, political and professional, that they could wield; T. Dan Smith[17] harnessed his enthusiasms to the imagination and technical skill of his Chief Planning Officer, Wilfred Burns.[18] Coventry established a similar member/officer relationship, and perhaps no city entirely lacks this experience.

Much of the evidence for what we have been hinting at is difficult to uncover. With professionals at least their record is more open; their books survive as do their Plans and they can be evaluated. The influence of Ebenezer Howard and other early figures in housing reform can be assessed with some accuracy. Howard's book *Tomorrow: a peaceful path to real reform* published in 1898 and reissued with slight revisions as *Garden Cities of Tomorrow* in 1902 proved timely and consequential. Earlier speculations on and proposals for the proper planning of big cities had been common enough, and Howard was not all that original in his prescription, but the Garden City Association took root in Britain and was paralleled by other imitations both at home and abroad. Other languages have been endowed with a new term (*cité-jardin, garten stadt*, for example) and the modern international town planning movement has been deeply affected by the garden city idea. In Britain, Letchworth and Welwyn were among the progenitors of the new towns and the ideal of a dispersed, low density form to urban spatial patterns has seemed peculiarly suited to British experience this century. Howard indeed deserves the title of 'pioneer', but in this volume at least Osborn is offered as a torch bearer of the movement which Howard founded.

But popular figures may unfairly eclipse others active at the same time, and in the same fields. A clutch of housing reformers at the turn of the century were tireless advocates for improved residential layouts, their work overlapping the garden city movement and the many low density experiments in garden suburbs. Further research is long overdue to reveal the considerable influence of these figures. Henry Vivian of the Co-partnership Tenants' Housing Council advocated Public Utility Companies to develop garden suburbs on co-partnership lines; Nettlefold's Harborne Garden Suburb at Birmingham was one example. The National Housing Reform Council had a tireless spokesman in Henry R. Aldridge, who bridged the gap between housing reform and town planning. So too did T. C. Horsfall, Chairman of the Manchester Citizens' Association, particularly influential through his advocacy of German forms of municipal planning. The years round the turn of the century threw up some fascinating cross-currents of interest and personality relationships. The way in which town planning actually took root in this period owed much to individual initiatives, as the lives of Unwin and Adams in particular in this volume indicate.

After these formative years town planning settled down into a relatively steady state; Pepler developed central-local relationships, Abercrombie worked on regional surveys, Geddes was the intellectual and Osborn propagated the garden city ideal. These are our chosen pioneers in this volume, but it would be quite wrong to overlook others. Consultancy practices such as that of W. R. Davidge, and Thompson, Maxwell and Fry laid important foundations. Furthermore, the great designers including Barry Parker, Stanley Adshead, Thomas Mawson and E. L. Lutyens established a reputation which linked town planning to civic and landscape design. These names simply introduce us to greater numbers still who it would be wrong to forget, and whose careers and influence deserve careful analysis.

But undoubtedly the most seriously under-researched period, with its own set of planning giants, is that of the war-time years of the 1940s. It is readily acknowledged that this was a most influential time, when the main features of the British post-war planning system took shape, but the people who were associated with that remarkable burst of energy have not yet been properly acknowledged and their work not yet evaluated. The work of Thomas Sharp is acknowledged in this volume, and the particular contribution of John Dower on the National Park movement is readily recalled. However, the official histories[19] have revealed the extent of political and professional dialogue at this time, and it is clear that much more work has to be done. Sadly, all too often the characters concerned have slipped into obscurity, and those exciting years have lost their sharpness. One of the key figures was William Holford. Research on his papers could not be undertaken in time for this volume, otherwise he would certainly have been included as a pioneer. His *Times* obituary described him as 'the most influential figure in town planning throughout the period during which town and country planning in Britain became transformed from a minor official regulatory activity into a major activity of central and local government departments'. He practised both as a town planner and an architect; he was a teacher, and a consultant with an international reputation. His personal charm and reasonableness naturally attracted people and he proved himself with gifts of diplomacy to be a committee man of genius. He was President of both the TPI and the RIBA and also received the Gold Medal of both Institutes. He was knighted in 1953 and made a life peer in 1965, the first architect or town planner to be so honoured.

He was born in 1907 in South Africa. He came to England to study architecture at Liverpool. After a brilliant student career he was appointed to the chair of Civic Design in that University at the age of 30, succeeding Abercrombie on his translation to London. (In due time, 1948, he succeeded him at London on Abercrombie's retirement.) During the war he became adviser to the Ministry of Town and Country Planning and was largely responsible for drawing up the 1947 Town and Country Planning Act. After the war followed his years of successful consultancy: adviser to Canberra, a plan for Durban, plans for Cambridge and the City of London, the replanning of the precincts of St Pauls and plans for Piccadilly Circus. He died in 1975 at the age of 68.

What is particularly missing from this brief sketch is his years of association with colleagues in the war years. A brilliant team was assembled and its influence was incalculable; tragically they quickly moved away to other things. Gordon Stephenson, for example, was a colleague of Holford at Liverpool. Coming to the Ministry, he was at first seconded to work with Abercrombie on the *Greater London Plan*: later he built up the Planning Techniques section of the Ministry. When Stephenson left he was Chief Planning Officer and succeeded Holford at the Lever Chair in Liverpool. Here the *Town Planning Review* was re-established and there was an important revision of the educational syllabus. Early in the 1950s he resigned his Liverpool chair to take up another academic appointment in Western Australia.

Terry Kennedy was Stephenson's second in command; ultimately he took a chair in New Zealand. Working in the same team were Peter Shepheard, Hugh Casson, McCaughan, Lovett, Buchanan, Johnson-Marshall and others. The Plan for Stevenage was prepared in 1946 (the first New Town in the world with a pedestrianised shopping centre) and a veritable outpouring of imaginative ideas marked this period. Myles Wright wrote the *Redevelopment of Central Areas* as a Ministry handbook where the idea of floor space indices and plot ratios appeared. H. D. Vincent was Head of Research, but later went to New York in charge of a British trade mission. A rich blend of expertise and experience was brought together: Lovett was Planning Officer for the City of London, Colquohuon was an engineer, Coote a planner who had worked with Adshead and Abercrombie, Pound came from the Ministry of Health and Reay took a chair at McGill after serving on new towns.

The liveliness of this period could not be maintained. The

enthusiasm for post-war reconstruction waned, bureaucracy blunted collective imagination, statutory planning drained the system of its impetus, and finally public support was eroded. The post-war years took on a more anonymous characteristic. However, the persistent, the flamboyant and the brilliant have continued to break through, and this volume offers Buchanan as an example of a person who has put his imprint on the course of planning. Naturally there are others too, though because we are dealing with a contemporary period it becomes almost invidious to draw attention to individual names. That of Robert Grieve, however, should be introduced as a persistent initiator in Scotland. The political input has been weak and uncertain, but one must acknowledge Duncan Sandys with his Green Belt circular, his work for the Civic Trust, and his Civic Amenities Act, 1967. Professionals have been circumscribed by local authority constraints, but the history of the post-war years has been featured by a number of outstanding contributions: at cities such as Coventry, Newcastle, and Liverpool for example, together with some of the larger counties. Outside the local authorities, educationalists have married academic work to practice, consultants have designed and created, lawyers have wrestled with planning legislation. Every planner in his own way has shaped the profession of which he is part, translating and interpreting the ideals to which he subscribes. It has become difficult for individuals to scale personal heights of eminence as in earlier years; those circumstances may come again, but in the meantime we can look back with no little instruction and acknowledge the work of the giants.

Notes

1 Papers from the First International Conference on the History of Urban and Regional Planning (London, 1977) have been published as follows:
Anthony Sutcliffe (Ed), *The Rise of Modern Town Planning 1800–1914*, Mansell, London, 1980
Gordon E. Cherry (Ed), *Shaping an Urban World: Planning in the Twentieth Century*, Mansell, London, 1980
Roger Kain, *Planning for Conservation*, Mansell, London, 1980
2 Geoffrey and Susan Jellicoe, *The Landscape of Man*, Thames and Hudson, London, 1975
3 Frederick R. Hiorns, *Town-Building in History*, Harrap, London, 1956
4 George Dangerfield, *The Strange Death of Liberal England*, London, 1935

5   Cynthia Cockburn, *The Local State: management of cities and people*, Pluto Press, London, 1977
6   Manuel Castells, 'Towards a Political Urban Sociology', in Michael Harloe, *Captive Cities: studies in the political economy of cities and regions*, John Wiley, London, 1977
7   Ralph Miliband, *The State in Capitalist Society*, Weidenfeld and Nicolson, London, 1969
8   Gordon E. Cherry, *Environmental Planning, Vol. II, National Parks and Recreation in the Countryside*, HMSO, London, 1975
9   Alan Bullock, 'Is History Becoming a Social Science?' The Leslie Stephen Lecture, CUP, 1976
10 Kenneth D. Brown, *John Burns*, Royal Historical Society, London, 1977
11 Gordon E. Cherry, *Factors in the Origins of Town Planning in Britain: the example of Birmingham, 1905–15*, Working Paper 36, Centre for Urban and Regional Studies, University of Birmingham, 1975
12 Gordon E. Cherry, 'The Place of Neville Chamberlain in British Town Planning' in Cherry (Ed) *Shaping an Urban World*, Mansell, London, 1980
13 E. D. Simon and J. Inman, *The Rebuilding of Manchester*, Longmans, London, 1935
14 Bernard Donoughue and G. W. Jones, *Herbert Morrison, Portrait of a Politician*, Weidenfeld and Nicolson, London, 1973
15 J. C. W. Reith, *Into the Wind*, Hodder and Stoughton, London, 1949
16 Michael Foot, *Aneurin Bevan*, Macgibbon & Kee, London, 1962
17 Dan Smith, *An Autobiography*, Oriel Press, Newcastle, 1970
18 Wilfred Burns, *Newcastle: a study in replanning at Newcastle upon Tyne*, Leonard Hill, London, 1967
19 J. B. Cullingworth, *Environmental Planning, Vol I, Reconstruction and Land Use Planning 1937–1947*, HMSO, London, 1975
    Gordon E. Cherry, *Environmental Planning Vol II, National Parks and Recreation in the Countryside*, HMSO, London, 1975
    J. B. Cullingworth, *Environmental Planning Vol III, New Towns*, HMSO, London, 1980

2

THOMAS ADAMS
1871–1940

Michael Simpson

Of the major pioneers of modern British planning, Thomas Adams is today probably the least known, yet in his lifetime (1871–1940), he was widely accepted as a leader of his profession in Britain, Canada and the United States. Spanning the years of genesis in North Atlantic planning history, his career, divided between three countries, had a diffused impact.

The eldest son of a dairy farmer, born at Corstorphine on the western outskirts of Edinburgh in September 1871, Adams spent the first thirty years of his life in the environs of Edinburgh, assisting in the family business and from 1893 to 1897 renting a farm at Carlops, just south of the city. The epitome of the sturdy yeoman, Adams's farming experiences nurtured lifelong beliefs in individualism, equality of opportunity and self-reliance besides a feel for the inherent possibilities of the environment, the interdependence of town and country and the ability to view the great city from a close but detached vantage point. Edinburgh itself offered him an excellent case study of both fine civic design and formless urban accretion. The 'New Town' was 'a heritage of incalculable wealth' but the disruptive railway-led Victorian expansion disturbed its symmetry and the city was 'woefully neglecting her duty today in the way she is allowing her suburbs to grow'.[1] Returning to his native village on his marriage in 1897, Adams 'became enthusiastic about writing rather than farming'. Identifying himself with Robert Burns's agrarianism, he championed in the local press a freeholding yeomanry, a free market in land and a more equitable land tax. His views and experiences led him into politics and he became secretary of the Midlothian Liberal Association and agent for its successful candidate, the Master of Elibank, in the General Election of 1900. Edinburgh Liberalism was Whiggish – suspicious of government and defending the rights of the individual – attitudes characteristic of Adams throughout his life. A founder of the home rulers' Young

19

Scots Society in November 1900, he left for London a month later. His parents having died and the family business resting in the capable hands of his sister Margaret, he felt no compulsion to stay; he had a family to support and London offered better prospects for an intending man of letters.

In London, he sought his destiny as a writer and found it as a planner. Ebenezer Howard's Garden City Association (founded 1899), struggling for members, money and respect, acquired a new chairman in the spring of 1901 – Ralph Neville, a barrister and former Liberal MP. Widely known and highly regarded as a man of drive, integrity and practicality, Neville immediately switched the GCA's emphasis from propaganda to action. One of the first fruits of this revolution was the recruitment in April 1901 of Thomas Adams as full-time secretary. Perhaps seeking security and the realisation of his agrarian views, Adams was well fitted for the post by his journalistic, speaking, political and environmental experience and a talent for dynamic yet practical organisation. Undergoing total conversion to Howard's ideas, he spoke and wrote extensively, helping to boost membership to over 2,000 by 1903 – many of them leading public figures. But his principal contributions were the supremely successful conferences at Bournville (September 1901) and Port Sunlight (July 1902). The GCA's association with widely-admired practical demonstrations of industrial decentralisation brought large attendances and widespread publicity. Adams summed up their effect accurately: 'At the Bournville conference, it began to be recognised that we had a definite aim, that there was a solid foundation for Mr. Howard's proposals, and that the central idea of the project was feasible'.[2] The Port Sunlight meeting coincided with the launching of the Garden City Pioneer Company, formed to select a site for Howard's experiment. That the movement had reached this stage by the summer of 1902 was due to the highly effective combination of Neville, Howard and Adams. Functioning smoothly, possessing confidence in each other and the Garden City idea, they were complementary – Neville the strategist, Howard the ceaseless, passionate evangelist and Adams the shrewd, aggressive organiser of victory.

Adams, Secretary of the Pioneer Company, inspected sites but had no part in the finding of Letchworth, though quickly endorsing the favourable opinion of Neville, Howard and Unwin.[3] Appointed Secretary-Manager of the succeeding First Garden City Company, his principal function from 1903 to 1906 was to launch Letchworth but he retained a supervisory role at the GCA. Indeed, in September 1905 he had to rescue it from the chaos left by the unsuccessful Organising Secretary of the past two years, G. J. H. Northcroft.

More importantly, he had also to solve its crisis of identity, 'for the objects of the Association were to some extent attained by the floating of the Company, and unless fresh objects can be given to the Association, it seems likely to languish'.[4] Recognising that garden cities were likely to be few and far between, he resolved to extend some at least of their benefits to conventional communities. He turned the GCA into the true predecessor of the Town and Country Planning Association, instituting a professional advisory group, revitalising the *Garden City* magazine and expanding the Association's scope to 'give general encouragement to manufacturers to move out of crowded centres, stimulate interest in and promote the scientific development of towns, and encourage the erection of sanitary and beautiful dwellings with adequate space for gardens and recreation'.[5]

Although he lacked managerial experience, a clear directive from the Board and adequate capital, Adams was given general responsibility for the establishment of a Garden City at Letchworth. Appreciating that industry would only locate there if essential facilities existed, he developed first a utilities and communications infrastructure and by the end of 1906 had helped persuade eight firms to settle. The hard-up company could not provide workers' homes and so Adams followed up an article on £150 cottages by J. St. Loe Strachey,[6] persuading both Strachey and the Board to sponsor a Cheap Cottages Exhibition.[7] The company, providing the site, would get 120 free houses, immense publicity and thousands of visitors. Held in 1905, the Exhibition brought the anticipated benefits but the design, construction and costing of the houses was criticised and they reinforced the garden rather than the city aspect of Letchworth.

It has been generally forgotten that to Howard, Adams and other pioneers, it was as important to solve rural as urban problems. Adams, who hoped for 'a democratic city of self-reliant citizens – surrounded by an agricultural belt occupied by a sturdy and independent yeomanry,' was the principal speaker at a conference on 'Garden City and Agriculture' (1905), advocating a comprehensive smallholdings programme. The urban aspect became dominant, however, the neglect of agriculture being a consequence of Letchworth's acute under-capitalisation. Adams wrote, sadly: 'The importance of the agricultural part of the scheme does not seem to be realised by some of those who are the warmest supporters of the industrial side of the movement'.[8] Made the scapegoat for Letchworth's failure to attain instant profitability, Adams was relieved of managerial responsibility in August 1905 by W. H. Gaunt, an experienced trading estate manager. The resignation in 1906 of his chief supporter, Neville, prompted his own regretful departure. Felt by many to have been the source of such success as the project had enjoyed, he was active in the town's frenetic social life and his wife was the unofficial social worker; with their going went much of the idealism. Launching an unprecedented venture on a tight budget, balancing economics with ideals, he was the victim of directoral irresolution and impatience.

From November 1906 to November 1909, Adams was in private practice as a 'land agent and consulting surveyor'; in effect, he was the first Briton to make his living entirely from planning, designing the following seven garden suburbs:

Fallings Park – 400 acres, 2 miles north east of Wolverhampton, for Sir Richard Paget, in association with the architects Detmar Blow and Fernand Billerey.

Knebworth – 800 acres, near Stevenage, Hertfordshire, for the Earl of Lytton, in association with Edwin Lutyens, related to the Lyttons by marriage.

Glyn Cory – 300 acres, 7 miles west of Cardiff, for John and Reginald Cory, taking over T. H. Mawson's design.

Childwall – on the eastern outskirts of Liverpool, for Lord Salisbury.

Newton Moor – 200 acres, near Hyde, Cheshire, for the Ashton Trustees.

Alkrington – 700 acres, 4 miles north of Manchester, for the Lees Trustees.

Shirehampton – 26.5 acres, on the western edge of Bristol, for Napier Miles.

In most cases, Adams worked for Garden City sympathisers who shared his desire to undertake object-lessons in low-density, topographically sympathetic residential estates, catering for all social classes, in the environs of great towns. Given ample garden, allotment and open space, extensive planting, service centres and making attractive and economical use of their sites, his designs were derivative, sharing common characteristics with similar schemes elsewhere in Britain. They also gave Adams the opportunity to express his social philosophy of voluntary co-operation between landowners and local authorities, co-partnership housing and ultimate management of the estates by the residents themselves. 'Associated individualism' was his compromise between the irresponsibility of complete *laissez-faire* and the state collectivism which he feared spelt the end of individual freedom and responsibility. All fell well short of their target populations (7,000–30,000), realisation being curbed by tight money and a depressed building industry. Of the seven (taken over by George Pepler and Ernest Allen in 1909), Childwall and Newton Moor never got beyond the drawing board, Fallings Park halted at 75 houses, Shirehampton at 50 and Glyn Cory at 25. Alkrington and Knebworth achieved modest fulfilment over long periods.

Though still unqualified, by the end of 1909 Thomas Adams was an experienced planner with a professional standing comparable to Unwin and Mawson. Playing a major part in the 1907 Cheap Cottages Exhibition, he organised one of his own at Fallings Park in 1908. He acted as an External Examiner in Civic Design at Liverpool University, served as a Smallholdings Commissioner and sat on the Council of the Garden City Association. The most interesting of his related activities was as spokesman for the Midland Towns Association, a consortium of 26 Black Country municipalities. Formed to co-ordinate highway construction, reclaim wasteland and improve municipal efficiency, it represented an early step towards regional planning.[9] Given his prominence, Liberal connections and acquaintance with John Burns since 1906, it was not surprising that Adams became Town Planning Advisor to the Local Government Board in December 1909, following passage of the Housing, Town Planning, etc., Act. The Act was a cautious, tortuous instrument of development control, the outcome of pressure upon successive Presidents of the Board – Walter Long and John Burns – by the Association of Municipal Corporations, the National Housing Reform Council and the Garden City Association between 1905 and 1907, who called for a Town and Village Development Commission and suggested 'that local authorities should have adoptive powers enabling them to prepare building plans definitely planning the lines of development of new areas,' acquire land and create model suburbs.[10] Adams, who claimed to have co-operated in framing the bill, and briefed both sides in Parliament,[11] had reason to be satisfied with it, but wished it had been made mandatory and had allowed public acquisition of development land at agricultural prices; however, it was more important to speedily enact an imperfect measure which could be amended in the light of experience and better public understanding of planning. Adams and the Board worked the Act with greater flexibility and intelligence than is sometimes supposed. Adams himself was as concerned to spread the gospel of planning as to encourage schemes and the Board pressed tardy authorities to proceed with their plans and stimulated regional planning, notably in the new Doncaster coalfield and the London Arterial Roads Conferences. The London meetings, begun in 1913, were regarded by Adams as the initial stage of a comprehensive regional planning exercise. Emphasising the contribution of forward planning to municipal efficiency and economy, he called for a central body to devise a flexible skeleton plan to cope with the expected doubling of the outer suburban population over thirty years and outlining land use zones, utility and transportation patterns, and the co-ordination of a hundred or more local plans. War halted the possible expansion of the Conference's remit. Though Adams was basically content with the Act, he became frustrated with 'the routine of planning control . . . the lack of opportunity to do constructive work in planning' and 'the subordination of the technical to the administrative branch' of the civil service.[12] Disillusionment with the Local Government Board's *modus operandi* left him open to the lucrative and challenging offer from Canada which he accepted in July 1914.

When Adams left Britain in October 1914 he was President of the Town Planning Institute, conceived by him during the passage of the 1909 Act, discussed with architects, engineers and surveyors from 1910 and launched in 1913 'to advance the study of Town Planning and Civic Design and to secure the association of those engaged or interested in the practice of town planning'.[13] Having had extensive contact with the environmental professions, Adams recognised that planning had a complex character, being a subtle combination of elements from each of them and beyond the capacity of any one of them to comprehend in its entirety. He envisaged the new Institute as a co-ordinating body, not as a rival to the existing professions. One of its principal functions would be to educate members of the professions to enable them to implement the new legislation. He also saw 'the need for an educational body to study and investigate the numerous problems to which Town Planning gives rise'.[14] While seeking the intellectual refinement of the subject and encouraging scientific research in the field, he was not yet articulating the case for a distinct discipline and profession. Alone among the founders in having no professional qualification of his own until 1913 (when he qualified as a surveyor, a logical choice given his agrarian background), he was nevertheless 'looked up to as the head of the profession in this country' and the natural choice as inaugural President of the Town Planning Institute.[15]

Between 1896 and 1913 Canada had experienced an immigrant-led urban and prairie boom, during which prevailing *laissez-faire* convictions were challenged only by a mild progressivism, one of the few national manifestations of which was the Commission of Conservation (1909–21). Headed by the able but enigmatic Clifford Sifton, it was to 'study, investigate and advise' on the use of Canada's human and natural resources. From its Medical Officer, Dr Charles Hodgetts, it derived an interest in planning, hosting the 1914 National Conference on City Planning at Toronto and drafting a model provincial planning act. Hodgetts, who had been impressed

by the practical Adams at a conference in 1911, attempted without success to 'borrow' him in 1912; he was finally captured in 1914, becoming Town Planning Advisor to the Commission.[16]
Arriving shortly after the outbreak of the Great War, Adams found it a disconcerting addition to an already challenging situation. Accentuating both rural and urban problems, it diverted attention, money and skilled personnel away from the nascent planning movement. Though Hodgetts' assertion that 'As for Town Planning, there has been none'[17] was not entirely accurate, there were no Canadian planners of note and (despite international conferences at Winnipeg in 1912 and Toronto in 1914) no national planning organisation. Three provinces had passed acts based on the British statute and several cities had commissioned plans, although none had been implemented. British influence, advocating primarily social goals, was evenly balanced by American, stressing aesthetic, 'City Beautiful' objectives. But these tentative steps merely highlighted the extent of Canada's environmental problems. In the countryside, Adams wrote, 'the necessarily crude methods of the pioneer stage of development' wasted land and resources; the American-style grid settlement, 'designed to promote speculation', ignored topography, and inadequate social and economic facilities prompted depopulation.[18] The cities, also plotted on the grid system, were congested at the centre and too diffuse on the perimeter; speculative sub-division had proceeded extravagantly far, to the point of sterilising land and inciting municipal bankruptcy. W. F. Burditt, sponsor of the St. John, New Brunswick, plan of 1914, expressed perfectly the nature of the wildcat urbanisation of the boom years:

So rapid was the development of Canada, so great were the opportunities for gain, that as individuals we became almost wholly absorbed in the acquisition of wealth and as communities, in the increase of population and the expansion of our commerce, while the amenities of life, health and the happiness of the masses received scant consideration.[19]

Adams brought to Canada development control planning, Garden City environmental standards and design principles, the Local Government Board's minimum standards for housing and public health, and the new conventional wisdom in North Atlantic planning circles, the 'City Efficient' or 'scientific town planning . . . and greater efficiency in the . . . use and development of land'.[20] Since planning was a provincial and municipal responsibility, he appreciated the need for tact and persuasion. Developing a rapid and thorough understanding of the Canadian environmental situation, the strategy he devised was the only realistic one – the simultaneous promotion of legislation, propaganda, advice, research and demonstration. Revising the Commission's draft model act, and existing legislation, he retained the development control basis of the British act but made it mandatory and applicable to rural areas, adopted the American appointive planning board and provided for a municipal planning surveyor. Recognising the need for provincial local government boards to spur and advise localities, he called also for departments of municipal affairs and planning comptrollers. Acknowledging the need for an informed constituency for planning, he drew on local and American examples in the formation of a national Civic Improvement League, acting as Secretary from its inception in 1915. Publicising environmental improvement through the Commission's quarterly, *Town Planning and Conservation of Life*, he wrote also for the professional and general press and spoke about twice weekly to universities and other groups. Initiating research projects into housing and rural and urban planning and development, he managed to complete only *Rural Planning and Development* (1917). Identifying accurately the countryside's problems, he suggested:

What is needed is the establishment of well-planned agricultural villages on good and accessible land. They must be planned in such a way that there will not be an entire absence of facilities for social intercourse, co-operatives, transport and ready means of marketing. They are necessary in combination to make farming pay, and unless we can make farming pay we cannot solve the problem of rural depopulation.

Though concerned to foster the family homestead, self-reliance and voluntary co-operation, Adams envisaged a dramatically expanded government role in rural development – cheap loans for pre-planned new towns and homesteaders, encouraging topographically sympathetic, compact settlement, improving agricultural education and advice, promoting rural industries and compelling speculators to disgorge accessible land held for profiteering, making landowners pay most improvement costs and licensing real estate operations.

In Canadian cities, Adams initiated planning schemes, undertook practical demonstrations and (in the 1920s) prepared comprehensive plans. Believing that 'The general objective to be kept in mind should be to do that which is best for the public welfare,' he assumed a unity of purpose in the city which could be satisfied by the objective application of scientific technique. Regarding the city as primarily an economic organism, he thought that 'Business interests – especially those concerned with productive enterprises – must have the first consideration' but, mindful of his reformist background, added that 'Closely identified with these interests is the health of the people'. Emphasising the vital need 'to secure that new growth will be properly regulated, that the evils which have resulted from haphazard growth in the past will be avoided in the future', he concentrated on development planning which would result in the most efficient distribution of land uses, compact growth and the avoidance of speculation. Aware of the financial embarrassment of many municipalities, he stressed the cost-effectiveness of planning – 'the exercise of forethought' meant 'no real increase in cost over what will have to be spent in any case'.

The need to pare costs ruled out urban renewal but, in the case of Halifax, he demonstrated what should be done. Halifax's Richmond district, 325 acres of hillside working class and waterfront industrial land, had been devastated by an explosion in December 1917. Adams, drafted in to replan it, was freed of the normal constraints on redevelopment – cost and the sanctity of private property. Subject only to the continued existence of some original streets and the restraining hand of the Relief Commission, he undertook a technical exercise in the destruction of the standard grid, breaking it up with diagonals, increasing accessibility, open and industrial space, establishing firm building lines and easing gradients. A successful, functional design, it was completed by George Ross's attractive low-cost housing.[21] Adams also had few opportunities to assist in the establishment of new communities but in 1917 he accepted an invitation to advise a lumber company on the building of a resource town at Kipawa (now Temiscaming) in western Quebec. Generally rough-and-ready places, resource towns needed an exemplar. A combination of welfare capitalism and skillful resolution of a scrub-covered hillside site-planning problem, Kipawa was laid out on garden city lines with a civic centre, extensive open space and community facilities, and cleverly integrated into the landscape.[22]

Having long stressed the interdependence of town and country, the need for industrial decentralisation and for the planning of a city's economic and social hinterland as well as its political entity, Adams came to believe that 'the most important, if not the most urgent, of our problems is to prepare schemes for large regions, embracing the large city, its adjacent satellite towns and the whole of the intervening lands that make up the metropolitan area'. To this end, he encouraged the Essex Border towns to co-ordinate utility, highway and park projects and in 1919 proposed a 1,000 square mile international regional plan for the Niagara district.[23]

Peace brought agitation for government-sponsored low-cost housing of publicly acceptable standard at prices affordable by working people for whom private enterprise was currently unable to provide. Adams argued that an emergency programme would effect a measure of social control in an unstable situation of unemployment, industrial unrest and 'serious discontent' among returning veterans, and would assist economic readjustment and efficiency; he recommended a Federal Development Board to co-operate with provinces and municipalities in the co-ordination of land development, transportation and housing.[24] Though not getting the powers he wanted, he was appointed housing advisor to a Cabinet Committee charged with the disbursement of a $26 million Federal loan. Envisaging a property-owning democracy, the programme called for planned schemes and the sale of houses at cost. This was in keeping with Adams's own philosophy, for he condemned British housing subsidies as 'a gratuity to those who will live in the houses' and as 'economically unsound',[25] describing the Canadian scheme as 'not like socialism – the antithesis of individualism – it is co-operative individualism'.[26] Adams himself designed a demonstration project at Lindenlea, Ottawa. On a rugged, accessible but countrified 22 acre site, he displayed his usual skill with an awkward location, turning ruggedness into a scenic asset, avoiding the traditional grid and providing an attractive garden suburb with ample open space and community facilities.[27] Intending it to be as much an example of social possibilities as of housing and planning, Adams hoped for residents' co-operative management on British co-partnership lines. Though 'Ottawa had an opportunity to make Lindenlea a model scheme of national importance . . . an ideal garden suburb', the housing, placed in other hands, was badly sited and unattractive. Unfairly made the scapegoat for this, Adams replied correctly that, 'as a town planning project, Lindenlea was a complete success'; others had reduced it to 'an ordinary real estate development'.[28] By the end of the war, Adams seems to have felt that his mission, and that of the Commission of Conservation, was running out of steam and he therefore prepared for his departure. Anticipating this and the rapid post-war expansion of planning, the 'grand seigneur' of Canadian planning set about creating an indigenous, self-sustaining profession. In December 1918 he initiated a series of meetings with members of the environmental professions, culminating in May 1919 with the formation of the Town Planning Institute of Canada, of which Adams was the two-term inaugural President. Like its British progenitor, it balanced neatly the constituent professions and sought the interchange of knowledge, the establishment of high professional standards, the encouragement of research and good public relations. Determined 'to built up the elements of something as nearly approaching an exact science as is possible with a subject so elastic', Adams coupled the Institute with his persistent campaign to establish diploma courses in the universities:

It is recognised that the most appropriate qualification might best come from the Universities and its is part of the object of the Canadian Town Planning Institute to promote educational courses in Canadian Universities and to make Town Planning a branch of applied science with the imprimatur of a University.[29]

Preparing further for his exit, Adams divided his time from February 1920 between the Commission and private practice. When the Commission was dissolved in 1921 – the victim of government jealousies, intrigues, parsimony and policy conflicts – he served out his time in the National Parks office, helping to design an administrative centre for the Jasper National Park on garden city lines and site plans for new Federal buildings in Ottawa. At the time of his departure in September 1923 he was making confident plans for the development of several Ontario cities. On leaving Canada, Adams could feel reasonably optimistic that planning was planted firmly in the dominion. Activity was greater than ever, lay interest was apparently increasing and the Town Planning Institute of Canada had over a hundred members. By 1926, only recalcitrant Quebec was without planning legislation and some provinces had even improved their original acts and planning machinery.

Canadian planning was, however, a tender plant. The bright façade hid disturbing tendencies. Though almost universal, 'the rather wheezy band of Canadian provincial town planning acts' varied greatly in comprehensiveness and effectiveness, lacking the machinery for implementation in some cases, the acts becoming dead letters. The demise of the Commission of Conservation substantially removed the Federal commitment to resource management and environmental improvement and took the pressure off backsliding provinces; the presence of a so-called Town Planning Advisor in the National Parks office was a totally inadequate substitute.[30] Nor had Adams created a firm, broadly-based constituency for planning; a fickle public remained suspicious of it – as Noulan Cauchon noted, 'It is an uphill fight for the cause'.[31] The Civic Improvement League had collapsed in 1918 – a casualty of the war and impenetrable Canadian indifference. The populist recommendations of Adams's *Rural Planning and Development* were too far removed from the freewheeling individualism characteristic of the Canadian frontier to be politically acceptable; post-war rural life went on much as before. The housing programme, a hasty reconstruction measure, was foredoomed to failure. Only two-thirds of the appropriation had been taken up and under 4,000 houses built by 1922 and the Federal Government's interest was casually terminated by Premier Meighen – 'The matter of house construction is not one with which the Federal Government has really any responsibility' – in May 1921.[32]

In fact the fear of Adams and the Canadian authorities of committing the sin of socialism by undertaking subsidised housing on British lines ruled out the solution of Canada's persistent low-cost housing problem. Given the reactionary attitude of Canadian business and the unreconstructed *laissez-faire* convictions of political leaders, other alternatives such as a substantial rise in working class real income and strict price controls were equally unlikely. The perceptive Burditt summed up the programme's shortcomings:

The general feeling seems to be that at the present excessive cost of building, the preferred loan by Government will be of little or no advantage as it will not be possible, even with capital at 5%, to build houses that can be rented at any figure which it is possible for workmen to pay, and unless the Government can do something in the way of reducing costs, I fear but little will be accomplished.[33]

Even more dispiriting to Adams was the general failure of Canadian universities to institute regular diploma courses on planning and the inability of his *protégés* in the TPIC to live up to his example in their practice. The lack of an adequate professional training led to a shortage of planners with the skill and confidence of Adams to undertake comprehensive planning and to a failure to establish the standing of the profession. Absence of self-confidence and the necessary skills and commitment compelled Canadian planners to accommodate themselves to the existing urban power structure and serve its ends. In effect, Canadian planning in the 1920s came to mean zoning, sub-division approval and the minimal co-ordination of real estate projects. The Regina Town Planning Association could safely claim that 'The object of a town planning scheme or by-law is principally protective . . . They are intended to ensure the permanence of investment in real property'.[34] Even this timid, socially-static approach was short-lived, for 'Canadian planning came to an abrupt and disastrous end in 1930, when Canada was crippled by economic depression.'[35] When the TPIC and its *Journal* folded in 1932, the destruction of Adams's system was complete.[36]

The failure of the Adams mission to Canada was due more to adverse circumstances than to his own limitiations. He was in tune with the Canadian psyche – suspicious of government, a champion of the individual and practical; crossing the Atlantic compelled no philosophical adjustment. Appreciating the conservative nature of Canadian society, he offered it nothing radical; as Gerecke has said, 'Canadian planning did not go beyond symptoms to basic changes in social structure'.[37] In general, Adams would have endorsed Carver's observation: 'The role of government in planning, whether in an economic or physical sense, is not to supply the initiative but to establish the limits and disciplines within which free enterprise can operate most efficiently'.[38] Sensitive to local needs and attitudes, Adams adapted his technique and proposals to the Canadian environment. Canadian planning would have developed, and on substantially the same lines, without him; his principal contribution was to speed up the process of codification and institutionalisation of law and practice. Considering the handicap of the Great War and his lack of adequate political and professional support, his short-term achievements were a testimony to his remarkable energy, enthusiasm and persuasive skills. What really defeated Thomas Adams was the hostility and indifference of an immature frontier society to the very notion of resource management and environmental planning, as he himself recognised:

The greatest difficulty in Canada was the strength of the resistance to the . . . proper use of land for healthful community use, even to the point of causing unhealthful conditions in town and country. This resistance is strong in other countries, but in Canada, still being exploited as a new country, it was exceptionally strong . . . the resistance came from real estate interests optimistically holding on to excessive land prices and wanting larger cities; unwilling that their profits should be lessened even when necessary for the public good.[39]

After 1920, Adams's career went into a melting pot. Though obliged until September 1923 to spend five months in each year on government work in Canada, his principal intention was to carry on a trans-Atlantic planning practice based on London, where in 1922 he formed a partnership with the engineer and surveyor Francis Longstreth Thompson. However, following his appointment as General Director of Plans and Surveys of the Regional Plan of New York and its Environs in October 1923, he spent most of the decade in America. His acquaintance with the United States had begun in 1911, when he attended the National Conference on City Planning at Philadelphia; thereafter, he was a frequent speaker to the NCCP. A founder of the American City Planning Institute (later the American Institute of Planners), he became a Vice-President. One of his most important services to American planning was in the initiation of professional education. In 1921, he was invited to launch a course at the Massachusetts Institute of Technology and taught it with pride and pleasure until 1936.[40] Concerned to provide America with an adequate supply of systematically trained planners, he took the initiative in 1928 which led to the Harvard School of City Planning, which he served as a research professor from 1930 to 1936. Although he regarded planning as an identifiable academic discipline, he contended that 'In its technical aspects, training in town planning should comprise a post-graduate course superimposed on a training in architecture (including landscape architecture), in engineering or surveying'. Planning was a co-ordinating discipline, composed of elements of these and also of sociology and economics. His teaching and textbooks contained a substantial historical background, as was the custom, a discussion of the relations between the professions, an outline of technique and a considerable amount of project work. Perhaps the moment of greatest pride for him was the award in 1932 of an honorary doctorate of engineering by New York University.[41]

Adams's principal achievement in American planning, the Regional Plan of New York, defined the metropolis as an area of 5,250 square miles and nine million people. Two major problems dominated the region – congestion and decentralisation. Congestion covered a multitude of urban sins – overcrowding at the centre, traffic paralysis (road, rail and water), shortage of open space and excessive height and bulk in buildings. In the late 19th century, it was countered by business and residential dispersal fueled by rising real incomes, real estate speculation and rapid transit, reinforced later by the automobile. However, unrestrained decentralisation was 'one of the principal causes of the worst evils in city growth,'[42] reducing population pressure but exacerbating traffic congestion and forming by 1920 an interlocking combination of dormitory suburbs, skyscraper offices and commuter transportation. Such reform as there was tended to be 'piece-meal planning and doing things when it was too late to do them right'.[43]

After a generation of Progressive reform, the architect Henry Wright commented sadly, 'cities are still fairly well messed up'.[44] It was this mess that the Regional Plan sought to clear up. It was sponsored entirely by the Russell Sage Foundation, whose trustees were Ivy League-educated, old-stock business and professional men with distinguished public service records. Patrician progressives, they stood for a responsible capitalist order with the state as referee. Imbued with a desire for urban health and beauty, they were interested too in municipal and economic efficiency and rationalisation. They were steered into the Regional Plan by a newcomer, Charles Dyer Norton. A self-made tycoon of unequalled dynamism, Norton had persuaded Daniel Burnham to undertake the Chicago plan of 1906–09 and carried the vision with him when he moved to New York in 1911: 'Let some Daniel Hudson Burnham do for this immense community what Burnham did for Chicago and its environs . . . Let him make a big daring imaginative plan'. The scheme was to be 'tendered as a free offering to the public of New York . . . designed to stimulate public interest in a subject of vital importance, and in the faith that it will be welcomed by public spirited citizens and officials'. Instigating studies of municipal taxation, planning and zoning law, physical conditions, recreation and open space, housing and social problems, transportation, the regional economy, architectural schemes and planning possibilities (Adams was chairman of the advisory group of planners), by his death in 1923 Norton was moving to clarify his aims, co-ordinate the studies and search for a 'supreme commander' – settling on Adams, who had 'qualities of practical sense,' to play the Burnham role.[45]

Adams's pragmatic liberalism matched perfectly the Plan Committee's progressivism. Accepting the region as defined, he described it as 'an area in which there is a family of communities having closely related physical, economic and social problems'.[46] Under no illusions that he either could or should produce a definitive plan, he confined himself to identifying problems and trends and providing an outline structure plan, encouraging public and private agencies to act upon its recommendations and fill in details:

The object of making the plan is to give guidance to the people of the Region and to the governing authorities that represent and act for them, to enable them to so direct urban growth in the future that the greatest practicable measure of health, safety, convenience and general welfare will be secured for the inhabitants.[47]

Assuming continued growth on lines already established, Adams's basic conundrum was how to fit into the area the projected 1965 population of 21 millions while reducing congestion, raising environmental standards and easing transportation burdens.[48]

To tackle central area population pressure, Adams proposed 'recentralisation', the encouragement of new, self-contained growth poles, where localised employment would reduce 'friction of space' or commuting. A co-ordinated regional transportation system in which railroads, rapid transit and highways would form a series of semicircles around the region, punctuated by radial spokes, would allow intersections to become the satellite centres and direct through traffic away from central districts. It would also permit the development of the rural webs between the spokes. A regional park system linked by parkways (which had vital roles as regional highways) would give one acre of open space for every acre of building. Adams felt little could be done about central area problems; reconstruction would have to await the pleasure of private owners. Redevelopment was costly and it was more important to prevent a repetition of inner-city mistakes in new growth. New skyscrapers were to be subject to stringent height and bulk zoning, relating them to the space about them. A believer in the free market for housing, Adams had little constructive to offer on low-cost housing and slum clearance, characteristically advocating low-interest government loans to co-operatives and the exploitation of new techniques and materials to reduce building costs; in general, workers should be persuaded to move to satellite towns.

Issued in two volumes (1929 and 1931), written mostly by Adams, and backed by eight subject reports, the Regional Plan represented the most comprehensive statement of the prevailing ameliorative planning tradition.[49] High priest of the ameliorative approach was Daniel Hudson Burnham, who recognised 'the fact that the American city is a centre of industry and traffic'.[50, 51] Accepting as fundamentally sound the existing social and economic structure, it sought to harness trends for community purposes while ensuring individual freedom of action. Sponsored by the business élite, mainstream American planning attempted to invest urban growth, which it deemed both inevitable and desirable, with humanity, efficiency and scientific management. Positing general socio-economic goals, it sought their attainment by rational environmental design. Predicated upon environmental determinism, it placed great faith in the technique of land use and resource allocation to combat society's problems. Rooted in classical liberalism, it distrusted positive government, confining it to a negative regulatory role.

Adams and the Regional Plan conformed faithfully to these precepts. Acknowledging that 'we cannot overcome the forces that make cities as large as New York,'[52] and that there was little prospect of 'any revolutionary change on the part of the public in favour of a more ideal system of city development',[53] they produced a trend-adjusting, project-oriented outline plan, endorsing many existing proposals, which went 'far in proposing restrictions on the rights of property but no further than it is reasonable to expect public opinion to go or government to authorise in the future'.[54] Its recommendations were thus conditioned by its readings of the public mood and its perception of the local power structures.

After the publication of the Plan, Adams retired to a consulting role and a Regional Plan Association was formed which, by persuasion and propaganda, secured the establishment of a regional park system, the acquisition of about half of the recommended open space and the construction of the greater part of the regional highway system – a fine record in comparison with other regional plans. Going to work at the outset of the Great Depression it was helped over it by the New Deal and Robert Moses. Its principal beneficiary was the mobile middle class but the poor gained little, for it sanctioned no feasible means of realising its low-cost housing and satellite town proposals. It failed to learn from previous experiences that reliance on private enterprise and philanthropy for the fulfilment of broad social ends was futile; only substantial state or Federal programmes could achieve these goals. All in all, it did little to solve the problems of congestion and dispersal. Its momentum was already waning before America's entry into war in 1941 killed it off.

Amid the general paean of praise which greeted the Plan's appearance, Lewis Mumford's was one of the few discordant voices. Heir to the alternative planning tradition, the radical strain, derived mainly from the self-confessed 'socialist-democrat' Frederick Law Olmsted, Senior, Mumford acknowledged also the civics of Geddes and Howard. Spokesman for the Regional Planning Association of America – an intellectual coterie as élitist as the Russell Sage Trustees – he attacked 'dinosaur cities' and their ameliorationist planners and publicised an alternative planning strategy. Set out in Henry Wright's New York State Plan (1926), this argued for a state-wide, government-sponsored approach to community building involving planned dispersal, applying modern technology which made industry footloose and people more mobile. In effect a state-financed new town programme, it was an enticing blend of nature and technology but politically unacceptable.[55]

In a root-and-branch condemnation of Adams's plan, Mumford criticised its 'attempt to remedy a few of the intolerable effects' and its acceptance of 'the fact of unregulated and unbounded growth as "given"' as fainthearted and conceptually inadequate. Regarding the whole huge effort as utterly misconceived, he believed it played into the hands of speculators for its opportunistic identification with trends would 'protect and tenderly cherish the one function that all American cities have traditionally looked upon as the main end of human activity, namely, gambling in real estate'. In effect calling for the substitution of a socialist for a capitalist ethic, Mumford attacked the Plan's timidity on the role of government, which meant that 'it carefully refrains from proposing measures which would lead to effective public control of land, property values, buildings and human institutions, and leaves the metropolitan district without the hope of any substantial change'.[56]

Adams communicated a vigorous defence of the Plan but he and Mumford 'sailed past each other in the night'[57] – despite a common inheritance and their co-operation at Radburn. Adams looked to the realisation of the full potential of metropolis, Mumford to its abandonment: 'Let Leviathan go hang!'[58] Adams worked with the grain of America's business civilisation; the radicals nagged away, more or less impotently, at its flanks. This, the most significant of ameliorative-radical clashes, divided on the old dilemma facing reformers; the issue, as Adams understood, was:

Whether we stand still and talk ideals or move forward and get as much realisation of our ideals as possible in a necessarily imperfect society, capable only of imperfect solutions to its problems.[59]

The publication of the Regional Plan marked the peak of Adams's career; no future planning task could approach its magnitude and significance. In his last decade, he became an elder statesman of the profession and spent most of his time in Britain, though continuing to teach, write and research in the United States until 1938. He founded the Town and Country Planning Summer School (1933), was elected a Fellow of the Royal Institute of British Architects, was active in the National Housing and Town Planning Council and served on the Council of the Town Planning Institute until 1936 and on its Competitions and Professional Practice Committee until his death. In 1936–37, he was a member of the TPI's Committee on a National Survey and Plan – a forerunner of the Barlow Commission. The most significant of his institutional commitments, however, was to the Institute of Landscape Architects (now the Landscape Institute), formed by a handful of young practitioners in 1928. From New York, Adams warmly endorsed the move and on his return in 1931 was elected a Fellow, becoming President in 1937–39, inspiring its title, supervising the drafting of its constitution and contributing to its *Journal*. Influenced by its high status in America as a major environmental discipline, he conceived of landscape architecture as the art of creating as well as preserving beauty. Advocating the integration of landscaping into plans at their inception, he called for 'design and planting that is adaptable to new conditions in addition to such preservation of good landscape as is possible', urging a National Parks programme, parkways and 'freeways for fast traffic on new sites'. Raising the sights of British landscape architects, he insisted that their function was design rather than gardening and gave them an intellectual rationale and professional standing.[60]

Adams's London practice with F. L. Thompson was joined about 1925 by the architect E. Maxwell Fry and was dissolved in 1936, following Adams's serious illness two years earlier. By 1919, as a result of his North American experience, Adams was identifying himself as a landscape architect and thus the firm was a practical manifestation of his oft-proclaimed view that planning should be a team effort by representatives of all of the environmental professions. Adams, Thompson and Fry's work was chiefly in the form of advisory regional plans for joint committees of local authorities in surburban and rural south-eastern England. The regions were arbitrarily defined and not always satisfactory for the planners and there were already trends towards county-wide planning. The scope of the

plans was limited by the legislative straitjacket of the 1919 Housing
and Town Planning (Addison) Act, which still confined planning to
the control of new development. Despite these acknowledged
deficiencies, Adams was a strong defender of advisory regional
plans. They had advantages over statutory plans of speed of production and greater flexibility and comprehensiveness and were 'a
greater factor in promoting town planning on sound lines than is
commonly realised. They have a great value in developing good
feeling between adjacent authorities, in giving them a wider outlook,
and in co-ordinating proposals for the improvement of circulation
and the control of land uses and densities throughout large regions'.[61] Conforming to the conventional wisdom of the profession,
these reports (of which there were about a dozen between 1923 and
1931) were trend-modifying, land use, amenity and communications
plans, based on thorough surveys, common sense and an eye for the
landscape.[62] Proposing zones founded upon physical divisions and
existing uses, they sought the containment of urban growth around
existing nodes, defined by 'green girdles', the discouragement of
development in agricultural zones and the prohibition of building
(except by special consent) in 'special rural zones,' or areas of
outstanding natural beauty. Particular emphasis was placed on the
improvement of arterial road systems by widenings, by-passes and
new connections. Protection of amenity was also a major concern,
involving the control of building lines, heights and elevations, gar-
ages and advertisements, the preservation and planting of trees, and
the protection of historic and attractive places. The substantial
public acquisition of open spaces and co-operation with landowners
to preserve private open spaces were also recommended. In many
cases, the proposals on highways and open spaces were
implemented, the chief beneficiaries being the car-owning middle
class and landowners with an interest in the preservation of rural
England and the protection of property values.

One of the firm's earliest commissions was for a resource town for
5,000 people at Corner Brook, Newfoundland (1923). Skillfully
exploiting a rugged upland site, the plan had attractive architectural
groupings and low-density residential provision; unfortunately,
economic adversity prevented its substantial realisation.[63] A similar
enterprise was Kemsley industrial village near Sittingbourne, Kent,
designed mainly by Thompson, an expert in site planning. Notable
here was the elaborate screening between village and paper mill.[64] A
somewhat different engagement was at Edinburgh (1929–31),
where the reports were educative in nature, selling planning in
backward country. Appropriately, since they were in Geddes's ter-
ritory, the firm recommended a thorough civic survey, suggested

major land use patterns, main road improvements, and seafront amenities, to be followed by detailed district plans.[65] After the break-up of the partnership, Adams had little opportuntiy for large-scale plans but remained active up to his death in March 1940 at his country home in Sussex, where he had enjoyed gardening and the company of his family.

Thomas Adams was a Victorian classical liberal. His was 'a concept of society in which the self-reliance of the individual is regarded as of vital importance'.[66] Cherishing individual freedom and equality of opportunity, he distrusted the state, allowing it the power only to curb the abuse of freedom (as, for example, by slum landlords and speculators) and, in exceptional circumstances, the function of promoting individual enterprise by loans and the provision of a planned physical infrastructure. While acknowledging the imperfections of *laissez-faire*, it was his conviction that it was possible to ameliorate these without recourse to collectivism; his preferred alternative he characterised as 'associated-individualism,' or the voluntary co-operation of individuals in a common enterprise. Socialism he abhorred as destructive of individual liberty, efficiency, initiative and self-reliance and he deplored the collectivist tendencies of reform in modern Britain. He had, too, the Social Darwinist's belief in the value of the struggle for existence. A self-made and largely self-educated man, he was exceptionally well-read, notably in philosophy, political economy and poetry. Nevertheless, it was ever a matter of regret to him that he was not a university man and he was, therefore, particularly anxious in later life to associate himself, and his chosen profession, with the academic world. He had the progressive's faith in the innate goodness of man, in the power of education and publicity to expose evils and raise civic standards, optimism about the future and belief in the inevitability of progress. A confirmed Utilitarian he declared that 'our vision of the future . . . cannot be worthy unless it includes the concept of the greatest good of the greatest number'.[67] Coupled with this was a firm attachment to the use of scientific analysis to discern an identifiable and indivisible public good which could be satisfied by the application of scientific method, disinterested and objective.

Given his philosophical predilections, it is scarcely surprising that the keynote of Adams's planning was practicality. Eschewing utopianism as futile, he maintained that 'the best plan is the one which presents the highest ideals that can be realised in practice'.[68] While acknowledging the feasibility of political and economic planning, his own milieu was the physical environment and he outlined the scope of planning as 'nothing less than the control and direction, on scientific principles, of all forms of civic growth and all kinds of land development in the country as well as in the town'.[69] His objectives, though constant, were but vaguely expressed as the securing of health, convenience, amenity and efficiency in physical growth. Addressing himself particularly to the problem of planning in a democratic society, he conceded that 'Town Planning will always be limited in its ideals by what the public will agree to' yet he counselled no servile acceptance of prevailing public attitudes, for a principal function of the planner was educative – the gradual raising of the public's environmental awareness and standards. Though such possibilist planning may have been short on boldness and imagination, it implied an intimate and harmonious relationship between professionals and the laity which he conceived to be essential not only for the successful realisation of plans but also to the establishment of planning as a normal social function.[70] He insisted, too, that planning was a team game, for 'It is not within the capacity of any one man to do well what needs to be done in every phase of town and country planning'. Envisaging the planning process as the coordination of contributions from the various environmental professions, he came in mid-career to a conviction that planning was 'a distinct profession' and an identifiable academic discipline.[71] Experiential in origin, Thomas Adams's philosophy of planning was entirely pragmatic and therefore well adjusted to the nature of North Atlantic society. If his goals were irritatingly imprecise and his vision disappointingly limited, resulting in cautious, opportunist, ameliorative, trend-modifying plans, it was nonetheless in tune with mainstream planning thought in all three countries. Of his contemporary professionals, only Raymond Unwin, with his warm, social-democratic, aesthetic humanism, Patrick Abercrombie, an outstanding creative intellect, and possibly the *enfant terrible* of the profession, Thomas Sharp, had wider, more positive conceptions of the planning function.

Thomas Adams had two major deficiencies. In the first place, he failed fully to understand the social consequences of modern economic life in that it created a set of competing and frequently hostile social groups and did not permit the existence of a readily-perceivable, widely accepted and easily attainable common good. He assumed too uncritically that the interests of 'the best men' – the political and economic élite – were unbiased and coincident with the interests of the community. In particular, having little direct acquaintance with the working class, his schemes made inadequate provision for their needs. This was a function also of his second great defect. His negative conception of the role of government and his persistence with patently unsuccessful notions of philanthropy, voluntarism and 'associated individualism' or co-operation led to his consistent unwillingness and inability to provide sufficient means to realise some of his social goals – notably decent housing for the low-paid. His rejection of any effective form of collectivism was almost total and so emotional that it blinded him to the limited nature of the results to be obtained from the mere imposition of land use controls and minimum standards without the incorporation of physical planning into a co-ordinated package of positive economic and social measures aimed at the redistribution of resources within society.

Adams's planning technique advanced rapidly to maturity between 1906, when he was still identified with Garden City and its theme of universal population dispersal and industrial decentralisation, and 1916, when he was the first to articulate in America the idea of regional planning, necessary to render city planning effective. His concept of the region was rudimentary by comparison with today's sophisticated definitions, consisting simply of the economic and social hinterland of a great city or an area having common economic and social features and problems for which outline zoning, land use, communications, utility and recreation plans should be made. Coupled with his perception of regional planning, which he derived from his experiences with the Midland Towns Association, the Local Government Board and the Canadian Commission of Conservation, was his refinement of Howard's Garden City, 'recentralisation,' or the scientific distribution about a region of satellite communities which would act as decongestants yet give the advantages of an economical degree of concentration and at the same time avoid the wasteful scattered development resulting from unplanned dispersal. His plans were founded upon meticulous and systematic surveys and accurate mapping, bespeaking his surveying background and though conformist, displayed a fine eye for scenery; he was particularly adroit in the planning of topographically difficult sites, always working with rather than against nature, so that man's contribution to the landscape blended with that of nature, a quality attributable to his agrarian background. In step with the drift of planning thought in the North Atlantic world, and in the wake of the Great Depression, he came to a final appreciation of the need for a hierarchy of surveys and plans, proceeding from the general to the particular, from the national inventory of resources, outline communications and power systems, and broad division of the nation into urban, rural and 'wild country' zones, to the specific, statutory, local plan. He was in a better position than anyone to provide a comparative perspective on planning on both sides of the Atlantic and scattered throughout his voluminous writings are many indications of this trans-Atlantic traffic in ideas. In North America a strong advocate of Garden City ideals and methods of planning, he brought back to Britain the American parkway. He gave to each side of the Atlantic a son who was to become the leader of the next generation of planners. In Britain, his eldest son James, County Planning Officer for Kent, was elected to the Presidency of the Town Planning Institute at the same time, 1948–49, as his younger brother Fred, Chairman of the Department of City Planning at MIT, became the head of the American Institute of Planners.

After his death in 1940, Adams slipped quickly into obscurity. Planning thought, technique and policy advanced rapidly far beyond the standards of the pioneer generation, yet Thomas Adams was responsible for many of the foundation stones upon which today's elaborate planning structure rests. His career would be memorable if only for his remarkable collection of 'firsts'. Beginning with the Presidency of the British Amateur Press Association in 1891, he was the first paid official of the Garden City Association, the first full-time planning consultant, the first Town Planning Inspector, and the founder and first President of both the British and Canadian Town Planning Institutes. Never out of the top half-dozen of British planners during his career, he was the undoubted giant of Canadian planning between 1914 and 1923 and in America between 1920 and 1930 he attained pre-eminence over indigenous practitioners. Vital to the early realisation of the Garden City idea, he later established the pattern of central government relations with local planning authorities. Though his impact on Canada was short-lived, it was, during his sojourn there, considerable and galvanised the infant Canadian planning movement into greater activity than it was to experience again until well after his death. The effective founder of modern American planning education, he directed the greatest planning venture in the union before the Tennessee Valley Authority and helped shape the American planning profession through his founding role in and Vice-Presidency of the American City Planning Institute. No one of his generation did more to institutionalise and professionalise planning in the North Atlantic area. His prolific speaking and writing career communicated the gospel of planning to an enormous number of people. His textbooks, monographs and planning reports were the basic diet of a whole generation of students on both sides of the Atlantic. Simply conceived and perhaps lacking in profundity, they represented the distillation of thirty years' practical experience and were couched in a dignified if occasionally ponderous Macaulayan prose (another trait from his Edinburgh background). It was in Adams's day an occupational hazard of the profession that many plans were totally or mainly unrealised and he had his share of disappointments.

Nevertheless, a substantial number of the features of the Regional Plan of New York were carried out, together with many of the highway and open space recommendations of his inter-war regional plans in Britain and the partial fulfilment of several of his garden suburb projects.

Thomas Adams's planning philosophy was rather ordinary, his plans conventional and he was rarely far ahead of his colleagues in technique and conception, but he was a first-rate publicist and organiser and a very capable synthesiser of the thought and practice of his day. Though much of his technique and many of his ideas have long ceased to be relevant, today's planners might remember that he was never a mere technician; planning for Thomas Adams was always a means towards the improvement of the quality of people's lives and environment. Moreover, he was ever mindful of the need for professionals to conduct a sympathetic dialogue with the people they served and not to plan in a vacuum, unaware of current social attitudes and possibilities. Thomas Adams well deserves his place in the pantheon of major pioneers of modern planning on both sides of the Atlantic.

Acknowledgements

I wish to acknowledge the assistance of the family of Dr Adams, my colleagues at Swansea, the Leverhulme Trust Fund, the Wolfson Foundation, the RIBA, and the United States International Communication Agency. I am particularly indebted to several Canadian scholars, notably Lloyd Evans, David Hulchanski and John Taylor. For permission to consult their archives, I would like to thank the National Housing and Town Planning Council, the Landscape Institute, the Town and Country Planning Association, the Royal Town Planning Institute and its Librarian, John Barrick, the Garden City Museum at Letchworth and its Curator, Doreen Cadwallader, and the Canadian Institute of Planners.

Notes

1 Adams, *The Garden City*, June 1907, p349
2 GCA, Memo. by Secretary, 8 January 1904 (Garden City Museum, Letchworth)
3 I am indebted to Mervyn Miller for information on this matter.

4   GCA, Secretary's Report on Organisation, 9 October 1905; Memo. by Herbert Warren, nd.
5   *Western Mail*, 17 September 1903
6   J. St. Loe Strachey, 'In Search of the £150 Cottage', *The County Gentleman*, 1 October 1904
7   Adams to Directors, 10 November 1904, *Adams Papers*
8   *The Garden City*, December 1906, January, February and May 1907
9   Adams, 'State, Regional and City Planning in America', p3, *Adams Papers*
10 Marquess of Salisbury to Adams, 15 October 1909, *Adams Papers*
11 File HLG 29/96, Public Record Office
12 Adams, 'State, Regional and City Planning in America', pp4–5, *Adams Papers*
13 Town Planning Institute (TPI), *Minute Book of Council*, 1913–32
14 Adams, 'Some Recent Developments in Town Planning', JTPI, 1914–15, p144
15 R. Unwin, L. P. Abercrombie, TPR, 1914, pp261–5
16 *Conservation of Life* (later *Town Planning and Conservation of Life*, TPCL), October 1914, pp27–8
17 C. A. Hodgetts, Commission of Conservation Annual Report (CCAR), 1912, p130
18 Adams, *Rural Planning and Development*, Ottawa, 1917, pp1–13, 44–9
19 Civic Improvement League, *Urban and Rural Development in Canada*, Ottawa, 1917, pp72–8
20 Sir Clifford Sifton, CCAR, 1917, pp10–12
21 J. C. Weaver, 'The Reconstruction of the Richmond District in Halifax', *Plan Canada*, March 1976, pp36–47
22 Adams, 'The Town of Kipawa', *Canadian Engineer*, 27 February 1919
23 Adams, 'Regional and Town Planning', NCCP, Niagara Falls/Buffalo. 1919, pp77–101
24 Adams, 'Report on Housing', 16 November 1918, *Adams Papers*
25 JTPIC, October 1920, p8
26 TPCL, October 1919, p75
27 JTPIC, April 1921, pp4–5
28 Adams, 'Ottawa Town Planning' and 'Lindenlea', vol 4, *Cauchon Papers*, National Archives of Canada
29 Town Planning Institute of Canada (now Canadian Institute of Planners), *Minute Book 1*
30 JTPIC, April 1926, pp1–5
31 N. Cauchon, 'President's Address', TPIC, 14 May 1925, vol 2, *Cauchon Papers*
32 Arthur Meighen to G. W. Fenwick, Prince George, B.C., 5 May 1921, vol 30, *Meighen Papers*, National Archives of Canada
33 Burditt to Adams, 26 February 1919, *Burditt Papers*
34 JTPIC, November 1923, p10
35 H. Carver, 'Town Planning in Canada', JTPI, 1957, pp13–14
36 K. Gerecke, 'The History of Canadian Planning', *City Magazine*, Summer 1976, p13

37 Gerecke, *op cit*, p20
38 Carver, *op cit*, pp13–14
39 Adams, 'State, Regional and City Planning in America', p7, *Adams Papers*
40 Correspondence between Adams and Dean Emerson of MIT, 1921
41 Adams, 'A Twentieth Century Career: Town and Country Planning, II', *Journal of Careers*, July–August 1937, p426
42 D. A. Johnson, *The Emergence of Metropolitan Regionalism: An Analysis of the 1929 Regional Plan of New York and Its Environs* (unpublished PhD, Cornell, 1974), pp26–95, 390
43 Adams, *The Regional Plan of New York: I, The Graphic Regional Plan* (New York, 1929), p358; *RPNY: II, The Building of the City* (1931), p42
44 H. Wright, 'To Plan or Not to Plan', *Survey Graphic*, 10 October 1932, p468
45 C. D. Norton, 'Proposal for the Creation of a Plan of New York', 31 January 1921; Norton to F. A. Delano, 24 November 1921; correspondence between Norton, Delano (later Chairman, Regional Plan Committee), J. M. Glenn (Director, Sage Foundation) and Adams, 21 August 1922, 9–20 June 1923, box 43, *RPNY Papers*
46 T. Adams, *Graphic Regional Plan*, pp126–8, 131, 312
47 T. Adams, 'Regional Planning in Relation to Public Health', *American Journal of Public Health*, November 1926, p1114
48 Johnson, *op cit*, pp506–16
49 Adams et al, *The Regional Survey of New York and Its Environs*, 8 vols, New York, 1924–31
50 D. H. Burnham and E. H. Bennett, *The Plan of Chicago*, Chicago, 1909, reprinted New York, 1970, p4
51 T. S. Hines, *Burnham of Chicago: Architect and Planner*, New York, 1974, p327
52 T. Adams, *Graphic Regional Plan*, p132; *Building of the City*, p35
53 T. Adams, 'A Communication in Defense of the Regional Plan', *New Republic*, 6 July 1932, p208
54 Adams to Lewis Mumford, 9 January 1930, box 30, *RPNY Papers*
55 State of New York, *Report of the Commission of Housing and Regional Planning*, Albany, NY, 1926
56 L. Mumford, 'The Plan of New York', *New Republic*, 15 and 22 June 1932
57 Johnson, *op cit*, pp365–83
58 L. Mumford, 'Wilt Thou Play with Leviathan?', *New Republic*, 24 January 1923
59 T. Adams, *New Republic*, 6 July 1932
60 *Landscape and Garden*, Summer 1935, Summer 1936, Autumn 1936, Winter 1938
61 T. Adams, *Recent Advances in Town Planning*, London, 1932, p64
62 For complete list see J. D. Hulchanski, *Thomas Adams: A Biographical and Bibliographical Guide*, Papers on Planning and Design, no15, Dept. of Urban and Regional Planning, University of Toronto, April 1978, pp38–40

63 T. Adams, *Recent Advances*, pp162–3
64 R. Whitten and Adams, *The Neighborhoods of Small Homes*, Cambridge, Mass., 1931, p135
65 T. Adams, Thompson and Fry, *Intermediate Report on Plan of Development of Granton-Cramond Area*, London, 1930; *Final Report on Town Planning*, 1931
66 T. Adams, 'State, Regional and City Planning in America', p3, *Adams Papers*
67 JTPIC, April 1921, p3
68 T. Adams, 'State, Regional and City Planning in America', p9
69 T. Adams, 'Town Planning in Canada', JTPI, 1917–18, p15
70 T. Adams, *Recent Advances*, p16
71 T. Adams, *Journal of Careers*, July–August 1937, p426

3

PATRICK GEDDES
1854–1932

Helen Meller

Sir Patrick Geddes is a well-known figure. Yet there are considerable difficulties involved in assessing the contribution he made to the town planning movement. He thought of himself, first and foremost, as a pioneer British sociologist who became caught up with the town planning movement, because it seemed to offer a practical way of implementing what he considered to be the purpose of sociology: discovering new laws of social development for the future. The concept of town planning, which he extended to a wider interpretation encompassing the direction of urban life as a whole, seemed to promise the possibility of reconciling the ways of evolution, the biological concept which had dominated Geddes's early training as a natural scientist, with the social progress of mankind.

As a sociologist, however, both then and now, Geddes was completely disregarded. His 'social philosophy' was a hotch-potch of ideas which he picked up and tried, though never succeeded, in welding into a satisfying whole.[1] His genius lay in another direction altogether. He looked for the practical implications of new knowledge and, in doing so, he opened up vistas of new possibilities to those engaged in concrete or practical disciplines.[2] Geographers and planners particularly, were greatly stimulated by his broader approach to specific problems. He made up for weaknesses in his theory and methodology by his acute powers of observation, and his individual stance, outside any of the social and political movements of his day, gave him the freedom to interpret his observations, like a field naturalist at large, observing natural phenomena. In this way, Geddes was able to make some discoveries about the 'human' organism and its environment, about modern society and the city, which gained him a cult following in his lifetime, and subsequently, a revered place amongst the founding fathers of the British town planning movement.

Yet the nature of his discoveries has been but rarely discussed. His central preoccupation, stimulated by his belief in the concept of evolution, was to discover more about the relationship between social processes and spatial form, between the social development of the individual and the cultural and physical environment most conducive to achieving the optimum in this respect. Geddes was nothing, if not ambitious. His overriding self-confidence and a belief in the importance of the natural sciences as the key to a whole new understanding of the human condition, were the twin supports that he leant on when tackling his mammoth task. But whilst he was prepared to rush headlong into the infinite complexities of his self-appointed life's work, he kept his feet on the ground by developing his ideas through practical work.

The activities he engaged in, in his attempt to establish a theory of life through a combination of theory with action, brought him into the town planning movement. His concern for the sociological implications of mass urbanisation and town planning, however, has to be seen especially against the background of developments in the natural and social sciences, and in contemporary concern over the slow rate of social progress and widespread evidence of social problems to be found in the growing cities from the 1870s and 1880s. It was always Geddes's preoccupation with the former that guided his responses to the latter. It was his overriding interest in the concept of evolution and its possible application to human development which directed his attention to the greatest social change of his lifetime, the movement of the majority of the population of Britain from the countryside into the cities.

Geddes became fascinated by the idea that the city was a social and cultural environment which could dictate the possibilities of the future because of its own inherent potential or limitations. This idea was part of a general framework of ideas on social evolution which Geddes shared with many of his contemporaries. There was a wide diversity in approaches to the development of sociological thought in the formative period of the social sciences from 1870–1914. But there was an overall dominance of biology as the most suitable guide for the study of the social sciences which Geddes was particularly receptive to, as a trained natural scientist. The term 'sociology' was used mostly to refer to attempts to define the laws of social development.[3]

This positivist legacy of Comte has been taken up and extended by the most influential late nineteenth century British social philosopher, Herbert Spencer. Spencer provided a new insight into the nature of society for eager young social evolutionists, such as Geddes became in the late 1870s and 1880s. Instead of seeking the facts of the historical development of human society which led to the present, Spencer sought the 'organic laws' which predetermined the course that development had taken.[4] If these could be identified, then it was possible not only to understand the present in a new way but also to predict the future. 'I take but little interest in what are called histories', Spencer wrote, 'but am interested only in Sociology, which stands related to these so-called histories much as a vast building stands related to the heaps of stones and bricks around it'.[5]

Spencer's attempt to create the 'vast building' of society became less influential with the passing of years, since the evidence rarely supported the elaborate structure he had created. Yet Spencer's failure did not deter others, including Geddes, from trying. Positivist thinking and the concept of evolution promised that such an exercise was possible, if only the method could be found.[6] Geddes's rival, L. T. Hobhouse, who beat him to the first Chair of Sociology in Britain, the Martin White Chair of Sociology at the London School of Economics, founded in 1907, shared this view. They, and many others, believed that great evolutionary forces were shaping society, regardless of all political attempts to control and direct changes, and despite the growth of new administrative machinery, and state and local bureaucracies. Even revolutionary movements were puny and powerless in comparison with such factors as the advances in scientific knowledge and technology which were unleashing new sources of energy; new means of production and transport; breakthroughs in agriculture and medicine. Change on this level was transforming every element of social existence.

Those concerned with social evolution had to take a proper view of these factors since they were the key to the future. To do this, however, was not easy. It required a general over-view of change, so that short-term contemporary concerns could be seen in the context of long-term change. Students of social development following the trails of Hobhouse and Geddes had, somehow, to distance themselves from the immediate scene and to place themselves on some Olympian height to observe change clearly. This was widely believed to be essential if humanity was ever to gain a measure of control over its destiny and good forces were to be cultivated to the detriment of the bad. Hobhouse, with more academic discipline and intellectual rigour than Geddes, produced a series of weighty monographs trying to achieve this vision and this objectivity.[7] His work provides a good basis for understanding Geddes's sociological perspective even though Geddes came independently to similar ideas and incorporated many theories from French social scientists and geographers in his intellectual rag-bag on evolutionary forces.[8]

Hobhouse, in fact, invented a concept of 'orthogenic evolution' which could well stand as the objective of Geddes's practical work, his 'applied sociology'. 'Orthogenic evolution' was a form of evolution compatible with Progress. In simple terms, evolutionary change could take place on three different levels. On the lowest level, the adjustment of action to the ends of the individual or the species was wholly instinctive, based on a pattern of inherited behaviour, determined by the operation of natural selection. At the next level, such instinctive action could be modified by learnt behaviour. At the highest level, self-conscious intelligence was a potentially determining factor. Only man was capable of this highest level. 'Orthogenic evolution' was thus the process of awakening and utilising the latent possibilities of the human mind, for the greater benefit of mankind.[9]

Two elements of Hobhouses's 'orthogenic evolution' were central to Geddes's way of thinking and working. The highest achievement produced by evolution was man's intelligence. Geddes had a lifelong interest in the nature of creativity and the nurture of intelligence, and he tried to approach the subject in an evolutionary way.[10] He was hostile to conventional forms of education because he believed they stifled instinct and intuition, of key importance to creativity. He sought for answers as to how to nurture intelligence by finding out the circumstances in which the greatest intellects of the past had flourished. An important, though rather dubious, element in Geddes's 'regional survey' technique was his willingness to mix historical data and environmental circumstances to provide evidence for his evolutionary approach.[11]

The second element of 'orthogenic evolution', which accounted for Geddes's missionary zeal in his work, was its rooting in moral values. As Dr Collini, Hobhouse's biographer points out, the concept of 'orthogenic evolution' 'rests on spiritual truth and must be applied by a moral force . . . universalistic humanitarianism is presented as the moral aspect of the stage of self-conscious development, the goal towards which "orthogenic evolution" is moving'.[12] It was no accident that one of Geddes's closest collaborators and disciples, V. V. Branford, tried to expound Geddes's social theory in a monograph entitled *Science and Sanctity: A Study in the Scientific Approach to Unity* (1923). If evolutionary forces were to be shaped by human intellect, or at least the intellect of the Olympians who could discern them, then common commitment to humanity was essential to the nurture of the good over the bad.

Geddes had to be Prophet and Priest as well, if he wanted to be a 'practical' social evolutionist.[13] It was a role he did not mind playing, his character and upbringing helping him to find it congenial.[14] Hobhouse wrote, of the role of the sociologist, that just as the botanist studies the development of plant species, seeking to understand the laws whereby it reaches perfection of form so 'does the sociologist with the human species; he treats it as something that has evolved and is evolving, and he seeks to discover what further developments it holds in germ. In this way, the study of growth, human evolution, is to the humanitarian spirit, what botany is to the gardener, who would not only bring the flowers that he has to the summit of their perfection, but would seek to derive from them new and more beautiful varieties'.[15] As gardener, natural scientist and practical sociologist, Geddes lived out this belief.

Neither Geddes nor Hobhouse questioned the teleological assumptions they were making to sustain these views, Hobhouse finding refuge in his understanding of liberalism as a political and social creed, Geddes seeking, not an intellectual haven, but the practical outcome of his sociological perspective. They both developed their ideas in the 1880s, in the great decade of national concern over the 'social question', though their differences in age and circumstances contributed greatly to the nature of their responses. Hobhouse went up to Oxford, aged 19 in 1883, and did not leave the academic world until 1897. Geddes however, much as he desired to acquire academic status with a chair in the natural sciences, consistently failed to get one. Between 1880 and 1889, aged 26 to 35, he remained a demonstrator in the Edinburgh School of Medicine and part-time lecturer in Zoology at the University.

During this time, Geddes published prolifically. In his own field in the natural sciences, he published a series of scientific papers and articles on evolution (some for the *Encyclopaedia Britannica* and *Chambers Encyclopaedia*) culminating in his first major work, a monograph aimed at the general reader, *The Evolution of Sex* which he wrote in collaboration with J. Arthur Thomson. This last work gained him a certain amount of notoriety, as Geddes allowed himself some discussion on human reproduction at the end of the volume. However, apart from a mild recommendation that the birth rate should be limited in favour of quality rather than quantity, the work was unexceptional.[16]

Geddes also, however, produced a series of articles on a variety of non-scientific subjects, such as his views on economics; on the contribution of John Ruskin; on the irrelevance of the debate between capitalism and socialism; even on art exhibitions in Glasgow and Manchester.[17] These were exercises in his own evolutionary development, breaking through his personal limitations as a scientist. They were also formative essays in which Geddes worked out his socio-biological approach to social problems. To test his ideas, Geddes undertook a number of practical activities, reacting spontaneously to the circumstances in which he found himself in Edinburgh. Although these activities were very varied, Geddes treated them as separate though related elements of his socio-biological approach. Theory and practice of these early days in the 1880s and early 1890 were thus welded together to become the system which Geddes labelled 'Civics: as applied sociology'.[18] It was to be the basis of his planning philosophy.

Geddes's path towards his goal was highly idiosyncratic. Whilst his activities led him step by step towards involvement with the British town planning movement, he had not started out with this objective in mind. His interest was in social evolution, his mission, to use his biological knowledge to improve organism and environment, people and the conditions they lived in, so that 'orthogenic evolution' could take place. The most original element in his approach was his belief that he was progressing in the right direction by testing his ideas out in practice, linking action with thought, though the link was sometimes sustained more by faith than fact. An early example, however, of how fruitful this could be, was Geddes's use of the geographical concept of the region, as a unit for the study of social, cultural and environmental factors.[19]

The elements which brought Geddes to an awareness of the region as an analytical unit were numerous. His early training in the natural sciences was perhaps the strongest. Botanists and zoologists, with an interest in the concept of evolution, had been studying flora and fauna in their natural habitat for many years; and T. H. Huxley, Geddes's teacher, had used a regional approach, particularly utilising the Thames basin, when writing his biological textbooks.[20] However, Geddes added to this his own personal response, part eccentric, part building on a wider experience of the possibilities of the regional concept. Eccentricity was foremost when, in 1883, he became fascinated by the 'golden age' of Edinburgh University, celebrating its tercentenary that year. Why had the University helped Edinburgh become, in the late eighteenth century, the 'Athens of the North'? Why had there been such a cultural flowering, and what factors had produced individual scholars of such calibre?

For answers, Geddes turned for guidance to the French social scientists, Comte and Le Play. He tried to utilise Le Play's formula for analysing society – Lieu, Travail, Famille – which he translated as 'Place, Work, Folk,' and interpreted as environment, function and organism. Since many of Edinburgh's greatest scholars had been drawn from different areas of Scotland, Geddes began to develop the idea of the special nature of particular regions, and then to relate the region with the city. He began to feel his way towards the idea that city and its region were intimately related and to understand one, it was necessary to understand the other. If the city was an organism, its region was its habitat. The basic idea behind Regional Survey was born.[21]

Whilst Geddes made this his idea, the concept of the region as a geographical and economic unit had already well penetrated intellectual circles on the continent, particularly in Germany and in France. The unification of Germany, and the wars which led up to it, had concentrated attention on the significance of the region, the location of raw materials and industries, even in political circles. In the aftermath of the Franco-Prussian war, renewed efforts were made to modernise the French economy, building on the newly established railway network. This had brought the great regions of that country into closer contact than ever before, creating national markets and encouraging regional development.[22] Geddes had witnessed some of this revitalisation process, having arrived in Paris in 1878 in time to attend the Paris Exhibition of that year, celebrating the progress that had been made since 1870. He was also aware of the new surge of activity in universities and agricultural institutes in France, with the creation and expansion of regional colleges and universities; and in Paris, the growing development of the social sciences as acceptable academic disciplines.

What he made of all this was the germ of the idea of Social Reconstruction which was to become his mission as his ideas on 'civics: an applied sociology' crystallised.[23] But in the 1890s, he pursued his interest in the geographical region as a key element in his socio-biological approach. His ability to attract famous geographers to his summer school, particularly on two occasions the veteran of the Paris Commune, M. Elisée Reclus, made his summer meetings a venue for those interested in geography, since it was a totally neglected subject in academic circles in Britain.[24] Geddes felt a certain rivalry with H. J. Mackinder, who was given the post of director of the first Geographical Institute at Oxford, supported by the Royal Geographical Society. Mackinder appointed A. J. Herbertson, one of Geddes's Edinburgh *protégés*, as a member of his staff. The Royal Scottish Geographical Society however, was firmly adamant in its refusal to support Geddes and make the Outlook Tower Scotland's first geographical institute.[25]

The Society, quite rightly, suspected that Geddes never had any real intentions to devote himself entirely to geography. He never lost sight of his initial objective, to discover the forces in social evolution. In the 1880s he had become aware of the great debate on poverty and the split which had opened up in philanthropic circles on the causes of poverty, between the moralists and the environmentalists.[26] The moralists, with their champion, C. S. Loch of the Charity Organisation Society, maintained that the poor were poor because of their moral failings. The environmentalists, amongst whom Canon S. A. Barnett of Toynbee Hall was one of the abler spokesmen, argued that the poor were poor because of their hostile urban environment.[27] At the centre of the debate was the problem of the housing of the poor, and in 1884 a Royal Commission was appointed to investigate the housing of the working classes. Barnett's mentor, Miss Octavia Hill, gave evidence to the Commission, based on her twenty years of effort to improve London's slums. Her message was that slums would always exist unless slum-dwellers were reformed, through the agency of caring landlords, who would reward good behaviour by renovating property and maintaining it in good condition. In her view, the personal relationship between lady rent-collector and tenants was the key to success or failure.[28]

It was a message with great appeal to Geddes (who made a visit to London to investigate Miss Hill's work) since it contained the promise of individual development with a close consideration of environment. Geddes, however, did not want to stop there. He was not so much interested in initiating Hill-type rent-collecting schemes in Edinburgh, as explaining to himself why the areas of the old city, which had housed the great men of the 'golden age' had now been reduced to slums, and, at the same time, Edinburgh was no longer the most glittering intellectual centre of north west Europe. Taking another leaf out of Miss Hill's book (whose sister had founded the Kyrle Society),[29] Geddes decided to make a practical start to arresting the decline by founding an Environment Society. Its aim was to beautify the old city by creating drinking fountains, adorning public places with pieces of sculpture, cultivating waste ground to make gardens and playgrounds, decorating elementary schools, and any other project which cost little and could be carried out with voluntary labour.

Geddes, however, could not work outside the realms of the philanthropic world since he constantly needed financial support. The Environment Society thus became transformed into the Edinburgh Social Union, a charitable organisation, based on the model of the London Charity Organisation Society. There was still support for Geddes's work in the old city. But the main aim of the Social Union was to relieve the needs of the poor by providing the most appropriate kind of relief, discovered through careful casework.[30] This was moving away from Geddes's interests. However, he continued to work on his renovating schemes, concentrating on the area of the city around the Royal Mile, which had plunged into a steady decline since the completion of Edinburgh's eighteenth century New Town. He went to live in a slum tenement with his wife and child, apparently echoing the work of Canon Barnett in the East End of London. Barnett, however, wanted the middle classes to live in the East End as a social bridge between the Two Nations, and his response to the physical environment of his parish was to flatten most of it, under powers given by the Cross Act of 1875.[31]

Geddes, however, was not concerned with the relationship between social classes. Living in a slum tenement was, in his case, a gesture to impress philanthropists, to encourage their continued support, and a way to gain first hand knowledge of what had to be done to renovate a slum and how to do it. He was very successful in raising money and with it he set about clearing up the tenements, repairing, renovating, whitewashing and lime-washing. He learnt by experience the techniques of reviving a run-down area, which he was to use again and again in his town planning reports. He found that revival was a slow, piecemeal activity, requiring constant attention, but mostly relatively low-cost. However, it was essential for success to involve the inhabitants and other volunteers in this ceaseless activity. Geddes, always trying to link theory with practice, was to seize on this as an indication of a pattern of social evolution, organism interacting with environment. It was to become a major plank of his planning philosophy.

The technique he based on this he called 'conservative surgery', a technique whereby place and people were left largely untouched, yet certain small adjustments were continually made here and there, with the active participation of inhabitants, to enhance the quality of the environment. It was a technique which worked well in old Edinburgh, where his work helped to reveal the great beauty and historic interest of the old houses which had become slums. However, Geddes was not wholly satisfied. The place improved but the people remained the uneducated inhabitants of slum tenements. How could they improve the cultural environment, a determining factor in the process of social evolution? Geddes decided that they could not, and practical as always, he hit upon the solution of buying up slum tenements and leasing them to university students as embryo halls of residence. In this way, he came to house university people within the same walls, or close by the same buildings, which had housed the great scholars of the 'golden age'.

This particular evolutionary experiment was to bring Geddes rich personal rewards. The English practice of providing student hostels or residential colleges for students had not spread to Scotland and Edinburgh students were scattered over the city in different lodgings. The first generation of students who came into Geddes's small halls of residence were thus deeply grateful to him, and some of them, particularly J. Arthur Thomson and Victor V. Branford, remained close friends, admirers and disciples of Geddes. The dedicated personal service they gave to him over the years was quite remarkable, Thomson collaborating with Geddes on all the articles and books the latter wrote in the natural sciences, Branford collaborating with him on sociological works and providing him with a platform in London, the British Sociologial Society,[32] from which to promote his views. Their help, and the help of Geddes's immediate family, especially his first wife, Anna, and their two sons, Alasdair and Arthur, was vital to his achievements in his publications, summer schools and exhibition work. In his town planning activities in India and Palestine he was greatly aided by H. V. Lanchester and F. C. Mears. It was, in fact, his chosen way of working. He liked to provide the ideas which other people then carried out.

He was never short of ideas. His evolutionist's concern over the quality of civilisation as he experienced it in Edinburgh set him on the path towards engineering a small cultural renaissance in the city in the 1890s. He established a publishing house, started a journal which lasted for four issues and encouraged the Edinburgh Art School, producing a rather contrived flowering of the Arts and Crafts movement in Edinburgh. Geddes's chosen artistic friend, John Duncan, was no Charles Rennie Mackintosh. However, Geddes's reputation for this work earned him the friendship of C. R. Ashbee, whom he was to come across again in Palestine in connection with his town planning activities there. Ashbee's Arts and Craft workshop in the East End was an attempt to provide an artistic spearhead for the kind of revolution so passionately advocated by William Morris.[33] Morris hoped that a socialist revolution would be accompanied by a raising of aesthetic standards and a return to the era of the highly skilled hand craftsman. Geddes, however, had no time for Morris's socialism. His revolution was to be socio-biological, a natural scientist's approach to the future. Not politics, but a proper use of resources was the Geddesian key to a better world.[34]

Geddes, in fact, was not entirely hostile to the economic forces unleashed by the industrial revolution. He welcomed the new means of transport, the railway and the steamship, which encouraged the movement of men and ideas; and the advances in knowledge of the environment and the human condition which were promising new wealth and new control over hunger, pain and suffering. But he was totally unsympathetic to the elements of the new system which led towards quantity rather than quality. He hated 'mass' production, the housing of the 'masses' in identical bye-law housing, the loss of individuality of place, as demolition removed old landmarks for the sake of new roads and railways. His own city, Edinburgh, had been barely touched by the methods of production brought by the Industrial Revolution. However, the railway had been built on the prime site of the filled-in loch which lay between the old city, dominated by the castle, and Prince's Street, which was the boundary of the

Georgian Edinburgh New Town. For Geddes, it was a salutary lesson on the need for greater control over the use of space and quality of the environment in the future.

The need to educate people to be more self-consciously in control of their own environment, however, was for Geddes more than a matter of straightforward conservation and rational planning for the future. Not content with his concern for 'place', as a true evolutionist he saw improvement in terms of 'higher and higher' individuation. Thus to educate people about their environment actually meant involving them in the process of control, as a crucial part of their own individual development. This was the link between the assorted activities, from his summer schools, the Outlook Tower museum, the Dunfermline Report, even the Cities and Town Planning Exhibition, all of which he himself saw as different ways of reaching this particular objective. To educate people about their environment was the most crucial element of a 'true' education. Education was defined, not in terms of academic achievements, but as a process of learning which was related to practical activity and engaged emotional responses.[35] This was the kind of learning which involved the 'whole man', stimulated creativity, and led to higher stages of evolution.

In his educational propaganda work, especially his summer school courses, in Britain and India, he reinforced the emotional impact of his approach by building his lecture programme in a special emotion-charged sequence. He began with a general low-key introduction to the idea of an evolutionary approach to cities and reached a climax at the end of the course with a consideration of the 'here and now' in the city in which the school was being held. In the 1890s it was Edinburgh. In 1900, it was Paris on the occasion of the World Fair. After the formation of the Cities and Town Planning Exhibition in 1910, it was whichever city invited him, from Edinburgh to Dublin, from Dublin to Madras, to many other cities in India, Palestine and in 1916, in Paris, at the famous Exposition Civique et Urbaniste: La Cité Réconstituée.

A good example of Geddes's approach can be illustrated by the syllabus of lectures he gave at Madras in 1915.

Cities in evolution
1.   CITIES IN GROWTH. – What is a Town, and what a City? the various answers to this question. What is the nature of Civic Growth and Progress? Theories of the City from Aristotle and Plato to Rousseau and Modern America; can we advance on these?
2.   CITIES IN DEVELOPMENT: (a) *as regards* MATERIAL CONDITIONS, of Situation, Industry and Population (*place, work, folk*).

Products of these, in 'Town', and in 'School', in 'People' and their immediate 'Governing class'. Historical and contemporary examples.
3.   CITIES IN DEVELOPMENT: (b) *as regards* PSYCHICAL CONDITIONS, of Ideals, Ideas, and Imagery, of Religions, Intellectual and Imaginative Arousal Products of these in 'Cloister', and of corresponding attainment, in 'City' proper. The City of the Muses.
4.   CITIES IN DETERIORATION. – Origin and Interaction of Evils: Unemployment and Misemployment, Poverty and Disease, Ignorance, Error and Folly, Vice and Crime, Indolence and Apathy, etc. The city plan as Chequer Board of good and evil.
5.   CITIES IN REVIVANCE AND RENEWAL.
Each City's life, viewed upon this Chequer Board, is thus an incessant and intricate strife of good and evil.
The City's plan viewed as a heritage from the past, is thus the record and resultant of these strifes. Viewed on the present, it is a dramatic situation, a theatre of struggles no less real than those of material wars, and in which we take varied and alternating parts. Viewed as a design, it is a plan of social campaign – that of the 'holy war' towards the 'City Beautiful,' the 'University of the Future,' or whatever other ideal we seek for. Examples from actual Cities.
What developments can we now plan, city by city, say definitely towards the post-industrial City, the post-Germanic University?
6.   MADRAS (Saturday morning, say 11 a.m.)
The City around us, viewed from the various view-points of the present course; and thus at once as centre of studies and of activities.

What Geddes hoped was that his lectures wouldstimulate the undertaking of a regional survey and that the data collected in the course of this work would be housed in a regional and 'civic' museum such as his Outlook Tower in Edinburgh. However no attempts were made anywhere to imitate the Outlook Tower,[36] probably because even the success of the Outlook Tower itself depended very largely on the presence of Geddes, inspiring his volunteers with his energy and enthusiasm. His ideas on how to carry out a regional survey were more successful in that his general approach was adopted by the loosely federated Regional Survey Association, founded in 1914 to promote regional surveys as an educational activity.
Geddes tried to convince people that his technique was more advanced than that of Booth and Rowntree,[37] even if there was no comparison in terms of the value of the data collected. He felt the collection of accurate data on social conditions was only a first step. The purpose of a survey should be to promote social service, though not in the conventional philanthropic sense of relieving needs.[38] Geddesian 'social service' was directed towards a better utilisation of the economic and social resources, revealed through survey work. Geddes had left the world of organised philanthropy behind even in

his Edinburgh days, in his quest for the evolutionary forces in modern society. He thankfully recognised in the town planning movement the kind of milieu in which his interpretation of social service might flourish. Geddesian 'applied sociology' was a form of social engineering, though without a specific objective like Howard's Garden City movement, the Bournville village experiment, or Hampstead Garden suburb's 'social mix'. Geddes could absorb all these ideas where he felt they fitted into his larger pattern of 'orthogenic' evolution. He always held fast, however, to the evolutionist's general overview.

Thus, when he did undertake any planning activity there was a curious remoteness in Geddes's approach. An early example of this was Geddes's venture to Cyprus in 1897, at the height of the troubles there, created by the Armenian refugees fleeing from the threat of genocide from the Turks. Here was a classic case when 'social peace' was threatened and Geddes set off for Cyprus, uninvited, but convinced he could offer some practical solutions. He and his wife toured the island, assessing in a rough fashion the extent of the problem, and attempting to initiate cottage industries and agricultural activities suited to the region. The provision of mulberry tree saplings and silk worms to start a cottage silk industry was a favourite solution as Geddes felt that making silk was the best method, in eugenic terms, of textile production, since it depended on good social practices with evolutionary potential. The relief funds he had raised for these projects, however, soon ran out and an attempt to form a commercial company to try and carry on the good work was not a success.

Geddes, however, regarded his approach as the sensible, practical way to bring about lasting solutions, and he tried to do the same kind of thing wherever 'social peace', the Le Playist objective, was threatened. One of his more impressive attempts at this was in Ireland in the years leading up to and including the First World War. Geddes was not uninvited this time, as by now his reputation had grown in stature. Between 1900 and 1910 his work had become increasingly well known, helped by the publicity of his International Summer School at the World Exposition in Paris in 1900; his papers on 'Civics: as applied Sociology' (the credo of the Geddesian sociobiological approach) given at the well-publicised first conferences of the British Sociological Society in 1904, 1905 and 1906; the publication of his planning report for Dunfermline in 1904; and finally his appointment as Director of the Cities and Town Planning Exhibition of 1910. The city of Dublin provided a favourable setting for a Geddesian social experiment since, as a colonial city, the free play of social and political factors was stifled and Geddes, with his non-political approach, was welcomed by all – the British officials and the Irish leaders.

He came at the invitation of the wife of the Viceroy, Lady Aberdeen, who was responsible, as President of the Women's National Health Association of Ireland, for organising the annual congress of the Institute of Public Health to be held in Dublin. Geddes found that an interest in public health by philanthropic persons proved an ideal audience for his socio-biological approach. He introduced them to the idea of the need for garden playgrounds for children to be made out of the derelict sites of the town's crowded quarters. Three were created in Dublin, sponsored and manned by volunteer labour of the Women's National Health Association. The members of the same Association enthusiastically supported the forming of a Housing and Town Planning Association for Ireland and the NHA itself began a collection of Housing and Town Planning Exhibits for its Health Exhibition.[39] Geddes became fascinated by the idea of initiating schemes which were an urban equivalent of Sir Horace Plunkett's Irish Agricultural Organisation Society. He hoped to undertake urban renewal along lines similar to Plunkett's ambition 'to consider the means, outside politics, by which the material prosperity of Ireland might be stimulated'.[40]

Geddes worked through his contacts with the Viceroy and his Lady, and the Women's NHA for whom he acted as expert advisor on Housing and related matters. His biggest coup in Ireland, the setting of the competition for a plan for the future of Dublin, subsequently won by Patrick Abercrombie, has received most publicity.[41] Yet the main thrust of his work in Dublin was in urban renewal schemes which he was able to promote with the help of the philanthropic sanitarians. His work in Ireland, however, was interrupted first by the First World War, and then the Easter Rising. Typically, Geddes held political and economic factors in such low esteem, that he believed he might have averted insurrection in 1916 if only he had devoted more time, energy and resources to his 'socio-biological' activities, improving the physical, social and cultural environment of the poor in Dublin.[42]

However, during the First World War, the vast new field of the Indian sub-continent opened up before him when Geddes received an invitation from Lord Pentland to go to Madras. What tempted him in this prospect was the possibility it held for exploring the evolutionary patterns of Indian cities formed by totally different, alien cultural traditions. In 1913 he had perfected his interpretation of 'Cities in Evolution' in exhibition form, winning the Gold Medal of the civic section at the International Exhibition at Ghent and he had already written his monograph of that title, even though it was not to be published until 1915.[43] India, politically and economically underdeveloped, offered him a chance that his socio-biological approach to urban problems might find a more fertile response than he had found even in Dublin. An optimist by nature, Geddes was very willing to give it a try.

His work, in what was to be his most productive decade in town planning (from 1914–24), was very varied and uneven in quality. He began as a propagandist for the town planning movement; progressed towards becoming a practical planner, and the products of his labour, his town planning reports became the basis for his subsequent reputation as an exponent of planning philosophy. The original Cities and Town Planning Exhibition was lost on its way to India, sunk by enemy action. However, friends in Britain, co-ordinated by H. V. Lanchester (then editor of *The Builder* and soon to join Geddes in India as the first town planning officer in Madras and assistant to Geddes elsewhere) were able to send further material to form a new exhibition, since anything could be incorporated into Geddes's evolutionary patterns.

Geddes then proceeded to take the second Cities and Town Planning Exhibition to the major presidency cities of Madras, Bombay and Calcutta, and to visit towns and cities, especially in the princely states, by special invitation. From this propaganda work was to spring Geddes's commissions for plans as he gained the reputation of being the expert on modern town planning in India, and everywhere he went, he always promised to cost less than the municipal surveyors, army engineers or medical officers who were the only other experts available for consultation on urban problems. New cities using Western urban forms, like the iron and steel centre of the Tata industrial empire, Jamshedpur, and the new imperial capital of the Raj, New Delhi, were still in their infancy. Colonial status had created special urban forms, particularly the addition of military and civil lines to older Indian cities.[44] But urban problems such as mounting traffic congestion and deteriorating standards of public health (the plague could not be completely confined to native quarters) had awakened governors and municipalities to the need for new measures.

Geddes had decided very quickly, within weeks of his arrival, what these should be, as he worked on his first town planning commission in India, which was to lecture to and instruct the borough surveyors of the state of Madras. In India, he was able to side-step the British 'housing and social reform' approach to planning which lay behind such experiments as Cadbury's Bournville and Ebenezer Howard's Garden City scheme. Instead he could go straight for solutions based on his 'biological' approach. In essence, what this amounted to was as follows: the physical environment had to be considered in terms of its location, climate, geological structure and historical use. Equally, the inhabitants had to be considered in terms of their economic activities, social structure and cultural heritage. Cities had to be viewed as 'whole' organisms and it was essential to preserve the best of the old features and traditions as it was to introduce new ones. Great respect must be given to cultural influences as these were crucial evolutionary factors, and for social evolution to be progressive, the best must survive and thrive.[45]

Starting from this theoretical, but highly generalised position, Geddes then exercised his considerable powers of observation and ingenuity to find solutions to the key problems which people were clamouring for him to solve. The latter were of three kinds: the problems of public health in a hot climate; congestion and over-crowding in central areas; and the layout of new areas for urban growth. All three he tried to approach by utilising the best solutions used in the past; by gaining the co-operation of the people; and by renovating and restoring central areas to what they had been before dereliction, decay and overcrowding had overtaken them. His favoured method was to deal with them all simultaneously.

Writing of Coimbatore, he suggests how this might be done. 'Here in old towns, we have undeniable overcrowding in crooked, narrow old lanes; but the solution is not by removing people into yet more monotonous roads and lanes, with house spaces often of smaller average area than before, and with their overcrowding also too commonly increased as well. How then shall we proceed? First by widening out these old lanes, here and there as occasion affords, into homely little thoroughfares, opening now and then into pleasant squares, with tree and shrine; also of housing the comparatively few displaced people, by helping them to help themselves to new and better houses, and bigger gardens than before. One is asked . . . "How can this pay?" First, with better town-planning, and the diminished waste of costly roads and more than proportional addi-tion, sometimes even doubling, of site-space which this allows. Sec-ond, with Housing Bank; and, thirdly, whenever possible, with Homely Labour.'[46] Geddes's approach to the need for capital and labour echoes Sir Horace Plunkett's Irish Agricultural Organisation Society. Yet besides such voluntary activities there were also State-sponsored schemes for rural renewal, such as those carried out in Denmark since the 1860s, and the extension of cooperative ventures in Germany and France,[47] all of which were possible models for the Geddesian version of urban renewal. Geddes wanted a combination of cooperative schemes and voluntary effort to maximise and improve the resources of the urban environment, since the most valuable crop of all, future generations of humanity, were to be produced there.

Geddes's 'biological' approach to urban problems was seen to best advantage in India.[48] In the mainly rural sub-continent, the cities were battlegrounds for the Western-trained engineers and surveyors, who found themselves struggling between their specialised knowledge and an alien physical and social environment in which to apply it.[49] For instance, the problem of a constant and pure water supply in some cities had completely defeated British engineers. In Indore, vast sums had been spent constructing reserve reservoirs to maintain the water supply during the dry season which did not yield a drop of water when required; whilst in other cities, like Lucknow, the monsoon brought damaging floods because insufficient attention had been paid to the need for storm drains and river control schemes. The age-old Indian custom in most towns and villages had been to build tanks or reservoirs which could be used for a multiplicity of purposes: as a source for water; for washing and bathing; as fish ponds; as safety valves to absorb the excess water during monsoons. Inevitably, however, such tanks sometimes became polluted and it was necessary to build new tanks, even to move the whole community to a new location. Meanwhile, the old tanks provided the ideal habitat for the mosquito.

When the mosquito was discovered to be the carrier of malaria, the solution adopted by the British was to fill in the tanks. It was the kind of solution to bring out the best in Geddes. His hatred of bureaucracy was confirmed by the insensitivity of this universal solution. It resulted in depriving some communities of their local facilities. It sometimes resulted in severe flooding during monsoons. It also destroyed some of the aesthetic charm of temple cities when the great temple tanks were filled in. Geddes was vociferous in his demand for the restoration of tanks and for effort to be expended on teaching the people how to keep the tanks clean and unpolluted, by stocking them with fish, planting their banks with the right kind of vegetation and encouraging the keeping of ducks which would feed on the mosquito larvae.

His solutions for problems of sewage disposal were equally 'biological' and unconventional.[50] He worked out a plan which he believed utilised an age-old practice and amended it in the light of modern knowledge. Indian custom was to commune daily with nature. Geddes suggested this should continue, but in an organised fashion. Rows of latrines should be placed in the fields and cash crops like tobacco, which required heavy fertilisation, could be subsequently grown there. This was a very cheap method of disposal compared with water-borne, piped sewerage and it would also actually increase the wealth of the community. What Geddes overlooked, however, was the difficulty of organising and maintaining such a scheme on a permanent basis among a people who might find it as hostile to their age-old traditions in this matter as a Western sewerage system.[51]

Geddes with his keen eye and strong practical sense, however, proved a useful man to consult on town planning schemes for the layout of new areas. But many of his town planning reports for existing cities were written in great haste after very brief visits. He wrote reports for towns in Madras and Bombay Presidencies after spending barely a day in any one of them. His Baroda Report was written after a couple of weekend visits. In his more lengthy reports, particularly the Indore Report, his *chef d'oeuvre*, more space is devoted, not to a detailed analysis of the city (no survey was carried out as Geddes pleaded lack of time and assistants) but to propaganda for the Geddesian biological approach to planning. It included a long section advocating a Geddesian style university for Central India (adopting an evolutionary approach to learning) to be located at Indore.[52]

In all his later reports, for Patiala or Colombo for instance, Geddes's idiosyncratic approach was reflected in his style and organisation of material. He did not organise his report around the solutions he put forward to the specific problems he had been asked to solve. Thus there were no chapters on traffic circulation or water supply, etc, on their own. Instead, his analysis followed the actual path he took on his visit to the city, starting with the approach, with comments on location and history, and arriving at the centre, slowly, dealing with problems on an *ad hoc* basis in what Geddes liked to think was the context of the city as a 'whole'. He was able to adopt this method because, wherever he went, he was rarely confronted by the problems of large scale urbanisation, or modern industrialisation, since there was very little modern industry to be found in the entire sub-continent.

The temple cities of the south,[53] the bazaar towns of the north, the carefully planned capital cities of the native states, gave Geddes patterns of Indian urbanisation which were rooted in history. One of his most important contributions was to try to open the eyes of the educated Indian and Briton alike to this precious legacy. Another was his expertise in renovating and beautifying the urban environment. Alongside his schemes for repairing the houses and streets of old quarters were schemes for gardens, parks, even in the case of Lucknow and Indore, of zoological gardens to enhance the beauty of the town and to offer better recreational facilities.

He tried always to be sensitive to the needs of the individual whilst still considering the city as a 'whole'. He attached as much importance to the siting of a tree in a small square for the benefit of local inhabitants as he did to a landscaping project for a zoo or university campus. He also considered that the cultural and religious functions of a city were of equal significance to its commercial and industrial activities. He was at his best, perhaps, in Lucknow, where, for his second report of 1916, he had the help of Lanchester to draft a detailed plan; and he could devote himself to his perambulations around the city, exploring every nook and cranny and meeting local officials and city worthies who became inspired by his enthusiasm. Lucknow was also a very beautiful old city, well-endowed with buildings of merit and untouched by modern industrialisation. Geddes's socio-biological approach, backed up by his personal energy and enthusiasm, was to achieve its greatest success there.

He tried to achieve his greatest personal success, however, at Indore. In a couple of visits lasting a few months, immediately after the death of his first wife, Anna, in the summer of 1917 and just a month or so after his eldest son was killed in action in France, he tried to put together a report which summed up his planning philosophy. In his letters he compared it with the Dunfermline Report of 1904 which had been a landmark in his 'action with theory' approach.[54] The Indore visits and report were an advanced exercise in initiating Geddesian style interaction between organism and environment, between place and people. The initial problem of Indore, the reason for his commission, was the incidence of plague. As a grain market for central India, Indore had more than her share of plague, carried by the black rats.

Geddes used a combination of practical commonsense and his flair for publicity to involve the people in his schemes, to overcome the problem. Control over the possible habitat for the rat was to be exercised by amalgamating the grain markets and locating them in one place where more stringent controls could be maintained over storage, and the keeping of cats could be encouraged. Education of the people on the need for cleanliness was carried out through a skilful use of their own customs and traditions. The religious festival of Diwali, which was a time for ritual cleansing, was made the occasion, in 1917 in Indore, of a big propaganda drive, mounted by Geddes, to encourage new standards of cleanliness in public places as well as private houses. Competitions were held, the support of the 'untouchable' sweepers enlisted, and, the climax of the proceedings, a massive procession mounted, dedicated to the elimination of the rat. A huge King Rat was carried in effigy, with plague fleas on its back, to be burnt at the end of the day in a large bonfire to the accompaniment of fireworks.[55] Geddes himself was Maharaja for the day, riding in the procession on a white elephant.

For Geddes, the Indore episode was the path towards 'orthogenic' evolution. However, he also sought the result, 'higher individuation' in a similarly self-conscious way, and he found it at that time, not in Indore, but in Calcutta, in the person of his closest Indian friend, Sir Jagadis Bose. Bose earned Geddes's great admiration, not only for his pioneering work in the natural sciences, but also for his struggle to establish and maintain his own research institute in Calcutta, against great odds. Geddes devoted some time to writing a biography of him, the chapters of which were organised to show the social evolution of the subject, from his rural childhood, urban education, to brilliant academic career, concluding with the opening of his research institute (at which Bose used a speech written by Geddes about India's double duty to preserve the best of its separate cultural identity and traditions whilst going forward into the future).[56] Geddes himself was the only European to be invited to attend the ceremony, which he did wearing Indian dress.

He was able to reach across the colonial barrier and even to make contacts with Indian nationalists such as Rabindranath Tagore and Mahatma Gandhi, with whom he corresponded. He could do this, partly because he was Scottish and not English, but mostly because he believed passionately that free individual development was essential for achieving higher levels of social evolution. He saw this higher stage in India, however, not in the political terms of the struggle against the British, but in social and cultural terms, relating to improvements in the physical and social environment. He was delighted when three hundred or so middle class Indians attending the annual Hindi Congress (one of Gandhi's publicity forums), held in Indore in 1918, gave their free time to helping Geddes with his civic activities.

Geddes and Gandhi respected each other, but their objectives were very different. Geddes however, continued his search for support for his ideas among British officials and Indian municipalities. He was to be continually disappointed. In vain were his efforts to point out that disturbances of the 'social peace', such as the rioting in the industrialising city of Cawnpore, were caused by the insensitivity of officialdom to social and cultural circumstances.[57] He felt that the time was ripe for his message but no-one would listen. The rapid changes occurring during the First World War encouraged him to transform his propaganda for 'civics: as applied sociology' into a crusade for social reconstruction.[58] It was a crusade which was to cut Geddes off from the town planning movement which, to succeed, had to come to terms with the political realities within which planners could operate.

Geddes threw himself into a publicity drive for the Geddesian programme of Social Reconstruction with his usual enthusiasm. He held a summer school in London on the war; he launched a series of monographs, with Victor Branford as co-editor, entitled *The Making of the Future*; he contributed, by using collaborators and copies of lectures he had given, two excruciatingly poor volumes to this series; he travelled to Europe in the summer of 1916 and went to Dublin, to involve himself in the renovations of the city after the Easter Rising; and to France, to give a paper at the morale-boosting 'Exposition Civique et Urbaniste: La Cité Réconstituée', held in Paris, with the German guns only seventy miles away. His enthusiasm was infectious but he chose emotional rather than intellectual methods to convert the world to the socio-biological eutopia of social reconstruction.

His town planning reports in India and Palestine were deeply coloured by this crusade. Unable to write a theoretical treatise to support his views, he validated them to himself by imbueing his practical work with theoretical significance. His friends could, and did, tease him for the absurdities this sometimes led to. H. J. Fleure wrote to him after receiving the second Lucknow Report: 'My dear Geddes, Your Lucknow Report is a source of much joy to me. Fancy getting such a fine exposition of civic philosophy, with religious considerations as well into the section on Latrines'.[59] However, there were some benefits. Geddes had a crucial influence on the town planning movement of his day because of his willingness to deal with the 'here and now' of contemporary conditions, rather than pursuing some Utopia. 'Eutopia', meaning a 'good place', the better utilisation of resources, was his slogan.[60]

In his view, there could be no blueprint for the future. Political revolutions may change governments. But the facts of everyday existence only changed slowly in response to a complex interaction of social, cultural and economic factors. An ecological understanding of place and people should be the starting point for better adjustment to the future. That was the message of his social reconstruction propaganda and the reward for believing it would be 'social peace'. Social conflict wasted valuable energies. As a natural scientist, Geddes wanted the human species to be united, to pool resources and effort in a Kropotkin-inspired programme of mutual aid. Applied sociologists trained in the Geddesian manner would provide the directives. Their special skills were needed because the way an organism responds to an environment can only be discovered by careful and sustained observation. No amount of theoretical analysis can be a substitute for this.

He wrote a series of articles, published in the *Indian Journal of*

Economics (1918) in which he put all these ideas forward together, calling them his 'theory of life' and explaining his special methodology, his notations. It was to be the precursor of the final statement of his philosophy which appeared as the end chapters of a general biological textbook prepared by J. Arthur Thomson, *Life: Outlines of Biology* (London, 1931). Geddes's efforts brought him the offer of the Chair of Sociology at Bombay in 1919, one of the first in India and one of only two teaching posts established as the university began the process of transforming itself from being an exclusively examining body.[61] However, Geddes did not capitalise on this chance. He was no longer deeply concerned with promoting a new academic discipline in the social sciences in India. Instead, he changed the name of his chair to Sociology and Civics and continued his planning and propaganda activities for three-quarters of the year.

He even arrived late to take up his post when he was first appointed. He had been held up in Jerusalem, which, with its illustrious history and mixture of races, provided him with a challenge for his socio-biological approach which he could not resist. He was not invited to be the Civic Advisor to the Government of Palestine. That post was given to C. R. Ashbee, his old friend from the Arts and Craft movement.[62] But his enthusiasm endeared him to some of the pioneer Zionists such as David Eder and Norman Bentwich, and Geddes brought his son-in-law, the architect Frank Mears, out to work on plans for a new University of Jerusalem. Geddes's last planning reports were to be for Jerusalem and future Israeli cities, the then quite small towns of Haifa and Tel Aviv. However, as Professor of Sociology and Civics at Bombay, Geddes did very little. When he found able students such as G. S. Ghurye and N. N. Toothi, he sent them to Europe for their education and expected them, on their return, to act as his lieutenants in the social reconstruction crusade.[63]

The lecture course he gave to his Bombay students, entitled 'Civilisation: a challenge' was an exercise in social reconstruction propaganda. Yet at the university and in his planning and propaganda activities, Geddes was doomed to failure. No interest group, economic, social or cultural, could wholly identify with his viewpoint and thus give him a base for his movement. His non-political stance had given him the freedom to perceive the significance of new knowledge in its bearing on social existence, especially the knowledge emanating from the life sciences. But, for all his 'practical' bent, Geddes was hopelessly out of touch with realities. His contemporaries may have erred in their neglect of economic and social factors, the Treaty of Versailles at the end of the First World War providing a classic example. However, he in his turn over-reacted by ignoring political factors completely.

When he returned from India in 1923, he was disappointed to find the excitement and response he had generated with his social reconstruction message, particularly in London and Paris in 1916, had gone. He tried to make an impact still by travelling to America, and inveigling any young man of talent, such as the youthful Lewis Mumford who showed an interest in his ideas, to work for the cause. He was not successful, nor was he when back at home again he held a symposium on the Coal Strike of 1926. In the volume of essays published afterwards, entitled *The Coal Crisis and the Future*, Geddes wrote: 'Medical men in their handling of disease increasingly have recourse to "team-work". Various specialists each make their own diagnosis of the patient, and set out a corresponding course of treatment. Then a physician of all-round competence, gathering the pooled resources of his specialised colleagues, brings to bear his wider experience, and his trained sense of unity, for the better understanding of the case and its more skilled treatment'. Geddes thought of himself as such a man, an 'orthogenic evolutionist', his subject 'civics' being a training in the 'unities of life, mind, morals and society'. He was the generalist, those who came to seek his advice, the specialists. It was not a position which he could justify theoretically, hence his inability to produce a monograph on his theory of life. His genius, for all his personal wishes, was not suited to the leadership of a mass movement. It lay instead in stimulating ideas in others by questioning preconceived assumptions. It was a valuable gift to the nascent British town planning movement, only counter-productive if Geddes himself was taken too seriously.

Notes

1 For the main sources of his ideas see H. E. Meller 'Cities in Evolution: Patrick Geddes as an international prophet of town planning before 1914' in A. Sutcliffe (ed), *The Rise of Modern Urban Planning 1800–1914*, Mansell Publishing Co Ltd, 1980

2 H. E. Meller (ed), *The Ideal City*, Leicester University Press, Leicester, 1979, pp9–39

3 J. W. Burrow, *Evolution and Society: A Study in Victorian Social Theory*, CUP, Cambridge, 1966, pp82–93

4 J. D. Y. Peel, *Herbert Spencer: the evolution of a sociologist*, Heinemann, London, 1971, pp166–191

5 H. Spencer, *Autobiography*, Volume II, p185

6 P. Abrams, *The Origins of British Sociology*, University of Chicago Press, Chicago, 1968, pp77–100

7 He concentrated mainly on social development of pre-literate societies. S. Collini, *Liberalism and Sociology: L. T. Hobhouse and Political Argument in England 1880–1914*, CUP, Cambridge, 1979, pp209–234

8 H. E. Meller 'Patrick Geddes: An Analysis of his Theory of Civics, 1880–1914' in *Victorian Studies* Vol XVI No 3, 1973, pp291–315

9 Collini, *op cit*, p180

10 One of his last comments on the subject 'Talent and Genius', was an article in the *Sociological Review*, July 1931

11 P. Geddes, 'Civics: as Applied Sociology I', *Sociological Papers*, 1904, reprinted in H. E. Meller (ed), *The Ideal City, op cit*, pp79–84

12 Collini, *op cit*, pp183–4

13 As was recognised by Geddes's first biographer, Amelia Defries, *The Interpreter Geddes: the Man and his Gospel*, Routledge, London, 1927

14 Biographical details of Geddes's life are fully documented in P. Boardman, *The Worlds of Patrick Geddes*, Routledge, London, 1978

15 Quoted in Collini, *op cit*, p184

16 J. Conway, 'Stereotypes of Femininity in a theory of sexual evolution' *Victorian Studies*, 14, 1970, pp47–62

17 There is a select bibliography of Geddes's works in P. Boardman, *op cit*, pp500–506

18 He tried to promote his view of 'civics' to a wider public at the first conferences of the British Sociological Society in 1904, 1905 and 1906. Papers I and II are reprinted in full in H. E. Meller (ed), *The Ideal City, op cit*

19 P. Geddes, 'Edinburgh and the region, Geographic and Historical' *Scottish Geographical Magazine*, XVIII, June 1902, pp302–12

20 T. H. Huxley *Physiography* 1877. For Geddes's comment on this see V. Branford and P. Geddes, *The Coming Polity*, Williams & Norgate, London, 1917 p5–11

21 P. Geddes 'Civics: an applied sociology', in H. E. Meller (ed) *op cit* pp76–79

22 A. Milward and S. B. Saul *The Development of the Economies of Continental Europe 1850–1914*, Allen & Unwin, London, 1977, pp71–138

23 P. Geddes and V. V. Branford, *Our Social Inheritance*, Williams & Norgate, London, 1919 pp344–345

24 P. Geddes, 'A Great Geographer: Elisée Reclus, 1830–1905' *Scottish Geographical Magazine* (September and October 1905)

25 Geddes campaigned for this in the pages of the *Scottish Geographical Magazine* in 1902

26 E. P. Hennock, 'Poverty and social theory in England: the experience of the 1880s', *Social History*, I, 1976, pp67–91

27 H. O. Barnett, *Canon Barnett, his life, work and friends*, London, 1921, pp655–660

28 O. Hill, *Homes of the London Poor*, London, reprinted 1970

29 Miss Hill worked to preserve places of outstanding natural beauty and was a founder member of the National Trust.

30 The Edinburgh Social and Sanitary Society, (1884) stated that its aims were 'to improve the dwellings and social conditions of the poorer

classes by (1st) Procuring information regarding their social habits and sanitary condition (2nd) Communicating the information obtained to the Authorities ... (3rd) Suggesting remedies in the interests of the comfort and health of the poor (4th) Endeavouring to get both landlords and tenants to co-operate in carrying out the objects of the society (5th) Specially endeavouring by practical advice, the diffusion of health literature, and kindly sympathy, to set people on ways of self-improvement, industry, thrift and cleanliness'. *Constitution and Rules.*

31   See H. E. Meller (ed), *The Ideal City, op cit*, Introduction, p12

32   Founded in 1904

33   Ashbee describes his work with the Guild of Handicraft in his book *An Endeavour Toward the Teaching of John Ruskin and William Morris*, Edward Arnold, London, 1900

34   As he explained in an early pamphlet *On the Conditions of Progress of the Capitalist and the Labourer*, Edinburgh Co-op Printing Co, 1886

35   Geddes shared with other hopeful ex-students of T. H. Huxley, such as C. Lloyd Morgan, an evolutionist's approach to education, which was seen, not as the transmission of knowledge, but the cultivation of instinct, intuition and intellect. Geddes was also influenced by the le Playist disciple, E. Demolins, who ran a school in the 1890s, the École des Roches, aimed at transmitting cultural values directly to gifted and responsive children.

36   Though some were impressed by it, including Charles Zueblin, sociologist from Chicago, who wrote a eulogy of his experiences in Edinburgh at the summer school of 1898, 'The World's First Socio-logical Laboratory,' *The American Journal of Sociology*, March, 1899, pp577–592

37   See discussion of survey techniques in R. Glass, 'Urban Sociology in Great Britain: a trend report', *Current Sociology*, IV, 1955

38   P. Geddes, 'Civics: as applied sociology' in H. E. Meller (ed), *The Ideal City, op cit*, p75

39   Countess of Aberdeen, *The Work of the Women's National Health Association of Ireland*, 1911–12, pp28–33

40   Quoted from R. Dunlop, 'Ireland and the Home Rule Movement', *Cambridge Modern History*, Vol XII, 1910, p88

41   M. J. Bannon, 'The Making of Irish Geography III: Patrick Geddes and the Emergence of Modern Town Planning in Dublin', *Irish Geography*, Vol II, 1978, pp141–148

42   A. Defries, *The Interpreter Geddes: the Man and his Gospel, op cit*, p181

43   Commissioned for the Home University Library series (ed. Herbert Fisher, Gilbert Murray and J. Arthur Thomson), it was considered inappropriate for the series and later appeared as a monograph.

44   See A. D. King, *Colonial Urban Development: Culture, Social Power and Environment*, Routledge, London, 1976

45   P. Geddes, 'Civics: as applied sociology II' in H. E. Meller (ed), *The Ideal City, op cit*

46   P. Geddes, *Reports on the Towns in the Madras Presidency*, Government

Press, Madras, 1915, p75

47 See M. Tracy, *Agriculture in Western Europe: crisis and adaptation since 1880*, Cape, London, 1964

48 H. E. Meller, 'Urbanisation and the Introduction of Modern Town Planning Ideas in India' in K. N. Chandhuri and C. J. Dewey (eds), *Economy and Society – Essays in Indian Economic and Social History* OUP, Delhi, 1979, pp300–330

49 A classic example of this is the work of the first Director of the Calcutta Improvement Trust, E. P. Richards, *Report on the Request of the Improvement Trust on the Condition, Improvement and Town Planning of the City of Calcutta and Contiguous Areas*, published privately, 1914

50 He was much indebted to a volume by a Dr Turner, *Sanitation in India*, 1914, which he acknowledged as the source for his main ideas.

51 The Agricultural Adviser for Central India, and the Principal of the Poona Agricultural College both make this point in their otherwise favourable response to Geddes's scheme Appendix II and III, in P. Geddes, *Town Planning towards City Development: A Report to the Durbar of Indore*, Vol II, Holkar State Press, Indore, 1918

52 The Sadler Commission on higher education in India happened to be in progress in Calcutta at that time. Geddes never missed opportunities for publicising his ideas.

53 Geddes published one of his lectures on 'The Temple Cities' in the *Modern Review*, Vol 25, 1919, pp213–22

54 P. Geddes, *City Development: A Study of Parks, Gardens and Culture Institutes: A Report to the Carnegie Dunfermline Trust*, P. G. & Colleagues, Edinburgh, 1904, which he used as the practical illustration to his lectures on 'Civics: as applied sociology'

55 Appendix VI, *Indore Report* (from circular of), Diwali Procession, 1917

56 Published as the last chapter of P. Geddes, *An Indian Pioneer: The Life and Work of Sir Jagadis Chandra Bose*, Longmans, London, 1920

57 Geddes in a letter to H. J. Fleure, 4 April 1917, MS 10572, Geddes Papers, National Library of Scotland, Edinburgh

58 He published the manifesto of his crusade 'The making of the future' in the *Sociological Review*, May 1917

59 H. J. Fleure to Geddes 25 February 1917, MS 10572, Geddes Papers, National Library of Scotland, Edinburgh

60 For discussion of this see H. E. Meller (ed), *The Ideal City, op cit*, Introduction, pp12–15

61 J. V. Ferreira and S. S. Jha (eds), *The Outlook Tower: Essays on Urbanisation in Memory of Patrick Geddes*, Popular Prakashan Private Ltd, Bombay, 1976, Introduction

62 C. R. Ashbee, *A Palestine Notebook 1918–1923*, Heinemann, London, 1923. There are many interesting parallels between the ideas and work of Ashbee and Geddes. Both had original ideas on education, both were skilled in propaganda work, both became involved in the town planning movement. Geddes awarded Ashbee second prize in his Dublin competition.

63 Interview with Professor G. S. Ghurye, Bombay, January 1973

4

RAYMOND UNWIN
1863–1940

Mervyn Miller

Raymond Unwin's life spanned almost eight decades, with the turn of the century as its pivotal point neatly dividing his socialist apprenticeship and the early years in partnership with his brother-in-law Barry Parker, from his tangible achievements in housing and town planning in the first decade of the 20th century. The First World War formed another watershed, and its munitions communities became a testing ground for state and municipal enterprise in housing and town planning. Unwin emerged in 1919 as an administrator rather than an initiator, and moved towards the broader scale of the city-region, an interest fostered through contact with Patrick Geddes (1854–1932) from 1910 onwards. In the 1930s he emerged as elder statesman of a discipline which he had helped to forge, a respected advocate passing on his breadth of experience through his Columbia University Lectures. His career encompassed a logical transition from the Arts and Crafts socialism of William Morris (1834–96), through the visionary specification of the Garden City set out by Ebenezer Howard (1850–1928) to the emergence of town and regional planning. This account seeks to summarise and evaluate the emergence of Unwin's ideology and his most significant achievements within the context of the development of the planning process itself.[1]

Apprenticeship
Raymond Unwin was born near Rotherham on 2 November 1863. His father, a small businessman with academic inclinations, moved to Oxford in the early 1870s, took his BA and MA and became an extra-collegiate tutor, an acquaintance of Arnold Toynbee and his circle. Unwin's Oxford boyhood left a profound impression – the quadrangle was to become one of his favourite layouts for co-operative housing, expanded to the blocks of *Nothing Gained by Overcrowding* (1912). Perhaps even more enduring was personal contact

72

with Ruskin and Morris. In 1937, at the presentation of the Gold Medal of the Royal Institute of British Architects – which Ruskin had declined – Unwin recalled that:

One who was privileged to hear the beautiful voice of John Ruskin declaiming against the degradation and disorder resulting from laissez faire theories of life, to know William Morris and his work; and to imbibe in his impressionable years thoughts and writings of men like James Hinton and Edward Carpenter, could hardly fail to follow after the ideals of a more ordered form of society, and a better planned environment than that which he saw around him in the 'seventies and 'eighties.[2]

Unwin turned initially to the 'ordering' or rather re-ordering of society through membership of Morris's Socialist League founded in 1884. In a lecture given the same year in Leicester, 'Art and Socialism', he hinted at the synthesis of social and environmental concern which would emerge as 'town planning' two decades later. Morris had specified the necessities for the good life as 'honourable and fitting work', 'decency of surroundings' and 'leisure' – remarkably modern-sounding objectives. 'Decency of Surroundings' was further subdivided to include:

1. good lodging; 2. ample space; 3. general order and beauty. That is: 1. Our houses must be well built, clean and healthy. 2. There must be abundant garden space in our towns, and our towns must not eat up the fields and natural features of the country. 3. Order and beauty means that not only our houses must be stoutly and properly built, but also that they be ornamented duly: that the fields be not only left for cultivation, but also that they be not spoilt by it any more than a garden is spoilt: no one for instance to be allowed to cut down, for mere profit, trees whose loss would spoil a landscape: neither on any pretext should people be allowed to darken the daylight with smoke, to befoul rivers, or to degrade any spot of earth with squalid litter and brutal wasteful disorder.[3]

Unwin embarked on a propaganda campaign for the League with evangelical fervour – indeed he had originally contemplated taking holy orders and consulted Samuel Barnett, who was enlisting support for the pioneer University Settlement which became Toynbee Hall. On learning that he was more concerned by human unhappiness than wickedness Barnett advised against the Church, and Unwin returned north to serve an engineering apprenticeship in Chesterfield.[4] Many years later Henrietta Barnett engaged him to plan Hampstead Garden Suburb. In 1885 Unwin moved to Manchester where he soon became branch secretary for the Socialist League, finding a sense of purpose lacking in his work. He also took an interest in the Ancoats Brotherhood, renewing acquaintance with Morris, hearing lectures by Walter Crane and Kropotkin and meeting T. C. Horsfall, the Manchester pioneer of housing reform and later an advocate of German 'town extension plans'.

Unwin also contributed prolifically to *Commonweal*, drawing on the writings of James Hinton (1822–75), an aural surgeon at Guys Hospital who had written anthropological studies emphasising the communal and co-operative basis of primitive societies.[5] He also brought out his dissatisfaction with the material motivation of capitalism which rewarded 'a few with enormous wealth living in luxury and idleness while the mass of people have to toil hard to live at all', and pointed forward to communal ownership of land, abolition of class interests and the enlightened life of the individual in a form which he followed until his death in 1940: 'The wants and comforts which are conducive to a happy life are comparatively few. A home to live in, furniture, clothes, books and a few works of art about comprise the list'.[6]

At this period he became firm friends with the Parker family, cousins through the second marriage of his paternal grandmother. His uncle, Robert Parker (1826–1901), was a Buxton bank manager, which provided a secure position and income with which to bring up his large family in comfort. Ethel Parker (1865–1949) began to exchange long letters with Raymond Unwin, and her younger brother Barry (1867–1947)also came under his influence from 1881. Barry Parker responded to Morris's reforms in the decorative arts and was articled to Faulkner Armitage of Altrincham whose studio included a craft workshop and smithy. When Unwin returned to Derbyshire in 1887 as an engineer for the Staveley Coal and Iron Company Robert Parker placed an embargo on further contact with his daughter.

Unwin formed a close liaison with Edward Carpenter (1844–1929), ascetic, philosopher, vegetarian, homosexual, advocate of the simple life, who had settled at Millthorpe in the Cordwell Valley, five miles south of Sheffield, in 1883. Carpenter's intellectual liberation stemmed from study of the American poets Emerson, Thoreau and Whitman whom he emulated in *Towards Democracy*, which set forth the necessity for a new, free relationship between man and environment. Contact with Carpenter completed Unwin's intellectual apprenticeship,[7] but he did not follow the older man's self-contained lifestyle, but continued to search for an opportunity to apply the simple models he had learnt, to order society through its environment, beginning with the individual home and family unit.

The artistic and practical 1890–1900

Unwin learnt the rudiments of housing layout through his work for the Staveley Company which was expanding into a combine of mining, iron and steel interests covering three counties.[8] Barrow

Hill, founded in the 1830s, had 600 stone cottages in blocks of three, a well designed school and managers' houses. By contrast the new communities which Unwin planned must have served as models for him to avoid in future. Typical was Poolsbrook (1891–3) a few miles from Barrow Hill stranded in countryside pock-marked by pit banks – 216 cottages in terraces of twelve, arranged in an unrelieved rectangle, divided by streets and the ubiquitous back alley. No private gardens were provided but a large plot outside the village was reserved for allotments. Public buildings included two chapels, a mission room, hotel, and a large school (1892–3) – a substantial two storey building with functional airy classrooms.

As early as 1891 partnership with Barry Parker was discussed, 'he (Parker) doing the artistic part and me (Unwin) the practical'.[9] Two years later another aspect of the partnership was completed by the marriage of Raymond Unwin and Ethel Parker after more than a decade of exchanging letters: a simple civil ceremony at Chapel-en-le-Frith attended by Barry and Stanley Parker, and Unwin's Socialist friends Bruce and Katherine Glasier.[10] Barry Parker commenced practice from 'Moorlands', the family home in Buxton in 1894, joined by his brother-in-law two years later. The partners initially undertook commissions for middle class houses, including the design of all interior fittings and furniture. As early as 1895 Parker boldly reversed the conventional relationship between house and street at 'The Shanty', Marple, to gain the benefit of a distant view of the Peaks, bringing the stables and coachhouse to flank the street frontage, a gesture which brought an outcry from the local council and began a process which led logically to the classic Radburn cul-de-sac. Each design in the 1890s represented an advance in internal planning and handling of space, accompanied by a simplification of detail and refinement of form. Design of such houses, however, lacked the social purpose sought by Unwin: the home might be the setting for the fuller life of an individual family but the principles required broadening to serve the community, with the same care given to the design of the workman's cottage as to the commission from the wealthy patron. This marked the beginning of what Frederic Osborn aptly characterised as 'the democratisation of architecture'.[11]

Unwin's interest in co-operative housing projects stemmed from memories of Oxford quadrangles with their common rooms. By June 1889 he was advocating the takeover of country estates to establish communal cells:

Small wonder that as we stood looking at the house and the splendid view it commands we should fall to talking about 'the days that are going to be' when this Hall and others like it will be the centre of a happy communal life. Plenty of room in this house for quite a small colony to live, each one having his own den upstairs where he could go to write or sulk . . . and downstairs would be common dining halls, smoking rooms – if indeed life still needed the weed to make it perfect. And we chatted on, each one adding a bit to our picture; how some would till the land around and others tend the cattle, while others perhaps would start some industry, working in the outbuildings or building workshops about the park, and taking care not to spoil our view with a hideous building or blight our trees with smoke. Others again would work in the mines bringing up coal . . . we all felt, I think, more than ever determined that what might be shall be.[12]

In the 1890s Unwin provided prototype designs to fit this concept. Barry Parker also turned towards the design of working class housing with a sketch for 'An Artisan's Living Room', with a traditional northern hob-grate, flanked by fitted settles and cupboards. The staircase led directly from the room, a feature of later designs often criticised by tenants. Publication of *The Art of Building a Home* in 1901 represented a significant land mark in the evolution of Unwin's approach to town planning.[13]

The book illustrated two simple concepts which were expanded through trial and error to form important elements of the Garden City approach to site planning. These were an urban quadrangle of co-operative housing and a village green scheme suitable for a rural context. Both had been designed in the late 1890s and represented a reaction against conventional bye-law terrace layouts. The quadrangle was designed for a site in Bradford, possibly influenced by pioneer experiments at Saltaire, and Akroydon, Halifax. The houses were turned inwards to face a quadrangle with communal gardens. Common rooms, laundries, and central kitchens represented a tentative step towards the neighbourhood concept which Unwin took further in later theoretical and practical examples leading to the block layout of *Nothing Gained by Overcrowding* (1912). The village green scheme was designed about 1898, with informally grouped houses facing a communal green, open to the south to command a distant view. A lightly metalled avenue ran around the green, but all through traffic not requiring access was excluded. A modified version was implemented as Westholm Green, Letchworth (1906), built by the Garden City Tenants' Housing Society. Unwin described the concepts in 'Co-operation in Building', stressing the notion of the village as an expression of corporate life, and advocating free association of families, middle class at first, to develop sites on a co-operative basis. Adoption of village green model would also help to relieve overcrowding in towns and could be developed by the state or municipality. The return to feudalism in order to find the design solution to the problems of the industrial city had distinct implications for the organisation of society and stemmed from Morris. Unwin stressed that 'the relationships of feudalism have gone, and democracy has yet to evolve some definite relationships of its own' but he concluded 'we could if we desired it even now so arrange a building site that it should . . . have some little of the charm of the old village'.[14]

A few weeks before publication of the book Unwin had participated in the first Garden City Association Conference, held at Bournville, and he made good use of this opportunity to present his material[15] —one of his outstanding characteristics was simply to be in the right place at the right time. Before discussing the two major commissions which seem to have been precipitated by his presence at Bournville, two further prototypes merit description. Unwin had initially been distressed by the break-up of the Socialist League in the early 1890s, but later joined the Fabian Society who, in 1902, published his *Cottage Plans and Common Sense* as a Tract. Unwin's deployment of a favourite Ruskin quotation advocating 'a cottage all of our own, with its little gardens, its healthy air, its clean kitchen, parlour and bedrooms' immediately evokes the Garden City, although the scheme illustrated was a development of the urban quadrangle, considerably simplified, and with a house plan identical to one built the same year in the first phase of New Earswick. At the same time Parker and Unwin prepared a pilot study for a small development at Starbeck on the outskirts of Harrogate, a chequerboard layout of semi-detatched cottages, with picturesque gables and dormers providing an anticipation of the Garden City. The project appears to have been abandoned following construction of the first pair, but was included in the Northern Artworkers Guild Exhibition at Manchester in 1903[16] – an indication of the fusion of the Arts and Crafts and Garden City movements in the emergent discipline of town planning. This pattern of development clearly fascinated Parker and Unwin and recurred in the first plans for Letchworth and Hampstead.

Opportunity grasped – New Earswick

Within three years, 1902–5, Barry Parker and Raymond Unwin became involved with three of the most influential projects incorporating low density, open development associated with the Garden City movement – New Earswick, Letchworth and Hampstead. Unwin's involvement with the Garden City Association acted as a catalyst. The Bournville delegates included George Bernard Shaw in the unusual role of a St. Pancras councillor, Frederick Lee Ackerman the American Garden City supporter, Councillor J. S. Nettlefold of

Birmingham, and Seebohm Rowntree (1871–1954).[17] His father Joseph Rowntree shortly afterwards embarked upon development of a model village on the northern outskirts of York following the pattern established by his fellow Quaker, George Cadbury, at Bournville.

New Earswick, undertaken shortly before Letchworth Garden City, proved a valuable testing ground for layout and cottage design. In 1902 Unwin prepared the initial plans indicating the first phases of development and sites for a wide range of social facilities – Library and Institute, Art School, Church and Chapel, Shops and Temperance Inn – greatly reduced during implementation but their location along Haxby Road remaining. A more detailed block plan showed the first phase of development – Western Terrace and Poplar Grove, to the south of Station Avenue, an east-west link between the Huntingdon and Haxby Roads, a microcosm of Unwin's more extensive and ambitious plans.[18] Development of this triangular tract was underway in 1902–3 and about 26 cottages had been completed by the 'official' foundation of the Joseph Rowntree Village Trust in December 1904.[19]

The designs provided an indication of the variety which could be generated from simple elements, with the picturesque pantiled roofs handled with increasing virtuosity until rising building costs forced the adoption of a simpler design.[20] Construction continued through 1905–8 of the south-east quarter of an irregularly shaped site which dictated the approach to site planning. Quadrangles and greens were distorted by existing site features and the layout was controversial in that cottages were often turned away from the road to give views over the River Foss and outlying countryside, with their out-buildings, coal houses and outside lavatories facing the lightly paved roads. Oddly enough this relationship enabled the Trust to fully Radburnise in 1972 with the conversion of the original internal roads to pedestrian ways and garage courts tucked round the original 'backs' on the riverside, though this involved a great reduction of private garden area. Interior design followed closely the sketches from *Cottage Plans and Common Sense*. Living room floors were quarry tiled, the fireplace including a cooking range and back boiler was flanked by dark-green stained dresser, cupboards and seats. Unwin's communal buildings included a remarkably progressive primary school (1912: completed 1920) with generous classrooms and large folding windows set in gardens facing the village green, in striking contrast to the closely hemmed-in urban board schools.

Unwin closely supervised the development at New Earswick until 1914. In 1904 he, Barry Parker and Seebohm Rowntree met a group of tenants to discuss criticism of the first cottages, out of which a

Village Council arose to participate in subsequent development. In 1919 Barry Parker was appointed to plan post-war construction, and he developed the short cul-de-sac into a minor art form in housing layout,[21] a pattern for the rapidly developing council estates. The small scale and phased development of New Earswick gave an opportunity to test and refine concepts in practice, and to recreate the village as advocated in *The Art of Building a Home*, a pursuit of innovation through tradition central to Unwin's work.

Utopia Ltd – the First Garden City, 1903

The development pattern of the first Garden City at Letchworth profoundly influenced urban form through its close relationship with the emergence of town planning. Publication of *Looking Backward* by Edward Bellamy, in 1888, a vision of Boston 2,000 AD transformed by technology and co-operation into a highly organised consumer society, provoked two starkly contrasting rejoinders. Morris shuddered and retreated into his mediaeval socialist dream-world and wrote *News from Nowhere*. Howard gloried in the vision as he walked through the City of London:

I realised as never before, the splendid possibilities of a new civilisation based on service to the community and not on self interest, at present the dominant motive. Then I determined to take such part as I could . . . in helping to bring the new civilisation into being.[22]

His own account of the ideal community, the Garden City, was published in 1898 as *Tomorrow: A Peaceful Path to Real Reform*.[23]
Howard had worked as a law reporter for many years, and seemed to be the archetypal city clerk, but remained an unorthodox and original character, apt to do the unexpected. He was also a compulsive inventor who returned doggedly to one pet project – the shorthand typewriter – throughout his life. He approached the Garden City with the clarity of an inventor, surveying the field to assess existing projects, and their merits and defects, describing and illustrating a prototype with the precision of a watchmaker. Howard was also politically astute enough to build upon existing achievement, however gradual, if it served his overall ends. Manuscript drafts for *Tomorrow* included a chapter, 'The Master Key', in which he summarily dismissed parliamentary procedure as a means of achieving the Garden City. This was, perhaps wisely, deleted and he also struck out the emotive command 'Go up and Possess the Land!' from the well-known 'Ward and Centre' diagram.[24] The gradualism of the housing reformers provided a useful model for implementation: 'five per cent philanthropy' was to be expanded to develop a complete

town, though Howard recognised that the resources of the development company would be stretched to the limit in the early years. The
building of the city would increase the value of the estate and the
limitation of dividends would ensure that such increments would be
used for the benefit of the residents – a neat adaptation of the
speculators means to serve communal ends.

There remained the important task of giving a convincing urban
form to the Garden City. Howard's concept is universally known:
the Garden City with population limited to 32,000, surrounded by a
permanent green belt, eventually forming part of a Social City
cluster of six Garden Cities and a larger Central City, linked by rapid
transit, with a total population of 250,000. Although the provision of
housing was a central objective, an examination of *Tomorrow* reveals
comparatively little detailed material on its provision and even less
on the urban form which would have evolved from a literal translation of his diagrams into built form. The 5,500 housing plots aver-
aged 20ft by 130ft each, long narrow plots which would have resulted
largely in terraced development. Howard's sketch diagram of 'Ward
and Centre'[25] was the most specific, showing grand crescents model-
led on the Royal Crescent, Bath or Regents Park, flanking the Grand
Avenue, with terrace quadrangles as developed at Akroyden and
Port Sunlight – two of the most publicised of the late 19th century
Model Villages – for the lower middle class and working class
housing.

Publication of *Tomorrow* initially provoked patronising dismissals of
the concept, but in October 1899 the Garden City Association was
formed and in 1901 the recruitment of Ralph Neville as Chairman
and Thomas Adams as secretary gave credibility to the organisation.
In September 1901 Thomas Adams organised the Bournville Conference of the Association and Unwin's paper 'On the Building of
Houses in the Garden City' transposed Howard's concepts in terms
of his own Morris-inspired ideology.[26]

He visualised the Garden City 'arranged in natural conformity with
the land . . . sites for our civil, religious and recreative public buildings have been determined, dominating the city . . . giving impressions of dignity to those who come, leaving with those who go a
rememberance of beauty'.[27] He firmly rejected speculatively built
suburb – 'no weak compound of town and country composed of
wandering suburban roads lined with semi-detached villas, set each
in a scrap of garden will ever deserve the name of "Garden City" '[28]
and turned to 'the quiet quadrangle with its expanse of grass, or the
square with its spacious garden'.[29] Garden citizens would become 'a
community inspired by some ideal of what their city should be; a
community moreover whose units will be bound together by com-

mon aspiration . . .'[30] A Garden City Pioneer Company, financed
among others by Cadbury and Lever, was formed in 1902 to acquire
a suitable development site. Adams prepared lists of estates for sale
and Howard and his fellow directors visited several to compile a
short list.[31] Unwin visited at least two sites and wrote enthusiastically to Howard of the potential of the Chartley Castle estate, eight
miles north-west of Stafford, which in spring 1903 appeared to be a
logical choice.[32] Eventually the Letchworth estate was selected and
although much too small by itself, only 1,014 acres, other land was
obtained on option totalling 3,818 acres. First Garden City Ltd was
formed in September 1903 to develop the site and organised a limited
competition for the Master Plan. Richard Norman Shaw, W. R.
Lethaby and Halsey Ricardo were approached to prepare plans; in
addition 'the name of Raymond Unwin was mentioned in connection with the Plan but no further action was taken'.[33] In October
1903 Lethaby and Ricardo were interviewed and requested to prepare a joint plan. Barry Parker was called to give a reference on
Unwin's behalf and committed the practice to prepare a preliminary
plan within five weeks.[34] A third plan was prepared by Geoffry
Lucas, an architect from nearby Hitchin, and Sidney Cranfield.
Assessment was unorthodox, seemingly undertaken by the Goods
Manager of the Great Northern Railway being called to advise
which of the alternatives showed the best arrangement of station and
sidings serving the factory area. On 28 January 1904 the Parker and
Unwin plan was provisionally accepted and on 11 February the
Board resolved 'that the plan be issued as the Company's Plan'.[35]
A glance at the plan might initially suggest an exercise in formal
geometry with emphasis on major and minor axes, but it was in fact
very carefully related to existing site characteristics. Unwin took
justifiable pride in incorporating many of the existing trees and
hedgerows, and the major axis led to a central plateau, whose
'position was so favourably placed . . . that it seemed to be desirable
to try and afford glimpses of the group of public buildings which
would one day adorn that centre to those approaching the town. . .'[36]
Buildings were shown diagrammatically, giving form to the street
layout, and outside the formality of the grand axis a number of
earlier ideas on site planning were recalled – 'urban' quadrangles on
the fringe of the town centre with a few 'village greens' and sites for
detached houses on the fringes of settlements. East and west of North
Common the neighbourhood concept was shown in embryo form –
Norton Glebe to the east retained the basic layout with its
north-south axis, completed largely as a pedestrian walk, and
east-west roads. Comparison between the 1904 layout and the form
in which it was implemented indicates that broad guidelines were

followed, with a significant reduction in road lengths: a central point in Unwin's argument for open development of a Garden City character and following practical experience gained at Letchworth and Hampstead he evolved a general theory of site planning in *Nothing Gained by Overcrowding* (1912).

Unwin had to defend the plan and its principles in the face of financial overcommitment by First Garden City Ltd. Early in 1905 Adams organised the Cheap Cottage Exhibition which drew 60,000 visitors to see 'Garden City in the Making' that summer. Unwin hastily prepared a layout for the area north of the railway, developed with predominantly detached cottages, giving little scope for the harmony and groupings he advocated. Through Building Regulations a degree of aesthetic control was exercised, requiring 'simple straightforward building . . . and the use of good harmonious materials'.[37] Roughcast brickwork and red tiled roofs were virtually standardised and an embargo was placed on the use of blue Welsh slate. The plan laid down broad zoning guidelines, roads were subdivided into building plots, with a 'building area' defined for each to avoid absolute rigidity of building line. A variety of road sections with planted and grass margins was one of the most characteristic features, maturing over the years to give a truly Garden City character.

Cottage Society development presented Unwin with the opportunity to develop his prototypes, and experiment in groupings and layouts. The Co-partnership Tenants under the chairmanship of Henry Vivian (1868–1930) played an important role in the development of Letchworth and Hampstead. Westholm Green (1906) closely resembled Unwin's early prototypes, flanked by grouped cottages, all excellent examples of early Parker and Unwin designs, giving the impression of a kit of parts, capable of almost infinite variety in the assembly of groups to fit individual site conditions.

The Birds Hill Estate (1906) added further elements – a short cul-de-sac off Ridge Road to enable development in depth, a tree belt as buffer zone to separate the housing from adjacent factory sites and a children's playground with footpath access. Design of the grouped housing followed Westholm with emphasis on a picturesque roofline with multiple gables and dormers. Rents began at 4s. 6d per week for a two bedroom non-parlour cottage and three and four bedroom parlour cottages for 'artisans' generally rented at 8s. 6d per week which provoked a fierce controversy in *The Garden City* magazine as it was claimed, with some justice, that the cottages were extravagantly constructed and excluded the poorer labourers. Unwin roundly refuted his critics in an article published in June 1906 and claimed that a wage rise of 9d per week for the unskilled labourer would solve the difficulty:

For if Garden City stands for anything surely it stands for this – a decent home and garden for every family that come there. This is the irreducible minimum. Let that go and we fail utterly. And if we succeed utterly, what then? A beautiful home in a beautiful garden and a beautiful city for all.[38]

He was wise enough to include designs for simpler, cheaper cottages in his article and set out the prerequisites for standardisation – a degree of repetition, a small range of door and window types. Grouping could help to make the best of simple buildings, following the vernacular precedent and anticipating the basis of the Tudor Walters *Report* (1918). A few of the simpler cottages were included in the ambitious Pixmore Estate built by Garden City Tenants (1906–9) which formed a pioneer neighbourhood unit complete with institute and recreational facilities. Unwin was almost too successful in serving the centre of the block by a single narrow track, now choked with parked cars, an unthinkable element in cottage housing estates at the time of its construction. One of the finest layouts, Rushby Mead (1911–12), built by the Howard Cottage Society, combined a Parker and Unwin plan with cottage designs by themselves, Bennett and Bidwell, and Courtenay Crickmer. The housing faced the landscaped valley of the Pix Brook – Howard Park – and the gently curving road followed the old stream bed. Effective use was made of setbacks from the street frontage and the layout incorporated a cul-de-sac which preserved original hedges.
Unwin built a house for himself in Letchworth Lane – 'Laneside' (1904), an enlarged version of the grouped cottages, with white roughcast walls and tall Yeoman Tudor Chimneys. In 1906 Barry Parker moved into the other half of the pair, 'Crabby Corner'. Shortly afterwards Unwin left to supervise the planning of Hampstead Garden Suburb. He anticipated an absence of a few months and Parker's design for the firm's new offices at 206 Norton Way South (1907: now First Garden City Museum) made provisions for the construction of an extra wing.[39] 'Wyldes,' an old weatherboarded farmhouse to the south of Hampstead Heath extension, became Unwin's home and office and he soon organised a group of assistants with the gentle skill of a mediaeval master craftsman.

The suburb salubrious 1905

Hampstead Garden Suburb elevated site planning to a major art form, and Unwin became deeply involved with the handling of the space outside the dwelling and with circulation patterns. Philosophically and physically Hampstead represented a considerable modification of the objectives of Ebenezer Howard, for despite its beauty and social goal of attracting a wide section of society it involved the outward spread of a great city. Unwin had attacked suburban development in *The Art of Building a Home* (1901) for its sprawling squalor and the loss of 'a refreshing glimpse of the cool green hillside from amongst our busy streets'.[40] The reservation of a large tract of land for the Hampstead Heath extension meant that Unwin could secure the 'refreshing glimpse' through his plan and he was also influenced by the fact that the creator of the Suburb, Henrietta Barnett (1851–1936) was motivated by social ideals close to his own, that the development should accomodate all kinds and conditions of men.

Although the suburb was not formally 'founded' until 1907 Unwin had been involved since his preparation of the first plan in February 1905, barely a year after receiving the Letchworth commission. It was a looser concept than Letchworth, perhaps reflecting Unwin's study of Camillo Sitte's *City Planning according to Artistic Principles*, but it included elements which were developed in definitive form through Unwin's direct involvement in the subsequent implementation, including the Central Square, the Great Wall and the entrance 'gateways' from Finchley Road and Temple Fortune Lane. Once again Unwin's early writing provided the seed from which the total concept grew:

In the old towns which we admire when we chance to come on them, we notice that the country comes up clean and fresh right to the point where the town proper begins . . . In the oldest cities we sometimes find a wall with the country coming right up to the gates, which adds to this effect.[41]

The early plan incorporated quadrangles, greens and even the old chequerboard layout, and also indicated how the narrow strip of land to the west of the Heath extension would be developed by the use of the cul-de-sac.

Hampstead achieved greater formality through the appointment of Edwin Lutyens as consulting architect to the Suburb Trust in 1906, at the same meeting which confirmed the appointment of Unwin to prepare the overall plan.[42] It was probably through Lutyens's influence that the central square became virtually pedestrianised in its final form, with the road deleted on the west, giving an opportunity to develop a pedestrian link to Hampstead Way and preparing the ground for similar innovations elsewhere. As implemented Hampstead represents a maturity in site planning with the relationship between houses and their setting more successfully and consistently realised than at Letchworth. Unwin was assisted by a special Act of Parliament, the Hampstead Garden Suburb Act, 1906, promoted by Vivian – the first town planning legislation operative in

Britain, which enabled the development of the cul-de-sac to the west of the Heath extension and elsewhere. It was this feature which so impressed the Danish architect and town planner Steen Eiler Rasmussen: 'the road net is differentiated . . . it is like a tree with branches, an organic pattern channelling traffic down to the smallest leaves of the plan'.[43] In Hampstead there is a distinct anticipation of Radburn principles, though naturally the separation of pedestrian and vehicular traffic was not so complete. The culs-de-sac of the western side of the Heath extension incorporated some internal footpaths and the area to the north of the Heath extension had a direct functional relationship between housing and open space which the studied picturesque of the Great Wall, intended to establish a clean break between suburb and Heath, seemingly contradicts at first sight. A careful analysis of such Unwin 'classics' as Reynolds Close or the layout of Linnell Drive, Linnell Close and Heathgate reveals a sophisticated concern for the space between dwellings comparable with the partners' ideas of handling internal space in the previous decade. Nor was such sophisticated site planning to be a preserve of the middle classes living near to the Heath extension, for the original 'artisans quarter' introduced a brilliant prototype cul-de-sac in Asmuns Place and included allotments, tennis courts, and communal gardens. Within the centre of the block defined by Temple Fortune Hill, Erskine Hill and Asmuns Hill, Unwin at last realised his ideal quadrangle scheme, 'The Orchard' originally built for old people's housing and now, alas, destroyed.

Unwin and his assistants developed a flowing relationship between house and garden, building groups and communal open spaces, residential areas and the Heath extension in a virtuoso manner. Hampstead received almost unstinted praise from the moment of its inception : H. E. von Berlepsch-Valendas, one of the leaders of the German town planning movement observed that 'the happy unison of art and calculation, as it is so typical of the social sense of the English people, has led at once to schemes of a similar nature in other parts of the country',[44] and dubbed its creator 'a worthy follower of Ruskin and Morris'.[45] The significance of Hampstead lay in its successful adoption of Garden City layout standards for suburban development, given statutory recognition in the Housing and Town Planning Act, 1909 which promoted 'the suburb salubrious'. It is debatable whether many politicians would have been prepared to support more fundamental measures such as the halting of suburban sprawl and the state development of garden cities. Hampstead was undoubtedly an easier option and, by its legitimisation of suburban development, a dangerous precedent – few of its imitators attained its visual coherence and its social objectives were soon lost through the workings of the housing market, in part by the very increase in property values promoted as one of the cardinal virtues of the new type of layout.

Town planning in practice

Unwin's early involvement with the Garden City Association confirmed his skill and effectiveness as a propagandist. From the early years of the century he would speak to any and every audience, developing his ideas into a set of simple, readily understood statements about the arrangement of towns in the broadest sense. He noted the advances of the German town extension plans, particularly the powers of land assembly, controlling individual rights in the communal cause. Civic Art – a form borrowed from Geddes – was 'the introduction of all that we do of that small margin of generosity and imaginative treatment which constitutes it well done'.[46] Letchworth formed the basis of his approach and plans were to be viewed as self-evident truths for which 'nothing at all is needed but that someone should think of them and suggest them at the right time'.[47] By 1906 he was freely using the term 'town planning' to describe the process of ordering the environment. Lobbying for national legislation mounted following the success of the Hampstead Act. John Burns, President of the local Government Board and a former labour supporter, introduced the Housing and Town Planning Bill in 1908, and in the following session it became the subject of a wrangle between the Liberal Commons and Conservative Lords, receiving assent two days before the fall of Asquith's government in December 1909.[48]

The content of the Act was scarcely revolutionary – virtually all the bye-law concessions of the earlier Hampstead Garden Suburb Act were incorporated, and permissive powers aimed at controlling suburban development – indeed the Act applied only to unbuilt land. Furthermore a cumbersome process ensured that long periods elapsed between the initial sanction to prepare a plan and its final statutory approval. Unwin immediately embarked on a practical exemplar, designed to give substance to planning: *Town Planning in Practice: An Introduction to the Art of Designing Cities and Suburbs*[49] was published in June 1909. The book remained in print for a quarter century, translated into French, German and Russian. In the 1930s Adams wrote that the book 'helped to raise the conception of town planning above the level of political discussions which centred around the problem of protecting property against alleged interference with private rights . . . It visualised town-planning as the art of town architecture'.[50] Unwin's homely philosophy ran through the book, calling upon his concept of community and love of the picturesque and vernacular, although he also presented more formal aspects of civic design. The chapters on housing layout, plots and placing of buildings and co-operation in site planning were a primer of Hampstead examples, and a necessary corrective to the mundane bye-law development. C. P. Wade, one of Unwin's best assistants, contributed drawings with a fairytale atmosphere, the most memorable elements rather than the drily presented Greek and Roman reconstructions or the plethora of views of Rothenburg. The art concealed Unwin's broad experience and empirical studies ranging from the simple models from *The Art of Building a Home*. He now set out general principles such as the density standard of 'twelve to the acre', based on long experience:

Twelve houses to the acre of building land, excluding all roads, has been proved to be about the right number to give gardens of sufficient size to be of commercial value to the tenants – large enough, that is, to be worth cultivating seriously for the sake of profits, and not too large to be worked by an ordinary labourer and his family.[51]

This standard also tied in with the important question of minimising, as far as possible, the amount of land to be devoted to roads and Unwin observed that 'it may often be wiser to reduce slightly the number of houses to the acre than to cut up the land with too many roads'.[52]

Unwin's career took on an increasingly public aspect. In 1910 he was one of the organisers of the International Town Planning Congress of the Royal Institute of British Architects, attended by 1,300 delegates, with forty-three major papers and visits to Bournville, Letchworth and Hampstead. The transactions were published as an eight hundred page volume – never before, or since, had town planning enjoyed such prestige and patronage. In 1911 he was unanimously elected a Fellow of the Institute, and participated in an international conference in Philadelphia. His first visit to the United States included three days in Chicago where the park belt and neighbourhood social centres impressed him as elements with which to articulate the sprawl of the great city region, by inducing 'crystalisation' into community cells.[53] This formed the basis for two decades of work on Greater London. In August 1911 – surely something of an *annus mirabilis* – he was invited by Sir Oliver Lodge to accept the newly created Cadbury Lectureship in Civic Design at Birmingham University. He also took an active role with Adams in the creation of the Town Planning Institute, founded in 1914.[54]

Nothing Gained by Overcrowding[55] (1912) was a slim pamphlet aimed at the presentation of an incontrovertible economic case for Garden City layout standards, distinctly tractarian in character, recalling his earlier Fabian work. The quadrangle was expanded to form a neighbourhood block from which roads were excluded, and compared with typical bye-law layouts in which a substantial area was occupied by roads and alleyways. At the general scale of the city as a whole Unwin published his observations on American city planning with a diagram to show the correct principles of town growth, with suburbs articulated by park reservations and natural features. He also sought to demonstrate that low density decentralisation would not significantly add to sprawl, using the theorem that the area of a circle increases proportionately to the square of its radius. This carried the implication – fulfilled in the interwar period – that London would be expanded to a vast amorphous suburban tract; Osborn and the Garden City supporters never liked the model.[56]

In December 1914 Herbert Samuel, who had succeeded Burns as President of the Local Government Board, appointed Raymond Unwin as his Chief Town Planning Inspector in succession to Adams. Unwin had achieved his most significant original contribution to the evolution of site planning and in the field of housing. His work had been widely published in Europe and the United States, a process which began with the issue of an American edition of *The Art of Building a Home* in 1902. Both *Town Planning in Practice* and *Nothing Gained by Overcrowding* received international recognition. His career as a civil servant placed emphasis on his administrative rather than his creative skills during fourteen years which included a world war and governments of the three major parties.

Housing for heroes

The First World War provided a stimulus to town planning: an unexpected consequence of the use of energy powers by the Ministry of Munitions initially under David Lloyd George, succeeded by Christopher Addison, and finally, in 1917, by Winston Churchill. Unwin was seconded to the explosives division of the Ministry of Munitions in July 1915, in charge of an ambitious programme of factory and house building. Already the Office of Works had commenced construction of the ambitious Well Hall Estate, Eltham,[57] and its emphasis on picturesque grouping and varied elevational treatment owed much to *Town Planning in Practice*. Ministerial policy subsequently promoted the construction of large munitions plants in remote areas. Most ambitious was Gretna, a State-developed new town on the banks of the Solway Firth. Its construction from 1915 onwards was shrouded in secrecy, and its wartime publication in the *Journal of the American Institute of Architects* provoked trouble with the censor.

The site of Gretna lay south-west of the old village, sloping gently to

Thomas Adams, c. 1920. (Author's collection)

(i)

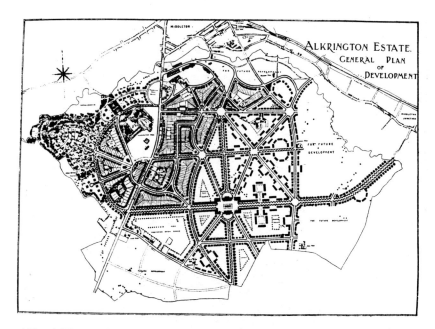

*(Above) Thomas Adams: Alkrington Garden Suburb, 1908–09 – typical of the genre. Villas were placed on the uplands to the west and on the flatter ground to the east is a more formal layout with a service centre on the grand avenue. Note the use of roundabouts and playgrounds in the interiors of blocks. (*Town Planning Review, *1910)*

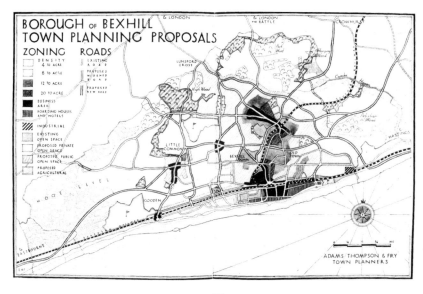

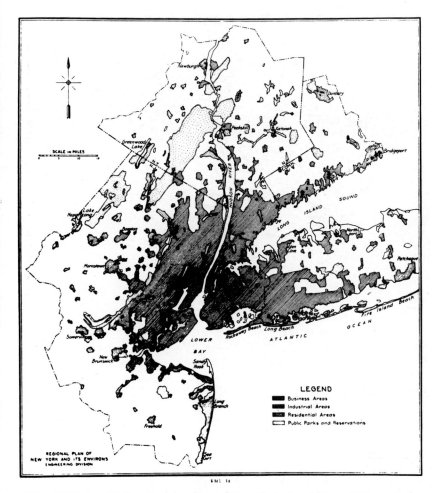

LEGEND

■ Business Areas
■ Industrial Areas
▨ Residential Areas
☐ Public Parks and Reservations

REGIONAL PLAN OF
NEW YORK AND ITS ENVIRONS
ENGINEERING DIVISION

(Above) Thomas Adams: Regional Plan of New York, Land Uses, 1929 – note the concentration of business and industry round navigable water-ways, the vast residential dispersion and the arc-like shape and great extent of the area. (Regional Plan Association, Inc., New York City, 1929)

(Left) Adams, Thompson and Fry: Bexhill, 1931 – densities decrease away from the urban core and a green belt preserves much fine country. Substantial road improvements are called for and several new stretches proposed. A typical inter-war development control plan, focusing on land uses, communications and amenity. (Recent Advances in Town Planning, *Churchill, London, 1932)*

(iii)

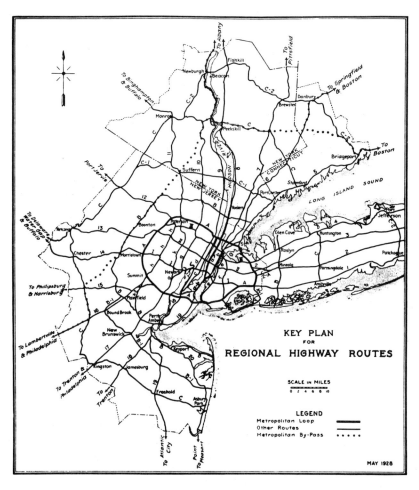

Thomas Adams: Regional Plan of New York, Highways, 1929 – all of the Plan's transportation proposals were designed on the same basis – intersecting radials and loops, directing Pennsylvania-New England traffic away from the congested centre. It was hoped that intersections would form new satellite centres. (Regional Plan Association, Inc., New York City, 1929)

Pencil drawing of Patrick Geddes, November 1916. (Author's collection)

(v)

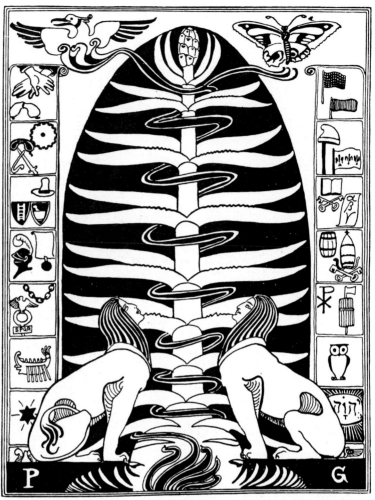

Arbor Sæculorum: 'A great tree and its branches, spreading right and left, suggest
the twofold aspects of each historic era, temporal on one side, spiritual on the other.
The tree has its roots amid the fires of life, and is perpetually renewed from them;
but the spirals of smoke which curl among its branches blind the thinkers and
workers each successive age to the thought and work of their precursors. While the
branches symbolise the past and passing developments of society, the bud at the
tree-top suggests the hope of the opening future. Two sphinxes guard the tree and
gaze upward in eternal questioning; their lion-bodies recalling man's origin in the
animal world, their human faces the ascent of man. Issuing from the smoke-wreaths
at the top of the tree are the phœnix of the ever-renewed body, and the butterfly
(Psyche) of the deathless soul of humanity. On either side of the window rises a
series of symbols, those on the right hand indicating the dominating spiritual forces
of the great historic periods, those on the left the corresponding temporal powers.
(Quotation from* A First Visit to The Outlook Tower, *Geddes and Colleagues,
Edinburgh, 1906)*

(vi)

Sir Raymond Unwin (1863–1940), photographed in New York, 1934. (Author's collection)

Barry Parker and Raymond Unwin: Sketch for a Village Green, c. 1899.
(Published in The Art of Building a Home, *Longmans, London, 1901)*

Unwin's Plan for the First Garden City, 1904. An early tracing from the
'Competition' Plan. Ebenezer Howard's Ward and Centre Diagram provided a
geometric basis which Unwin developed, taking his arrangment of radiating and
circumferential roads around the Central Square from the Exchange in Wren's City
of London Plan (1666). He related the formal arrangement brilliantly to existing
topography and landscaping, and provided the basis for land use zoning. (First
Garden City Museum, Letchworth)

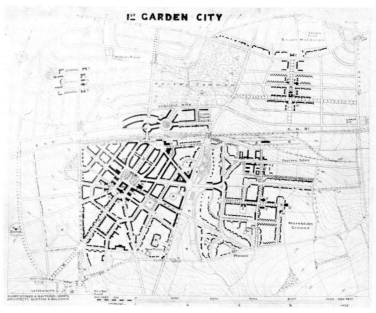

*'Westholm', Wilbury Road, Letchworth, developed by Garden City Tenants, 1906.
Parker and Unwin were at last able to implement their ideal Village Green scheme
(see illustration above) for a site overlooking Norton Common, developed by one of
the pioneer housing societies. The groupings were developed with gables and dormers
with virtuoso flair, breaking away from all vestiges of bye-law development.
Criticism of the cost of construction and its effect on rent levels led to Unwin's
spirited defence of the firm's determination to provide the best standards for cottage
housing*

*Hampstead Garden Suburb, Plan, c. 1909. The Hampstead layout was conceived in
looser and more informal terms by Unwin in 1905, but it was tightened up following
the appointment of Lutyens as consultant in 1906. Lutyens was largely responsible
for the Central Square with its 'trinity' of religion and knowledge. To the
north-west the 'Artisans' quarter was a classic Unwin layout with the cul-de-sac
Asmuns Place, the quadrangle of The Orchard, and subtly varied groupings and
setbacks along Asmuns Hill, Hampstead Way and Temple Fortune Hill. West of
the Heath Extension the distinctive pattern of culs-de-sac made possible by the HGS
Act may be seen*

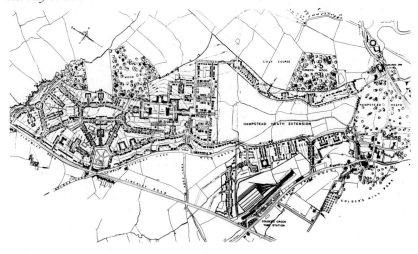

The Garden City Method of Development.

FRONT GARDENS TO HOUSES UNDER TOWN PLANNING.

The By-Law Method of Development.

ORDINARY SUBURBAN VILLAS, SHOWING AMOUNT OF SPACE FOR FRONT GARDEN.

Nothing Gained by Overcrowding, *1912. The contrast between Hampstead Garden Suburb and speculative development. This pamphlet was one of the most effective propaganda exercises by the planning lobby, using photographs and diagrams to press the point that garden city standards paid in aesthetic, social and economic terms. The view of Hampstead Way, originally built 1907, testifies to the almost Arcadian quality which the Suburb attained within a few years*

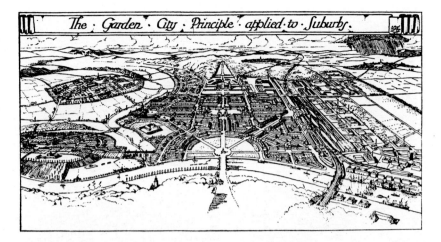

Nothing Gained by Overcrowding, *1912. The Garden City Principle applied to Suburbs. Unwin was acutely aware of the need to attain a recognisable overall form for urban development, as well as for its component parts. The urban cluster with belts of open space following existing physical features was a model which he ultimately expanded to serve as the basis for his work on Greater London*

Nothing Gained by Overcrowding, *1912. The two systems of development contrasted. Unwin's persuasive argument held out the promise of lower road and service costs and the benefit of increased garden size and communal open spaces. There is little evidence of builders adopting the principles prior to 1914 but the argument came into its own during the First World War reconstruction debate on housing*

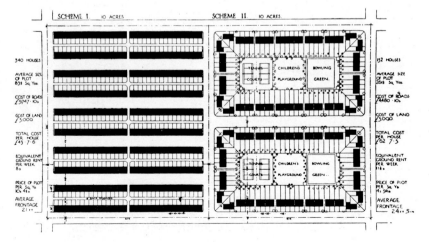

Nº5   CLASS   B4 URBAN
SOUTHERLY ASPECT

FRONT ELEVATION

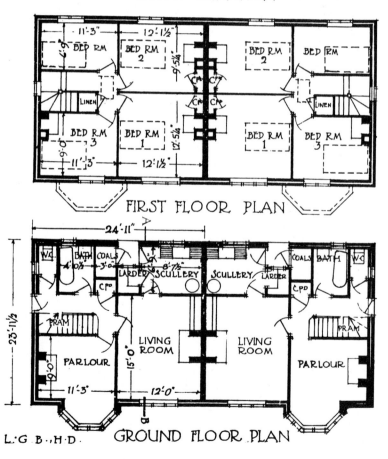

FIRST FLOOR PLAN

GROUND FLOOR PLAN

L·G·B··H·D·

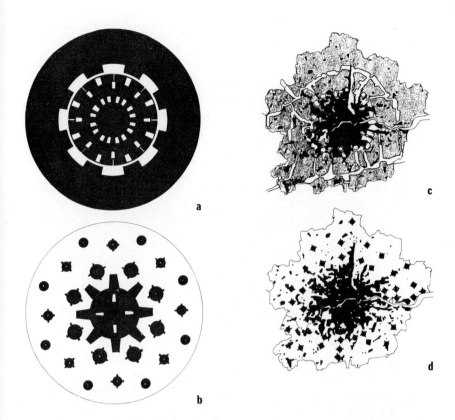

(Above) The Greater London Development Plan, *1929. The pattern and the background. (a) Open space designed on a background of potential building land (b) Building areas designed on a background of open land (c) Green Girdle reserved on a background of land with unlimited potential for building (d) Diagram of satellites and areas for development on a background of open-land. Unwin's simple diagrams encapsulated a dual strategy for the Greater London region: in the 1944 Abercrombie Plan the more ambitious became the basis for the post-war contained metropolis with new towns to accomodate growth*

(Left) The Housing Manual, *1919. Four Bedroom Parlour Type and Three Bedroom Non-Parlour Type. The Manual presented a series of standard types, originating from a list drawn up by Unwin for discussion with the reconstruction panel on housing. The new Ministry of Health under Addison, with Unwin as Chief Architect, seemed determined to prove that the State and Local Authorities could promote housing standards which were little short of revolutionary*

(xiii)

Sir Patrick Abercrombie as President of the Town Planning Institute, 1925. (Royal Town Planning Institute)

GREATER LONDON PLAN

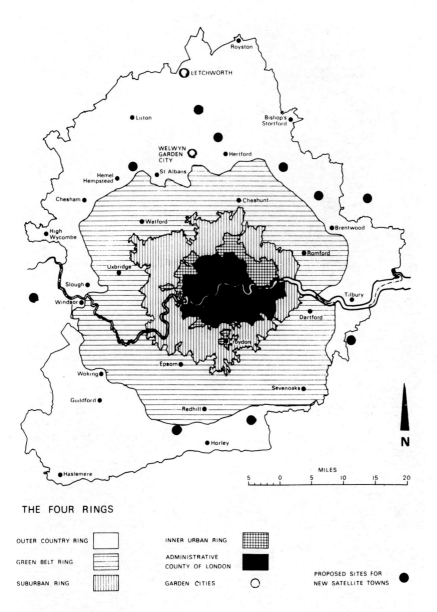

Royston
○ LETCHWORTH
● Luton
Bishop's ●
Stortford
WELWYN
GARDEN
CITY ○
● Hertford
Hemel
Hempstead
St Albans
Chesham ●
● Cheshunt
● Watford
High
Wycombe
● Brentwood
Uxbridge
● Romford
Slough ●
Tilbury
Windsor ●
Dartford
Croydon
Epsom ●
Woking ●
Sevenoaks ●
Guildford ●
Redhill ●
● Horley
● Haslemere

N

MILES
5   0   5   10   15   20

THE FOUR RINGS

OUTER COUNTRY RING	□
GREEN BELT RING	▤
SUBURBAN RING	▥

INNER URBAN RING	▦
ADMINISTRATIVE COUNTY OF LONDON	■
GARDEN CITIES	○

PROPOSED SITES FOR
NEW SATELLITE TOWNS   ●

*The Greater London Plan,
1944: the four rings. The
practical application of the
new town and green belt to
metropolitan scale
planning. (Town and
Country Planning
Association)*

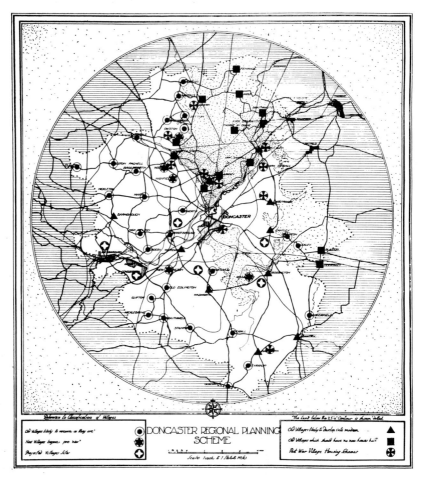

Classification of villages in the Doncaster Region: concern for community in the first regional plan prepared by Abercrombie and T. H. Johnson, 1920–22. (The Doncaster Regional Planning Scheme, *Liverpool University Press*)

Woodbridge, Suffolk: villages and landscape were again of concern in a plan for a predominantly rural region prepared by Abercrombie with Sydney Kelly between 1931 and 1934 (East Suffolk Regional Planning Scheme, *Liverpool University Press, 1935*)

The County of London Plan, 1943: social and functional analysis. Concern with community reaches maturity. (*Adapted from* County of London Plan, *Macmillan and London County Council, 1943*) the Solway, with an impressive view towards Skiddaw and the Lake District, which Unwin incorporated on the long axis of the plan. On one of his site visits Unwin checked the alignment and to the consternation of the surveyors asked them to correct it: 'it was', they groused, 'the first day in three months that it had been possible to see that far'.[58] The existing Annan Road formed a division between a modified grid layout to the south, developed with temporary timber buildings, and a more informal layout to the north along Victory Road. Courtenay Crickmer (1879–1971) acted as resident architect in charge of a team with considerable Garden City experience, and housing designs ranged from roughcast informality to a more austere brick neo-Georgian style which became a prototype for many inter-war council estates. Unlike inter-war estates Gretna and the smaller community of Eastriggs a few miles away were provided with churches, shops, schools, institutes and cinemas, whilst large central canteens were also established in connection with the hostel accommodation. The developments clearly demonstrated the benefits of a planned provision of housing, and were ready models for post-war reconstruction.[59]

Asquith took the first initiative in this direction but the pace quickened under Lloyd George's administration, with a Ministry of Reconstruction under Addison and a Reconstruction Committee divided into panels – Seebohm Rowntree, Lord Salisbury and Unwin were involved with housing.[60] It was concluded that immediate provision of 300,000 houses in England and Wales must be made within twelve months after the war, and that the State must intervene, with subsidies to cover abnormal post-war building costs. In July 1917 Hayes Fisher, President of the Local Government Board, convened a committee of inquiry under the chairmanship of Sir John Tudor Walters to examine the whole question of the provision of working class housing.[61] Members included Unwin, Sir Aston Webb and Frank Baines. Unwin threw his whole energy into the work and the published report bears the imprint of his concepts of housing design, garden suburbs, site selection and survey. Thus the fragmentary experimentation of Letchworth and Hampstead crystalised into statutory house types and area standards, and a density of twelve houses to the acre, paving the way for an unprecedented municipal intervention into the provision of housing: Unwin and the committee were determined to demonstrate that state and local authorities in partnership could fulfil the ideal of 'homes for heroes', but the harsh post-war economic climate soon brought retrenchment.

Political infighting modified the commitment to reconstruction, but a strong Housing and Town Planning Act emerged in July 1919, incorporating many of the findings of the Tudor Walters Committee, requiring local authorities to submit proposals for housing schemes within three months, imposing a statutory duty to provide working class housing, and offering the incentive of a subsidy of 75% of abnormal costs. The town planning provisions were less dramatic, but simplified the cumbersome procedure of 1909, and required every local authority with a population greater than 20,000 to prepare a planning scheme for development land within three years. In June 1919 the Ministry of Health was created under Addison, with Raymond Unwin as Chief Housing Architect, and later Chief Technical Officer for Building and Town Planning. George Pepler was also recruited to the Ministry.

Initially hopes were high as local authorities embarked upon their schemes with varying degrees of competence and enthusiasm. Barry Parker became one of the foremost consultants, in effect still in partnership with Unwin by assisting local government to implement schemes which demonstrated Tudor Walters and Garden City principles in practice. House types were standardised but Parker's ingenuity came to the fore in layout, particularly the short cul-de-sac and the use of octagonal groupings to frame road junctions. Letchworth had acquired urban district status in 1919 and two early estates – Jackmans Place (Bennett and Bidwell) and The Crescent (Crickmer) represented continuity from the pioneering housing society schemes. The Treasury soon began to count the cost and in April 1921 Addison resigned and Sir Alfred Mond soon terminated the generous subsidies, restricting local authorities to stereotyped copies of the simplest dwelling-types from the Housing Manual. The Housing Acts were periodically modified bringing an increasingly partisan approach to provision of housing – further tightening of controls under Baldwin, more liberal subsidies under the short-lived Macdonald government. A period of stability from 1924 with the Ministry under the control of Neville Chamberlain enabled consolidation. Unwin remained a constant factor, promoting good housing design wherever possible, and taking a keen interest in the development of new techniques and materials through the Building Research Station. As a town planning inspector on behalf of the Ministry he became involved with the initiation of Wythenshawe, the Manchester satellite, in 1926, reviewing the city's application for loan sanction to acquire the Tatton Estate, and recommending the purchase of additional land. The following year the Town Clerk approached him requesting the recommendation of a suitable consultant, and the subsequent appointment of Barry Parker suggests that the old partnership was still alive, both men oblivious of the accusation of collusion which critics of a more cynical era would have been only too ready to have levelled.[62] Parker's plan (1927–31) provided the prototype satellite community, with neighbourhood planning, density zoning, and articulation of the whole by parkways, a bold updating of Howard's concept to suit the motor age, and highly regarded by American observers such as Mumford. Regrettably implementation was inhibited by the long battle to incorporate the land within the city boundary, and the economic crisis of the early 1930s.

The Tudor Walters standards, amplified in detail by the Housing Manual, 1919, which illustrated a range of house plans and model layouts, established a basic approach which was re-affirmed by the Dudley Report in 1944, and not seriously questioned until the Parker Morris Report of 1961. The effect on urban form and housing design was revolutionary and encompassed both public and private sectors. The narrow frontage terrace house had long been the norm for all except the most prestigious middle-class suburbs, and was now ousted in favour of the wide frontage cottage, built in groups of two, four and six, with generous gardens and tree lined roads, curving around contours or forming complex geometrical patterns, many of which could only be appreciated from the air or from maps. The speculative developer soon selected the semi-detached house as the most effective compromise between economy and individuality. The pattern of low density suburbs spread to all major cities, towns and even to villages, often little more than feeble copies of the original high design standards, but meeting the aspirations particularly of the growing members of lower-middle class white collar workers, a surprisingly high percentage of whom were tenants in large council estates. The Ruskinian ideal of 'a home of our own' was promoted through acceptance of Tudor Walters standards, but planning controls were ill-suited to secure preservation of natural features, articulation of form and prevention of the urban development which inexorably followed the construction of the new arterial roads of the 1920s. Unwin was already in 1919 conscious of the need to control the overall pattern of development as well as the detail but a decade elapsed before he was given the opportunity to apply his simple logic to the complexities of the metropolitan region.

Regional perspectives 1921–40

Unwin's interest in the city region appears to have been stimulated by contact with Geddes during the organisation of the 1910 Town Planning Congress, where a section was devoted to the latter's work on the subject. In 1911 Unwin attended the Third National Town Planning Conference in Philadelphia with Adams and Thomas Mawson and was impressed by the advance of the 'City Beautiful' movement. A three day visit to Chicago, where the Burnham plan of 1909 formed the basis of a comprehensive physical plan, revealed an approach to the articulation of the large city in terms of the spacious park reservations to deal with the overall form – 'this green-girdle is indeed a wonderful creation'[63] he declared in a lecture at Manchester the following year. He also endorsed the grass-roots policy of provision of neighbourhood community centres and playgrounds within a half-mile of each home which would result in 'the amorphous mass of humanity . . . beginning to take on a definite relation to the centre . . . as particles in a chemical solution group themselves into beautiful crystalline form about some central point of attraction'.[64] These simple concepts formed the basis of his twenty year involvement with the problems of Greater London.

Pepler had proposed the designation of a parkway green-girdle around London as early as 1911 related to recommendations of the Royal Commission on Traffic, and the 1913 Arterial Roads Conference agreed on the need for north and south circular roads. Unwin became a member of the London Society, a group of eminent professionals who during the First World War prepared a plan, published as a large-scale atlas with traffic proposals, open space and recreation zones superimposed on the base map.[65] Under the editorship of Sir Aston Webb a collection of essays, *The Future of London*, was published in 1921.[66] Unwin's contribution dealt with the control of growth by 'a green belt . . . preserved around London to protect its inhabitants from disease, by providing fresh air, fresh fruit and vegetables, space for recreation',[67] secured 'by the development of satellite towns, largely self-supporting having their own industries, garden cities, and perhaps also by detached dormitory suburbs'.[68] This represented a re-statement of Howard's original concept, and coincided with the views of younger advocates of the garden city movement – C. B. Purdom and Frederic Osborn. A quarter century was to elapse before the concept received full statutory recognition through the New Town Act, 1946 – the legal framework for the implementation of the detailed proposals of Abercrombie's Greater London Plan (1944). Unwin recognised the key problem of development values which he felt could be approached following the example of Letchworth, with local authorities buying outlying land, planning development, and ultimately recovering the increase in value for the community. Perhaps no single planning-related issue has provoked such lengthy controversy: Unwin could look back to the German town extension plans where the municipality had long been able to assemble and redistribute ownership patterns according to a prescribed plan and reflect upon the inability of the 1909 and 1919 legislation to deal with the problem. The matter remained in abeyance until the Second World War, and the most comprehensive attempt to grasp the issue was incorporated into the 1947 Town and Country Planning Act, which involved the nationalisation of development values.

Unwin continued to press the broader scale of planning through the International Federation for Housing and Town Planning, at whose conferences he was a key figure throughout the 1920s, taking over chairmanship following Howard's death in 1928. In 1922 he had been consulted by the Russell Sage Foundation on the New York Regional Plan which Thomas Adams was invited to prepare, and the Federation meetings, which included New York in 1925,[69] presented an opportunity to evaluate progress on an international basis. Although beyond the scope of statutory town planning, the regional scale emerged in the 1920s as a useful vehicle for advisory plans, promoted by joint committees: Patrick Abercrombie was particularly active as a consultant in this respect.

In November 1927 Neville Chamberlain, then Minister of Health, convened the Greater London Regional Planning Committee, forty-five members representing the London County Council and the complex tiers of authority from rural districts to metropolitan boroughs. Unwin was appointed as Technical Advisor on 1 January 1929, following his retirement from the Ministry of Health. The area of concern was the London and the Home Counties Traffic Area, 1,846 square miles within 25 miles of Charing Cross. Whilst the committee appeared to be high-powered and comprehensive in its aims the practical reality was rather different, and outgoings were initially minute. Unwin rented offices and he was driven by his son Edward through the metropolitan fringe to survey the consequences of unplanned sprawl, ribbon development, haphazard shacklands and spreading glass-houses which pock-marked the countryside before it was totally overwhelmed by low-density speculatively built suburbs which must have appeared as grotesque shades of Hampstead. Unwin wrote the major part of the *First Report* published in December 1929[70] – a slim and hastily written document which established a frame of reference later taken up by Abercrombie. Unwin drew four rings from the County of London to the Greater London Region, analysing population trends within each. Decentralisation had gathered momentum since 1921 and a means of articulation had to be sought to give some perceptible overall form to development. Unwin seized on open space, to fulfil social needs for recreation in addition to the overall physical objective, assigning narrow belts to separate the four rings in widths proportional to the population – recalling Pepler's 1911 green girdle.

Unwin developed his proposals in terms of alternative strategies, characteristically presented as balanced opposites conceived in terms of a 'pattern' and 'background',[71] completing a continuum of physical design which had begun with the individual object. A major initiative would have been required to attain the more radical model of self-contained satellites in a green setting. A more limited view was based upon the assumption that virtually all land had development potential and the planning process should be confined to reservation of public open space, resulting in suburban tracts articulated by green wedges following river valleys, linked to form a green girdle about fifteen miles from the centre of London – a model based on Unwin's earlier enthusiastic response to the Chicago park belt in 1911.

Agreement on even the lesser alternative required immediate steps to protect 62 square miles of recreational open space and 142 square miles of additional open land. Unwin diagramatically superimposed the alternatives on the map of the region, but stated that the patterns did not represent an agreed spatial allocation. He recommended the creation of an executive regional body with land acquisition powers, or at the least a voluntary pooling of interests by major landowners and uniform use of planning powers throughout the region. In the event the committee did nothing and many local authorities withdrew or reduced their contributions. Unwin continued to press the proposals in public engagements and subsidised the publication of a *Second Report* in 1933 which included the Radburn plan and a detailed proposal for a narrow green girdle around London. The committee was reconstituted under the 1932 Town and Country Planning Act and in 1935 the LCC resolved to contribute £2 million towards the formation of a green belt, given statutory recognition in 1938. Slowly Unwin's recommendations were adopted, but in the context of a rearguard action, rather than in the ordering of the inter-war development which earlier initiative could have promoted. Unwin also served on the Marley committee which reported in 1935[72] on steps to promote a state garden cities programme and he gave evidence to the Barlow commission, appointed by Chamberlain as Prime Minister in 1937 to enquire into physical, social and economic aspects connected with the distribution of the industrial population, which laid foundations for post-war new towns and co-ordinated regional policies and planning.[73] In the early 1930s Unwin may have seemed to be working for an inactive committee convened by a Ministry not geared towards policy and research, and with few staff with a cutting edge,[74] but even from these unpromising surroundings key concepts emerged which were to be developed in post-1945 planning.

Elder statesman

Unwin served as President of the RIBA 1931–3, and was knighted in 1932. Academic honours from British, European and American universities indicated recognition of his pioneer role in environmental design and emergence as an elder statesman of town planning. On public occasions he would look back over half a century to his memories of Ruskin and Morris, re-affirming their philosophy. Younger colleagues would seek him out – the Danish architect Steen Eiler Rasmussen described one such occasion when Unwin hosted a group of students at 'Wyldes': 'as he stirred up the fire with a few movements of the poker, he could bring new life to the discussion by means of a Socratic question now and then'.[75] His activities in the cause of housing and town planning continued unabated, particularly in the United States. His daughter Peggy had married an American publisher in 1920, and transatlantic visits became more frequent.

In 1934 he was invited to join the Rockefeller International Housing Commission with the National Association of Housing Officials, which forwarded a national policy in the context of Roosevelt's 'New Deal'.[76] Two years later he was appointed visiting Professor of Architecture at Columbia University, returning each session until 1939–40. His lectures represented a distillation of his personal involvement with all levels of planning. Carl Feiss acted as his assistant and recalled that

Unwin always spent hours in the studio . . . students liked him right away . . . he was always genial and friendly and relaxed . . . Mumford, Stein, Ascher . . . would wander into the drafting room and we would have several hours of informal discussion . . . Unknowingly the students were being exposed to a unique assembly of geniuses dedicated to the public interest.[77]

Unwin was both fascinated and appalled by the scale and pace of urban development in the USA:[78] as early as 1924 he had analysed the congestion resulting from skyscraper office development and at the very end of his life turned to the related problems of derelict land bordering the central business districts of the great American cities. His solution was to invoke the tried and tested principles of low density residential development which would provide a speedier and more equitable, though lower, rate of return than would the selection of small parcels for high density development whereby the owner would recoup all, and many nothing at all.[79] Such proposals were, after all, logical updating of Morris and Howard.

He arrived in the United States on his last trip shortly before the outbreak of the Second World War. He had been working on the agenda for an international planning forum, subsequently cancelled. The overall theme posed the question 'Can planning raise the general standard of living?' Unwin had no hesitation in affirming this proposition and the process which he had done much to initiate:

1. Planning improves homelife by providing better living places in pleasanter surroundings with increased security for their amenity values.
2. It enlarges the economic basis of life by affording more adequate opportunities for the fishing industry and agriculture.
3. It enhances the effective value of all production by promoting rapid and convenient means of transport for persons and food and thus aiding efficient and economical distribution, both wholesale and retail.
4. It adds to the enjoyment of life by increasing the opportunities for every kind of healthy recreation and culture for all.
5. It adds to the richness and quality of life by preserving the natural beauty of the country and by securing orderly and comely urban development, thus satisfying the natural aesthetic hunger of mankind.[80]

Raymond Unwin died in Lyme, Connecticut on 28 June 1940 after a two-month illness.[81] Much of the work he had campaigned for became the basis for the planned post-war reconstruction of Britain.

Evaluation

Unwin's career evolved naturally from the broad views of the new society which his socialist apprenticeship provided. His practical experience, by contrast, led from the particular to the general, from the grass roots of home, hearth and family to the community, the Garden City and ultimately to the region. He accomplished a transition from the reformist tradition to a broader strategy of environmental management, concerned with forging a balanced relationship between housing and employment, education, leisure and open space. Although largely concerned with physical design Unwin did not neglect social factors: indeed concern for a fuller life and a more just society underlay the projects with which he was most closely identified – Earswick, Letchworth and Hampstead, which set standards for post-1919 housing and town planning, themselves promoted through his wartime work for the Ministry of Munitions and service on the housing panel and Tudor Walters Committee. Unwin moved easily towards the larger scale:

No matter how intricate the problem or all embracing his proposals, he never outgrew his confidence in and human affection for open space and the land, his faith in beauty as a positive element in human affairs, his expectation that a planner should be committed and concerned, a social artist before he was a social scientist, and, above all that he should not lose his head . . . should have common sense.[82]

This latter quality shone throughout. His tweed clad figure appeared like a backwoodsman among the immaculately clad academics at Harvard and MIT where he received honorary degrees. His clear, direct philosophy was founded upon a bedrock of sincerity, an ability to see both sides of an issue, to take a balanced view where 'everything matters but nothing overmuch'.[83] His personal lifestyle and designs are aptly summed up by a quotation from Barry Parker's 'Our Homes' (1895): 'plain, simple and ungarnished if necessary, but honest'.[84] Old fashioned virtues became outdated in the febrile inter-war period and the Garden City lost ground to the alternative vision 'La Ville Radieuse', which gloried in the growing mechanisation of life. Unwin perhaps seemed to be 'a bit of a Quaker'[85] but the intervening half century has served to emphasise the robustness of his simple concepts.

His civil service career is more difficult to evaluate than his pre-1914 projects. Clearly he played a central role in the adoption of his approach to housing design and layout in post-1919 housing legislation. Success of the policy depended on the initiative and competence of the individual local authority, the financial and political climate and the quality of architect, designer and, subsequently, housing manager. Unwin remained loyal to the low density cottage estate, defending it in the face of greater emphasis on flats in the 1930s, prophesying that:

England will rue the day . . . the housing movement of half a century is sacrificed for the makeshift expedience of congestion, the futility of which has been proved whenever it has been adopted.[86]

Although few schemes achieved the co-ordinated approach advocated by Tudor Walters and official adoption of town planning was slow and sporadic, the public sector made a significant contribution to housing provision in a comparatively short time and most estates incorporated the principles of layout and planning to serve as models for the private sector. Politicians of all governmental levels and parties soon realised the power of housing statistics; even Unwin was not averse to playing the numbers game, particularly at Columbia University where he commended 'England's Housing Example': 1,800,000 houses, 19% of the 1932 stock, built between 1919–32 under the various Housing Acts.

Present-day distrust of statistics and the uncertainty of the future of public housing has again focused attention on the quality of life, the individual hearth and home, the field where Unwin's contribution was most sure and original, where he matched need and aspiration, aesthetics and economics, reviving traditional forms to invoke potent and enduring images of the family and its activities as the rational and human basis for planning.

Notes

1 The author has developed this theme at greater length in his forthcoming book *An Environment for Everyman*
2 The Royal Gold Medal – Presentation to Sir Raymond Unwin, Monday 12 April 1937 – extracts from Sir Raymond Unwin's address', *RIBAJ*, 24 April 1937, p582
3 William Morris 'Art and Socialism: The aims and ideals of the English Socialist of Today', a lecture delivered before the Secular Society of Leicester, 23 January 1884; *Collected Works*, Vol XXIII, p127
4 Walter Creese recounts this in *The Search for Environment*, Yale, 1966. Christy Booth (Unwin's cousin) and Peggy Curtice Hitchcock (Unwin's daughter) also independently told the author of this
5 At this time Unwin wrote to Ethel Parker of his vocation to undertake a detailed study of Hinton's work and drafts are in Unwin Coll, Manchester Univ.
6 Raymond Unwin, 'The Dawn of a Happier Day', ms lecture, January 1886, Unwin Papers, BAL (RIBA)
7 In his memoirs, *My Days and Dreams*, Allen and Unwin, London, 1916, Carpenter characterised Unwin of this period as 'a young man of cultured antecedents . . . healthy, democratic vegetarian'
8 Information on Barrow Hill and Staveley is held by Sheffield Reference Library. Directors' minutes which record the Company's increasing involvement with housing are in British Steel Corporation Archives, Irthlingborough, Northants
9 Unwin to Ethel Parker, 9 August 1891, Hitchcock Coll.
10 Bruce Glasier underwent a similar training to Unwin, who would have liked to include him in the practice: see Lawrence Thompson, *The Enthusiasts: A biography of John and Katherine Bruce Glasier*, Gollancz, London, 1971, p135
11 Osborn stressed this point as Unwin's most significant achievement in conversation with the author, May 1976
12 Raymond Unwin, 'Sutton Hall', *Commonweal*, 15 June 1889, p160
13 'An Artisan's Living Room' was first published in Barry Parker's 'Our Homes', *Building News*, 19/26 July 1895, and privately reprinted, Buxton, 1895. Much of the original material survives in Parker Coll, FGC Mus, and can confidently be dated several years earlier than its 'definitive' publication in Barry Parker and Raymond Unwin, *The Art of Building a Home*, Longmans, London, 1901
14 Raymond Unwin, 'Co-operation in Building' in *The Art of Building a Home, ibid*, pp92–5

15 *The Garden City Conference at Bournville . . . Report of Proceedings*, Garden City Association, London, 1901 contains a paper by Unwin, 'On Building Houses in the Garden City', which began the process of reworking Howard's prototype with Arts and Crafts overtones

16 The proposals were described by Parker and Unwin in 'Cottages Near a Town', pp34–43 in *Catalogue of the Northern Artworkers Guild Exhibition, Aug 10–31, 1903*, Mayfield Press, Manchester, 1903

17 List of Delegates, *The Garden City Conference at Bournville, op cit*

18 The early Earswick plan was reproduced in L. Waddilove, *One Man's Vision: The Story of the Joseph Rowntree Village Trust*, Allen and Unwin, London, 1954. The initial layout for the area south of Station Road was held by the former Flaxton RDC. Both originals have subsequently disappeared

19 A detailed sequence of building was compiled by Keiji Makino in 'New Earswick: A Study for Conservation', unpub dissertation, Institute of Advanced Architectural Studies, University of York, 1979

20 The minutes of the Joseph Rowntree Village Trust give a fascinating account of the conflict between Unwin's picturesque ideals and their philistine dismissal as 'fads' by the resident clerk-of-works W. J. Swain.

21 Described in detail by Parker in 'Site Planning as Exemplified at New Earswick', *Town Planning Review*, Vol XXVII, No 3, February 1937, pp79–102

22 As recounted in Dugald Macfadayan, *Sir Ebenezer Howard and the Town Planning Movement*, Manchester University Press, Manchester, 1933, p20

23 Published by Swan Sonnestein, London, a firm noted for socialist literature including Marx's *Das Kapital*. Howard's book is much more accessible today in the text of the 1902 revision, *Garden Cities of Tomorrow*, edited by F. J. Osborn for a new edition published by Faber, London, 1946

24 A number of interesting drafts and diagrams survive in Howard Papers, Herfordshire County Council Record Office

25 Original in Howard Papers (HCC)

26 Published in *The Garden City Conference at Bournville, op cit*

27 *Ibid*, pp69–70

28 *Ibid*, pp70–72

29 *Ibid*, p71

30 *Ibid*, p72

31 Archives, FGC Ltd, Letchworth Garden City Corporation

32 Unwin to Ebenezer Howard, 13 January 1903, LGC Corp Archives

33 Engineering Committee Minutes, 5 October 1903, FGC Ltd, LGC Corp Archives

34 *Ibid*, 20 October 1903

35 FGC Ltd, Board Minutes, 11 February 1904, LGC Corp Archives

36 Raymond Unwin, 'The Planning of Garden City', Appendix 8 in W. C. B. Purdom, *The Garden City*, Dent, London, 1913, p228

37 *General Suggestions and Instructions regulating buildings other than Factories on the Garden City Estate*, FGC Ltd, 1904. Unwin's authorship is confirmed

by a typescript draft of his in Unwin Coll, BAL (RIBA). His Hampstead Building Regulations later followed this format.

38 Raymond Unwin, 'Cottage Building in the Garden City', *The Garden City*, June 1906, pp107–11

39 Drawings showing the total proposal are in Parker Coll, FGC Mus, Letchworth

40 Raymond Unwin, 'on Building and Natural Beauty', in *The Art of Building a Home, op cit*, p84

41 *Ibid*, p84

42 HGS Trust Ltd, Board of Directors Meeting, 28 May 1906, Minute No 74, HGS Archives

43 Steen Eiler Rasmussen, 'A great planning achievement', *Town and Country Planning*, Vol XXV, No 7, July 1957, p286

44 H. E. von Berlepsch–Valendas, *Die Gartenstadtbewegung in England*, 1912, cited by Sir Nikolaus Pevsner in his foreword to *Hampstead Garden Suburb: the Care and Appreciation of its Architectural Heritage*, HGS Design and Study Group, London, 1977. The translation is by Sir Nikolaus.

45 *Ibid*, p135

46 Raymond Unwin, 'The Improvement of Towns', a paper read at the Conference of the National Union of Women Workers of Great Britain and Northern Ireland, 8 November 1904, p2

47 *Ibid*, p5

48 For a detailed account see John Minett, 'The Housing and Town Planning Act, 1909', *The Planner* (Journal of the Royal Town Planning Institute), Vol 60, No 5, May 1974, pp676–80

49 Raymond Unwin, *Town Planning in Practice: An Introduction to the Art of Designing Cities and Suburbs*, Fisher Unwin, London and Leipzig, 1909

50 Thomas Adams, *Recent Advances in Town Planning*, Churchill, London 1932, pp54–5. Significantly Adams chose a view of Hampstead as his frontispiece.

51 *Town Planning in Practice, op cit*, p320

52 *Ibid*, p327

53 Unwin's impromptu impressions of Chicago were included in the *City Club Bulletin*, Vol 4, No 13, 1911

54 See Gordon E. Cherry, *The Evolution of British Town Planning*, Leonard Hill, London, 1974

55 Published by the Garden Cities and Town Planning Association, London, 1912

56 Typescript notes by Sir Frederick Osborn, Parker Coll, FGC Mus, Letchworth

57 See S. L. G. Beaufoy 'Well Hall Estate, Eltham', *Town Planning Review*, October 1950, pp259–71; and Simon Pepper and Mark Swenarton, 'Home Front', *Architectural Review*, Vol CLXIII, No 976, June 1978, pp364–75

58 Peggy Curtice Hitchcock to the author, 5 August 1979.

59 The complete list of Ministry of Munitions schemes was given in Appendix I (chapter III) *History of the Ministry of Munitions*, Vol V, Part V, HMSO, London, 1922

60 Paul Barton Johnson gave a comprehensive account of planning for post-war reconstruction in *A Land fit for Heroes*, University of Chicago Press, Chicago and London, 1968

61 Published as *Report of the Committee appointed by the President of the Local Government Board and the Secretary for Scotland to consider questions of Building Construction in connection with the provision of dwellings for the working classes in England Wales and Scotland and to report upon the methods for securing economy and despatch in the provision of such dwellings*, Cmnd 9191, 1918

62 Wythenshawe Estate Special Committee, Minutes, City of Manchester Archives

63 See Note 53 above for Unwin's initial impressions; also Raymond Unwin, *The Town Extension Plan*, Warburton Lecture for 1912, Manchester University Press, Manchester, 1912, p44

64 *Ibid*, p45

65 London Society, *Development Plan of Greater London . . . prepared during the Great War 1914–1918*, London, 1919

66 Published by Dutton, London, 1921. Unwin's contribution was entitled 'Some Thoughts on the Development of London', pp177–92

67 *Ibid*, p181

68 *Ibid*, pp181–2

69 The visit of the party, which also included Ebenezer Howard and Barry Parker, had a significant impact on Lewis Mumford and the younger generation of American planners including Henry Wright and Clarence Stein. The occasion was vividly recalled by Mumford, in conversation with the author, June 1978.

70 Greater London Regional Planning Committee, *First Report*, Knapp Drewett, London 1929

71 A theme developed by Unwin and published separately as 'Urban Development: The Pattern and the Background', *Journal of the Town Planning Institute*, Vol XXI, No 10, August, 1935.

72 *Garden Cities and Satellite Towns*, Report on the Departmental Committee, HMSO, London, 1935

73 *Report of the Royal Commission on the Distribution of the Industrial Population*, Cmnd 6153, HMSO, London 1940

74 Information from Blaise Gillie, former Under Secretary of the Welsh Office

75 Steen Eiler Rasmussen, 'Unwin: The Man and the Planner', *Town and Country Planning*, Vol XXI, Nov 1953, p433

76 For greater detail see Carl Feiss, 'Unwin's American Journeys', *Town and Country Planning*, Vol XXXI, Nov and Dec 1963, pp422–7 and pp471–3

77 Carl Feiss in a letter to the author, May 1979

78 Unwin presented his first detailed arguments against skyscraper office development in 'Higher Building in Relation to Town Planning', *RIBAJ*, Vol XXX, No 5, 12 January 1924, pp125–49

79 Raymond Unwin, 'Land Values in Relation to Planning and Housing in the United States', *Journal of Land and Public Utility Economics*, Vol XVII, No 1, February 1941

80 'Sir Raymond Unwin's Suggestions for a Proposed Forum: Unwin-Tugwell-Moses-Heydecker', Lyme, Connecticut, 9 September 1939, Unwin Coll, UN 16/59, BAL (RIBA)

81 The principal obituaries appeared in *New York Times* (30 June 1940); *RIBAJ* (15 July 1940); *JTPI* Vol XXVI, No 5, (July/August 1940). Both the latter included memoirs by Barry Parker.

82 Walter L. Creese, *The Legacy of Raymond Unwin: A Human Pattern for Planning*, MIT, Cambridge Mass, and London, 1967, p34

83 Recounted by Christy Booth to the author.

84 Barry Parker, 'Our Homes', *Building News*, 19/26 July, 1895, p105

85 Lewis Mumford to the author, June 1978. Unwin was characterised as 'politically gifted, dispassionate, reasoned, always a bit of a Quaker – a sound, practical man due to his apprenticeship as an engineer'. By contrast Parker was 'the complete artist from head to foot – I felt drawn to his personality, he was one of the most loveable men I ever met'.

86 Raymond Unwin, 'Cottage Homes Better than Flats: Congestion and Discontent', *Daily Telegraph* Housing Supplement, 26 November 1934, pvii

5

PATRICK ABERCROMBIE
1879–1957

Gerald Dix

Professor Sir Patrick Abercrombie enjoyed a professional career of extraordinary duration and enduring durability coinciding almost exactly with the first half century of statutory planning in Britain. At the time of his death, in 1957, he had been thinking, teaching and practising planning for over fifty years with a zeal and devotion that carried him forward from a junior architectural assistantship in a Liverpool office to being the world's foremost prophet and practitioner of town and country planning. No mere theoretical 'paper-planner' with pet ideas and pat formulae to thrust down people's throats, or with any high-handed 'take-it-or-leave-it' attitude, he was a patient striver for a true appreciation of a problem and then for its most logical, beneficial and just solution in the light of all the special circumstances, taking a wide bifocal view of planning that was new at the time and characteristic of all his work.[1]

Leslie Patrick Abercrombie was born in Ashton-on-Mersey in 1879, the ninth child of a Manchester businessman. He was educated at Uppingham and on the continent before being articled on 11 May 1897, for four years, at a premium of £300, to Charles Henry Heathcote, a Manchester architect. Soon after his apprenticeship was over the young architect made the most complete break in his life when he moved to Merseyside.[2] He came to know and love Birkenhead and Wirral and became an admirer of Chester, where he went to work for a firm of architects in which he hoped for an early partnership. Abercrombie's Chester days formed an unconscious preparation for planning, for he maintained that he learned more from the complexity of that ancient city and the way its form reflected different influences in its long history than he did from any other town.[3] When, after a year there, it became clear that his partnership chances remained firmly in the future, Abercrombie was happy to accept an invitation from Professor C. H. Reilly to a lectureship in the Liverpool School of Architecture. Receiving the invitation was a complete surprise to Abercrombie for he had never been a student in a school of architecture, but once in Liverpool it was not long before the opportunity arose for him to apply and further develop his interest in the new subject of town planning which had been hovering before him for years.[4]

The first ten years of this century were remarkable for an increasing awareness of the need to pay more attention to the design of our surroundings, and in 1909 when the first Housing and Planning Bill was before Parliament, William Hesketh Lever, later first Viscount Leverhulme, gave Liverpool University the funds to create a Department of Civic Design. As well as endowing the Chair that bears his name, Lever provided sufficient money to establish a research fellowship and the *Town Planning Review*. The first Lever Professor was Stanley Adshead and Reilly could think of no one better suited to complement him in the research fellowship than Patrick Abercrombie. As Lever Research Fellow, he had access to a travel fund and was able to visit Vienna, Paris, Berlin, Brussels and other cities, publishing his studies in the *Town Planning Review*, of which he was founder editor. In 1915 when Adshead resigned Abercrombie was appointed in his place to the chair he was to occupy for twenty years, during which time he was to play the principal role in establishing the reputation of the Department of Civic Design. It was Abercrombie's ambition to produce students with a breadth of outlook and technical skill, adopting Geddes's fundamental triad of 'Place:Folk:Work' as the basis of his teaching.[5]

Whilst consolidating the work of the young department, Abercrombie became prominent as a practitioner, especially in the field of regional planning. 'Perhaps I should explain', said Abercrombie in an autobiographical note, 'that the University allows its town planning staff to engage in private practice, which roughly corresponds to the external work done in writing or consultation by members of the professorial and junior staff in other departments'.[6] He attached great importance to this for, as he said, 'without these external contacts and experience, teaching (in planning and architecture) would gradually be etiolated into a pallid enunciation of theory based on second-hand information'.[7] This approach was important for it contributed substantially to the development of the subject and to the strength and reputation of the Department. Through professional contacts and those developed through the *Town Planning Review*, the department became a 'sort of information bureau',[8] which people visited for consultation and where there was a valuable library collection of books on planning and allied subjects. It was 'very much what Lord Leverhulme had in mind in founding the department and in financing the *Town Planning Review*',[9] and Abercrombie's many activities helped to establish the department as a centre of planning activity more all-embracing than simply the conduct of professionally orientated courses.

Abercrombie shared Geddes's view of the nature and purpose of town planning. 'Planning simply means proposing to do, and then doing, certain things in an orderly, pre-meditated, related and rational way, having in view some definite end that is expected to be beneficial.'[10] Town and country planning applies this principle to the use of land and buildings and Abercrombie had a clearer idea of what this involved than did most of his contemporaries: he summarised his views of the subject in his London Inaugural Lecture[11] and in a slim volume called, simply, *Town and Country Planning*[12] that remains as elegantly refreshing and relevant today as when it was first written more than forty years ago. 'Town and Country Planning', he said, 'seeks to proffer a guiding hand to the trend of natural evolution as a result of a careful study of the place itself, and its external relationships. The result is to be more than a piece of skilful engineering or satisfactory hygiene or successful economics: it should be a social organism and a work of art'.[13]

The start of private practice

Abercrombie's extensive private practice began modestly enough with the occasional commission to design housing schemes and cottages, as at Chester and Mouldsworth, or a country house, such as Hownhall, Ross-on-Wye[14] and through winning some of the architectural competitions for which he entered, for although his architectural practice formed only a small element in his long career, it was important as a foundation to his later work, showing clearly many of the influences to be found, often subtly concealed, in his approach to planning problems. One essential ability his architectural work gave him was that of considering concurrently and then mastering a range of functional and aesthetic requirements.

It was Patrick Abercrombie's success, in association with Sydney and Arthur Kelly, in the Dublin Town Planning Competition in 1914 that marked his entry into the leading ranks of the young planning profession. The assessors were John Nolen of Cambridge, Massachusetts, Charles McCarthy of Dublin, and Geddes. They were unanimous in their decision to award the first prize to Entry G, that prepared by Abercrombie and the Kellys, commenting on its magnitude and comprehensiveness.[15] Geddes, in fact, regarded the plan as impractical, and maintained that the survey was less adequate than it should have been.[16] He did not then know of Abercrombie's eighty pages of minutely handwritten notes from a personal survey *in ambulando*, lasting two weeks, undertaken to supplement published information, and 'characteristically' (as Abercrombie says) the survey was not published until some time after the plan was made.[17] Although the plan as such was never carried out, its authors enjoyed a long and continuing association with Dublin, for their proposals were not forgotten as the city developed. More importantly, the competition drew national and international attention to Abercrombie and to his application of a Geddesian approach, associating the town and its surrounding region in a way quite belying the superficially *beaux arts* appearance of much of the plan.

Doncaster and the start of regional planning

Abercrombie's work now began to take him further afield and with Adshead, he designed Dormanstown, a small 'workstown' near Redcar, and later with Henry Johnson of Doncaster, worked for Pilkington Brothers on the village of Kirk Sandall.[18]

In 1920 through the instrumentality of George Pepler of the Ministry of Health,[19] Abercrombie and Johnson were asked to make a regional planning scheme for the whole of the Doncaster area, covering 169 square miles and having a population of 139,940,[20] with the expectation of future growth. The report, approved in July 1922,[21] was the first comprehensive regional plan to be prepared in this country and became the model to be followed by Abercrombie and other planners,[22] even though it had to be prepared in the absence of any guidance about nationwide planning policy. Abercrombie had earlier advocated the carrying out of a survey of national resources[23] as a precursor for a comprehensive plan for development on a national, regional and local scale.[24] 'Doubtless', he had written in 1918, tongue in cheek, 'the Minister of Reconstruction has a general Plan in front of him, whether it has taken graphic shape or not; but there is no sign yet of a comprehensive survey of our resources upon which to base it'.[25] There was no sign of such a survey in 1921 at the time of the Doncaster plan; nor was there two decades later when Abercrombie was Chairman of a drafting committee to press for precisely the kind of survey that he had been proposing so long before.[26]

The importance of the Doncaster regional scheme may be considered under three headings: organisation, survey, recommendations. While the authors 'plunged boldly into concrete proposals affecting in definite ways the future growth of every local Authority'[27] in the area, they were at some pains to comply with the principle that their proposals should be of regional rather than purely local significance; local affairs should be dealt with locally and were none of their concern. A village by-pass which might open up a long distance route would clearly have regional significance, but local open spaces, for instance, being in Abercrombie's conception 'static', were considered to lie outside the scope of regional planning. It was thought that if the various district councils co-ordinated their plans and acted in accord with one another it would be possible to bring the regional proposals into operation piece by piece under the fairly rudimentary planning laws then operative. Events showed this view to be unrealistically optimistic.

Abercrombie considered it undesirable that there should be a single major centre and instead proposed the development of 'ten more communities, new or so changed as to rank as new, towns complete in themselves but of moderate size, manageable in their loose texture'. Central to them would be Doncaster, 'a city neither swollen nor tentacular, but in the truest sense of the word, metropolitan'.[28]

Topography and the dangers of subsidence were carefully considered and all residential development was to be kept away from low-lying land, the new communities being separated from one another by a green belt consisting partly of land liable to occasional flooding – as good a way as any, one might suppose, to ensure its respect by developers. And what better place than the proposed green belt for the line of the main A1 route north in a 120 ft reservation to allow room for planting within fencelines, well away from residential development? The advice was not heeded and although one community built a housing scheme on marshland, the planners were vindicated by nature when the site quickly became flooded. Later, too, narrow road reservations, adopted against their advice, had to be widened at great expense.

Here, then, were Geddes's lessons being applied in close association with Howard's garden city ideals in a scheme that perhaps also owed something to Arthur Crow's ten cities of health that Abercrombie had known from the Royal Institute of British Architects' Conference on Town Planning in 1910.[29] Here, too, are the first indications of some of those ideas that were to reach fruition in the great London plans and those for the Clyde Valley and the West Midlands, then still twenty years into the future. Despite Abercrombie's suggestion that the Doncaster plan might be considered deficient in formal research,[30] any weakness in this direction was overcome by the super-abundance of information available to him, largely through Johnson's encyclopaedic local knowledge which produced a flood from which overflows branched, meandering afar.[31] Although neither their experience nor their resources enabled the planners fully to organise and utilise all their material, it did ensure (as with the Dublin plan) that their proposals, the visible tips of the iceberg, were properly and substantially supported in a report that attracted attention far beyond immediate local and professional circles. John

Burns, a former President of the Local Government Board, offered his congratulations on 'such excellent work',[32] a sentiment shared by the reviewer in *The Architect* who regarded the Doncaster plan as 'a model of the manner in which such problems should be dealt with and which if applied to other districts in the course of development, would enable us to avoid the errors of the past and leave our successors an infinitely finer country'.[33]

Abercrombie considered the scheme the 'best piece of constructive regional planning'[34] that he had done and certainly with Dublin and Doncaster behind him, his professional reputation was assured.

The Sheffield City Survey

If there were doubts, other than those expressed privately by Geddes, that Abercrombie's early approach was inadequately supported by a proper survey, the Sheffield Civic Survey of 1924[35] must have gone a long way to assuage them. It is important methodologically and as an example of the way Abercrombie learned from experience. This report arose from a proposal that a committee be appointed to develop mutual municipal and industrial interests for the benefit of the city. What was required was a broadly conceived development plan based on a civic survey and relating the needs of the inhabitants and their access to work, and the provision of utilities and other services, considering at the same time the appearance of their surroundings.[36] The problem, said Abercrombie, was to arrange the 'parts of the city so that they form one satisfactory mechanism, each part performing its functions in the best way' and he emphasised the need for flexibility.[37] The Development Committee was spelling out in slightly different terms Geddes's belief in the relationship between Folk, Work and Place. This relationship would be achieved, as Geddes would have wished, through a survey and its analysis as a preliminary for the preparation of a plan, the Civic Survey being one of those things 'which always must be carry'd on, and still be doing, never done'.[38] The Sheffield survey certainly found favour with the *Sociological Review* which thought it was 'by far the most interesting of Professor Abercrombie's Reports; for the Survey, merely suggested in others, is here carried out in detail'.[39] 'I look upon the Dublin competition design, the Doncaster Regional Report and Sheffield Civic Survey as the foundation of all my town and regional planning work', wrote Abercrombie in 1940, adding that the 'landscape aspect was still to be developed'.[40]

The East Kent Regional Plan

If any one among the sixteen regional schemes prepared collaboratively in the period between 1923 and 1935[41] can be said to mark a single large step forward, it was that prepared in 1925 for East Kent.[42] It was not to be an attempt to improve an area already largely spoiled, but of planning to prevent the destruction of a region untouched by industrialisation; it was to be preventive medicine rather than surgery.

The presence of coal in Kent had been confirmed in 1890 and the coal measures were illustrated in a superb cross-section that Abercrombie drew and which was subsequently reproduced in the East Kent report.[43] It was suggested in the planning report that other industries should be encouraged and that they should be located within the as yet undetermined pit head zones. What was needed was a settlement pattern that could cater for mining and industrial needs and would also fit in to the chalk landscape of Kent. The solution to the planning problem in Kent was in many ways very different from that for Doncaster, although the parentage is fairly clear. Abercrombie's appreciation of environment and his Doncaster experience led him to propose the modest expansion of some existing centres and the building of eight small towns, between them serving eighteen pits, each settlement to be situated in a fold in the chalkland.[44] Abercrombie thought that small concentrations of carefully sited development, combined with a stout-hearted defence of the spaces between, was the only real way to reconcile mining and landscape considerations. Although the Kent plan gave careful consideration of the availability of building materials in sufficient quantities to maintain a steady rate of house building,[45] it did not adequately emphasise the organisational and social requirements necessary to translate plans into programmes and thence into development in which the completion of houses, schools, shops and places of work is co-ordinated. There were lessons to be learned here about programming development that would have been useful to those planning the new towns after the Second World War, but there were no monitoring procedures and the opportunity was missed. In East Kent, despite the Minister's exhortations, each of the local authorities went its own way, looking only after its own interests, leaving Abercrombie's bold plan as an inspiration and as a model for what might have been, and raising questions about whether or not the planner is to blame for the timidity, lack of courage or self-interestedness of those who seek his views.

The protection of the countryside
The countryside and country towns always interested Abercrombie and from his earliest days he had been concerned with the assimilation of buildings into the landscape. In October 1900, when he first visited the Cotswolds, he thought Tewkesbury 'quite lovely with

scarce a note out of tune – the fresh and red-tiled houses with half timbered ones between . . . quite charming', while at Chipping Campden, he wrote that 'every village contains houses that are not only architectural but individual'.[46] His sketches record what he saw of his 'beloved Cotswolds' and incidentally demonstrate his technical ability, for with Stanley Adshead and Sir Albert Richardson he was arguably one of the three best architectural draughtsmen of his day.[47]

Following planning commissions in a number of rural regions and consequent upon his observation of the vulnerability of the Wirral to the pressures of urbanisation, he became increasingly aware of the harm that was being done to the countryside as cheap transport encouraged the spread of 'Blasphemous Bungalows':[48] greater attention should be paid to the choice of building materials in the countryside. He was convinced that town and country must be planned together, but that the distinction between them must be kept clear. Dependent they might be, but the advantages of each would be destroyed if they were to be combined in an amorphous town-country. And yet he saw that perhaps all was not then lost. 'Ten years would convert the derelict desert between Birmingham and Wolverhampton into an incipient jungle',[49] he wrote in his 'Epistola Epilogica' to Clough Williams-Ellis' England and the Octopus, if only a more responsible and more sympathetic attitude could be encouraged. His idea was to protect and sensibly use the countryside, welcoming evolution and change in a landscape modified by the adoption of new agricultural methods. In 1926 he published in the Town Planning Review[50] a major essay which led directly to the establishment that year of the Council for the Preservation of Rural England (CPRE) with himself, the Earl of Crawford and Balcarres and Sir Guy Dawber as co-founders.[51] In his work for the CPRE, as in his planning reports and in his general planning advocacy, Abercrombie was at pains to emphasise that rural planning was not a simple matter and should not 'be embarked on casually by a country district with an under-staffed and over-worked surveyor and a quiescent Council'.[52] What he was after was the continuous study of the principles of landscape design[53] and the accompaniment of statutory power by persuasive planning; 'there should be, above all, a light hand in compulsion but a heavy hand on outrage'.[54]

Although he elaborated some of his ideas about rural planning in a series of accomplished but largely unrealised plans, Abercrombie never developed his many ideas in the theoretical basis of this aspect of his work. Perhaps it was best that way, for he was not by nature a theoretician. No man can do everything and, in Abercrombie's case, once the idea had been floated others might carry it on while he moved to new places with new ideas and fresh chains of activity. Time, the dimension that in its historical and future context was never forgotten in his reports, was forever driving Abercrombie to new developments in rural, urban and regional planning. The Bristol and Bath Plan of 1930 introduced a methodical notation of landscape character and values based on geology, topography, vegetation, architecture, population, services, natural history and traffic.[55] The Cumbrian Regional Report, prepared with Kelly in 1932, drew attention to many important planning problems in a potential national park area.[56] Although Abercrombie was subsequently to quote this plan as an example of the failure of local authorities to co-operate even to the extent of not having a single joint committee for the whole of the plan area,[57] Pepler thought the plan an excellent example of regional planning, worthy of display in an international exhibition.[58] Abercrombie himself drew many of the illustrations. The Gloucester report included village analyses based on techniques using photography to supplement mapping and notes.[59] A survey of the Thames Valley incorporated assessments of the importance of the protection of rural and riverside land from untoward development[60] and the East Suffolk regional scheme applied similar techniques to creeks and estuaries as well as to villages and market towns.[61]

Practice and purpose

The passage of time saw some standardisation of approach, which was both understandable and desirable. First there was a survey using published data and specially collected information on the basis of the detailed knowledge of Abercrombie's local collaborator, who was often selected because of the local background that he could contribute. Then there would be development proposals which might require the operation of several Acts of Parliament (not merely Town Planning Acts) as well as a deal of friendly persuasion. A third section was usually included to elaborate methods of implementation which always required co-operation and goodwill between neighbouring authorities. Thus, the schemes followed the Geddesian functional triad of survey, analysis and plan, which forms the basis of most subsequent planning methods.

Many of the reports were intended to help groups of authorities form planning policies. They were slim documents, but by no means lacking ideas. By present standards, many would be considered short of survey information and analysis, although often none the worse for that, especially as jargon was non-existent: they demonstrated Abercrombie's lightness of touch. It was accepted that plans would not suddenly be put into operation as if one were letting a building contract, but that they would guide development that would take place in any case. Detailed plans elaborated in accordance with an advisory scheme would be prepared to cope with growth shortly before it occurred, rather than in an attempt to forecast what that growth should be, all plans being sufficiently flexible to allow for adjustment as circumstances changed during the life of the plan.[62] And, of course, character, place and time dictated the degree of detail appropriate in plans prepared for different purposes. Each set of circumstances demanded an appropriate planning response. In all of this, be it in a coalfield or the Cotswolds, 'place' was predominant and the 'work' of 'folk' as manifest in the 'place'.[63] Although considering all three of the Geddesian elements Abercrombie was concerned primarily with 'place', with the built environment: folk alone, and their activities, he regarded as being primarily the concern of the sociologist and not the business of planners such as himself, nor of his department.[64]

It may well be, in the judgement of planners of later generations, that Abercrombie's major contribution to planning to the time he left Liverpool in 1935 (apart from his university teaching and his outstanding work in establishing and for many years editing the *Town Planning Review*) lay in the way in which he gave a practical reality to the long term possibilities of planning at a regional level. There were few who consistently demonstrated their ability to refine their planning techniques with each completed plan, as Abercrombie did; but perhaps few had his capacity for learning or for work: he was apparently indefatigable.

Industrial location and the Barlow Commission

In the aftermath of the economic depression of the 1930s a Royal Commission was appointed (in 1937) under the chairmanship of Sir Montague Barlow, to enquire into the causes which had influenced the geographical distribution of the industrial population, to consider possible changes in that distribution and to report what remedial action, if any, should be taken.[65] Service on the Commission enlarged Abercrombie's range of contacts, particularly within government; it also prompted him to write a Dissentient Memorandum[66] in which he developed some of his ideas about town and regional planning, its practice and administration. This important planning document was based on lessons learned from practice in many parts of the country and Abercrombie regarded it as a fairly full account of his views on the defects of the Town and Country Planning Act of 1932 and 'the general state of diarchy between the Ministries of Health and Transport'.[67] He was concerned that planning should be represented at the highest level in central government and that there should be an outline of general development giving positive policy guidance at national and regional level. There was a wide divergence between the regional plans prepared at the request of the joint committees and the statutory plans that were intended to put the proposals into effect: when it came to preparing statutory plans expressing positive actions rather than pious aspirations local authorities got cold feet; they were not interested in commitments that involved individual sacrifice.

'Clearly', stated Abercrombie in his Memorandum, 'however enlightened and far seeing a regional outlook can be, there must be some national guidance in the background'.[68] It was left to the lone voice of the practitioner to appeal for positive action going far beyond the 'accommodation of trends and expectations'[69] and embracing specific planning measures, including industrial and commercial location, agriculture and forestry, the location of population, including all their associated requirements, and transport, utilities and other services and recreation, as well as national parks and green belts and rural zones separating centres large and small, new towns and old settlements. What was required was an outline of general development on a national and regional basis, prepared by a research commission reporting to and forming part of a department or ministry. 'It need not be emphasised', wrote Abercrombie, giving much needed emphasis, 'that such a plan will not resemble a Statutory Scheme . . . it will be rather a policy than a plan, something flexible and continually evolving, based upon research, surveys and experience'.[70] The Ministry should have the power, *inter alia*, of the Minister of Health under the Town and Country Planning Act and the planning (but not construction and management) powers of the Ministry of Transport under the Restriction of Ribbon Development Act and the Trunk Roads Act.[71] Dressed up in the kind of planning jargon that Abercrombie abhorred, it would resemble very closely the practice of planning subsequent to the Planning Advisory Group Report of 1965.[72] We do not seem to have advanced far in forty years.

The early war years

Completion of the Barlow Report coincided with the outbreak of war in 1939 and with the evacuation of the Department of Town and Country Planning from London University to St. Catherine's College, Cambridge. Abercrombie, then aged 60, saw the disruption of his life as teacher and practitioner as perhaps marking the end of his major contribution to planning in Britain. How wrong can one be? Staying only long enough to see his small department settled in its new surroundings, Abercrombie left in May 1940 for Ceylon where, with Clifford Holliday, his former pupil and erstwhile colleague from the days when they had worked together in Tel-Aviv, he was to revert to a primarily architectural role in designing the University of Ceylon at Peradinya. He clearly enjoyed Ceylon and the long sea journey home provided the opportunity to review an eventful career and to look forward with interest, but not overmuch enthusiasm, to continuing work advising the Air Ministry on the location of air fields and the Ministry of Health on the design of mental hospitals.

The planning of London

When Patrick Abercrombie got back to England the first phase of bombing was over, the critical need for re-planning was evident and Lord Reith, Minister of Works, was 'considering the methods and machinery for the planning and carrying out of the reconstruction of town and country'.[73] The County of London Plan was not only to indicate proposals for the future development of the capital, but to assist Reith's Ministry in its deliberations; 'it was to be a plan capable of necessary adjustment', the proposals, believed by the authors to be practicable though 'involving works of great magnitude and expenditure' being indicative only, precise routes and boundaries to be decided in the light of later investigations.[74] Lord Latham, Leader of the London County Council, warned of obstacles ahead – 'conflicting interests, private rights, an outworn and different scale of values and lack of vision'[75] – giants that stood, too, in the way of the Greater London Plan[76] prepared by Abercrombie at the invitation of the Minister of Town and Country Planning.

The two London Plans were without doubt the most significant of contributions to planning practice in this country, for they brought together in realisable form not just the lessons of Abercrombie's experience over the years in Dublin and Doncaster, Sheffield and Kent and other places, but also ideas previously tried out separately elsewhere, here united in a single grand ensemble.

Whilst Abercrombie had not previously been concerned in any official way with the planning of London, he had for years taken a more than academic interest in the subject. As early as 1912 he had argued for the replacement of piecemeal topsy-turveydom by a plan for Greater London as a whole[77] and over the next thirty years he regularly analysed the planning – or lack of it – in the capital. He was a member of the Royal Academy Planning Committee under the Chairmanship of Sir Edwin Lutyens, which in 1942 produced a singularly unrealistic civic architecture London Plan.[78] In that year Abercrombie commended Alker Tripp's development of the idea of the precinct as a practical contribution to the planning of towns. He had earlier noted that the grid iron road plan, 'that least elevated but most honourably ancient form', was 'immeasurably superior to the

no-plan haphazard'.[79] It had been the basis for the development of
the London squares and now in his hands, combined with Tripp's
traffic ideas, its advantages were turned to good use in the precinct
development of Bloomsbury proposed in the *County of London Plan*,[80]
only to be ignored for 20 years until Colin Buchanan revived it in his
study of *Traffic in Towns*.[81]

The four major defects which any plan for the County would have to
overcome were traffic congestion, depressed housing, inadequacy
and maldistribution of open space and the jumble of indeterminate
zoning.[82] There was confusion over road planning: the Bressey
Report on roads in the London area[83] dealt with roads without
reference to land uses, whereas a contemporary LCC Scheme apparently ignored traffic needs and road plans in its land use proposals.[84]
The County Plan attempted to get the balance right. The principal
defect over housing was seen to be its general drabness rather than
the extremely high density found in some other cities: there was a
lack of industry to parallel the social individualism of the separate
communities that, in Rasmussen's view, make London unique.[85]
This could be overcome by the social and functional identification of
the various centres, each based on a former village or market town,
from which by coalescence London had developed, and by developing further to acceptable new standards from the old nucleii.[86]
Abercrombie thought that this concentration on community was the
most distinctive single contribution of the County Plan.[87]

Work on the Greater London Plan, prepared for the Standing Conference on London Regional Planning at the request of the Minister
of Town and Country Planning, began during the later part of the
preparation of the geographically smaller County plan, compared
with which this was extensive rather than intensive, consisting of
general ideas rather than detailed proposals.[88] In it Abercrombie
and his team proposed the definition of four rings beyond the
County. There would be, first, an inner urban ring, not in fact a ring
at all but a logical completion of some of the closer-in developed
areas. Outside this came a suburban ring and beyond that the Green
Belt; finally an outer country ring.

Abercrombie was careful to point out that although there was consultation with all the authorities concerned, the Regional Plan was
not the sum of the wishes and proposals of the multitude of separate
authorities concerned with planning in the Greater London area.[89]
Decentralisation, adapting and adopting Howard's concept of the
satellite town was the Plan's salient feature and the five major
assumptions on which the plan was based were clearly spelled out:
that the Barlow report recommending restriction of industrial
growth in London and the Home Counties would be accepted; that

more than a million people and their associated employment would be decentralised; that the total population of the area would be somewhat reduced; that London would continue as one of the world's great ports; and perhaps most important, that new planning powers would include the control of land values.[90] These were not unreasonable expectations at a time when there was a new Ministry charged exclusively with responsibility for town and country planning, with the Barlow, Scott and Uthwatt reports[91] before it. The tools for the job, or at least their specifications, were available. 'All things are ready', quotes Sir Patrick at the head of his report, 'if our minds be so'.[92] Evidently, most of our minds were not so, for although the plan was welcomed as 'the town planning classic for which the time [was] ripe, and the world has been waiting'[93] implementation was slow and it did not become the nucleus of the vital comprehensive planning many desired.[94] And yet although London is probably not as Abercrombie saw it in his mind's eye[95] the influence of the plan has been profound and Peter Self could write 35 years later that his plan 'was timeless and it was costless, and yet it was largely achieved over 20 years ago'.[96] The new towns are an achievement to be proud of even though all but two are on different sites from those proposed.

The idea of the Green Belt is widely accepted albeit frequently misapplied, and many of the elements of the plan are now standard in the better examples of planning practice in this country and abroad. Whilst the London plans can be criticised for regarding 'industry' as being primarily manufacturing and for their failure to anticipate the growth of office employment[97] or road traffic, they must be assessed against the conditions anticipated at the time of preparation. What F. J. Osborn characterised as the *definiteness*[98] of the plan in relation to land uses, new town sites and so on was necessary to make planning 'real', to demonstrate the principles, the arithmetic of which could be checked later. It is the element lacking from so much of our planning today and one that is perhaps necessary if a plan is really to capture the public imagination – or perhaps to have the long term influence of the London plans. Osborn, who regarded Abercrombie as the only philosophic or sociological planner in the country, had at first been bitterly disappointed with the County of London Plan[99] only later coming to appreciate some of the constraints under which Abercrombie worked, but he had a warm regard for the Greater London Plan from the start, regarding it as a classic, gathering up all the threads and weaving them together in brilliant fashion as a garment for a great metropolis[100] – and great it certainly was in area and population, 2,599 square miles and six and a quarter million people. Such a plan must seize the public imagination, said Osborn,[101] yet the government of the day was opposed to any change in London government that would unite the 131 authorities concerned: Sir Patrick was likely to go down in history as the second man who was not allowed to rebuild London.[102] Lewis Mumford described the plan as the mature form of the organism whereof *Garden Cities of Tomorrow* was the embryo, to be admired for its intellectual penetration and its political skill as well as for its all round comprehension of the planner's and the citizen's job.[103]

The Clyde Valley

As concentrated work on the London Plans came to a close, Abercrombie was appointed Principal Consultant to the Clyde Valley Regional Planning Committee which had been constituted in 1943.[104] He accepted the new and daunting challenge with characteristic enthusiasm and agreed to present an interim report on housing within six months. Abercrombie and his team began the plan early in 1944 and completed it just over two years later, although it was not published until 1949.[105] The plan was to form the basis for statutory plans to be produced by the individual local authorities,[106] many of whom, perhaps inevitably, later acted independently, to the detriment of the plan and the region. Early in their report Abercrombie and Robert Matthew, his deputy, stressed that physical planning was not an end in itself, but must go hand in hand with economic and social planning if it was effectively to meet human needs. For almost a century and a half, Glasgow had grown at the expense of the rest of Scotland, so that by 1939 two-thirds of the national population lived in the Clyde Valley region with all but a quarter in Glasgow itself; 700,000 people living in less than three square miles.[107] There was a corresponding intensity of industrial and commercial uses with much obsolescence and ageing dock facilities. And yet half the region is moorland and heath, with Ben Lomond but twenty-five miles from the centre of Glasgow and the Clyde resorts even closer.

The amelioration of the housing situation, the attraction of new industry and the redistribution of employment opportunities were the most important considerations for the planning team. To bring the general housing standard up to an acceptable level would involve the replacement of the major proportion of existing communities in the ensuing quarter century.[108] Most of the industry in the region was approaching the end of its useful life. There was no definite information about the future of the iron and steel industry that provided much of the region's engineering employment and the vagueness of the industry's policies meant that the planners had to provide for considerable revision of their proposals when a final decision was made. New industry was required for purposes of diversification and balance and to absorb anticipated unemployment in the declining basic industries dependent upon coal and iron.[109] Decentralisation of population was to be provided for by town expansion and by the construction of new towns, at East Kilbride, Cumbernauld and Bishopton with the possibility of a fourth one at Houston, if the steel industry were to be resited far from its existing location. The importance of village and rural planning was stressed,[110] particular attention being paid to the development of settlements of a size adequate to support social, educational and shopping facilities. The green belt contained practically all the agricultural land in the middle and lower Clyde basins and it was recommended that this land be bought by a proposed regional planning authority, which should be established with positive planning powers in respect of the area within the outer limits of the green belt surrounding the central conurbation.[111] Two areas beyond the green belt, Loch Lomond and the Trossachs, and St. Mary's Lake, were recommended as National Parks.[112]

The speed of the production of the plan and the range of consultations about the proposals showed Abercrombie at his best. During his first visit, in January 1944, staff were appointed and 'general understanding' reached about terms of reference[113] and by August 1944 the draft interim housing report covering 321 specific sites was being considered prior to presentation to the full Clyde Valley Planning Committee in October.[114] The pace was gruelling, especially for Abercrombie himself, engaged as he was with other plans in other places at the same time. An overnight train journey from London – first class by sleeper £8.12s.2d return – would be followed by a series of office meetings on a wide range of subjects, extending to late in the evening, then days of site inspection and meetings with engineers and agriculturalists, often with Provosts and occasionally with the Press; preparing for and attending committees, discussing the next month's work with his team, Matthew, Grieve, MacFarlane and the rest, before darting off again, overnight as often as not, to repeat the whole process with different colleagues elsewhere.

Like so many other plans, that for the Clyde Valley seems on the face of it to have been largely ignored. To a great extent this may be so, for delays in publication and in decision-making and failure of nerve in high places – especially as we now realise over some important issues concerning basic industries – and the absence of a positive regional authority made its accomplishment difficult. But Cumbernauld, although almost certainly not as Abercrombie would have visualised it, and East Kilbride, where he might have felt much more at home, are built, and in more general terms the ideas behind the plan permeate all subsequent schemes for the region. It was never intended to be a finite Master Plan, but rather to lay down in broad terms an outline pattern of regional development.[115] In this connection the consultants thought it would be advantageous for there to be a university chair of regional planning in Scotland to provide the research background so important to the continuity of planning,[116] a recommendation undoubtedly based on Abercrombie's own experience in Liverpool and London. One wonders, however, to what extent the undoubted research capabilities of the Scottish universities in the field of town and country planning are utilised by the regional planning authorities and what opportunities for cross-fertilisation of ideas remain to be realised.

Birmingham and the West Midlands

The publication in 1948 of *Conurbation*,[117] a survey of Birmingham and the Black Country prepared by the unofficial but authoritative West Midlands Group was intended to supply the basic facts that would be required in the preparation of a regional plan for the West Midlands. Abercrombie was commissioned by the Minister of Town and Country Planning to prepare the regional plan, this time working with Herbert Jackson. It was the hope that the plan would 'encourage co-operative organisation in the Region, and that the plan [would] be carried out on a Regional level'.[118] Once again a report, complementing *Conurbation*'s survey and analysis, was produced with all reasonable expedition, but was never generally available.[119] Like the London plans and that for the Clyde Valley it was based on the best available assumptions and the most reliable anticipations of population growth. But as in the earlier plans the best estimates were not very accurate, the plan review and monitoring procedures, where they existed at all, were too slow and cumbersome: above all there was a failure by government to ensure co-operation between local authorities. Another planning opportunity was lost, by default, and without general consideration of the proposals by the public. Whilst these great regional studies were being prepared Abercrombie was working in other places with different planning teams.

Two city plans

Patrick Abercrombie's wartime activity was by no means restricted to regional planning and two town plans, for Plymouth and Hull, preceded a radical plan for Edinburgh and later schemes for Warwick and Bournemouth. His approach in each case showed the strength of his conviction that a town could not be considered in isolation from its hinterland, any more than one could plan without clearly defined objectives.

In the autumn of 1941 Viscount Astor, Lord Mayor of Plymouth, invited Abercrombie to prepare a plan for the redevelopment of that badly bombed city in co-operation with J. Paton Watson, the City Engineer. In proportion to its size Plymouth had suffered more bomb damage than any other British city and provided a rare opportunity to introduce a new street pattern appropriate to antici- pated future needs. Here was a challenge, indeed. Yet Abercrombie noted that 'the absolutely frightful time that Plymouth and sur- roundings have passed through has not had the slightest effect on the petty jealousies and meanness of surrounding authorities'.[120] In Abercrombie's view the plan for Plymouth should treat the whole of an area extending six miles and more beyond the town centre as a single unit, irrespective of the incidence of artificial boundaries,[121] and he was not prepared to piece together patches of a plan prepared at Liskeard on one side and Exeter on the other.[122] More important, however, was the determination of objectives and he was anxious to talk with Astor and others, not necessarily councillors or officials, about the kind of future for which they should be planning.[123]

In the event, although the Council followed the Minister of Works' advice that it should go ahead planning boldly and comprehen- sively[124] 'the adjoining authorities failed to take advantage of the offer . . . to participate actively' in the plan.[125] Abercrombie saw this as an opportunity missed. The plan was characterised by the usual systematic Abercrombie approach, the opportunity being taken to integrate the former separate towns of Devonport, Stonehouse and Plymouth.

In the city centre Abercrombie replaced the haphazard mediaeval street pattern with a road layout, superficially reminiscent of that of his Dublin plan, displaying his love of the *beaux arts* solution for the grand occasion where topography did not dictate otherwise. Whether the various uses could possibly justify the provision made for them is in many instances arguable, as for example a 40% increase in shopping area,[126] unrelated to turnover per square foot. In this form of layout there was less flexibility than in many Aber- crombie plans, particularly when the design was dependent on the continuity resulting from a unified scheme of architectural treat- ment.[127] Elsewhere in the city, in the Barbican for example, the Abercrombie Watson plan emphasised the need to retain both tradi- tional scale and materials, for as Abercrombie later wrote, 'the narrow streets and the intimate urban atmosphere are exactly what we miss in our New Towns and slick housing schemes'.[128]

There was in the Plymouth plan a failure to anticipate changes in employment, especially in the dockyards, but this was perhaps understandable. Although in the event the Abercrombie central area road pattern, owing much to the ideas of Alker Tripp, was adopted and has been successfully adapted to later conditions, the architecturally unified precincts which the roads were to serve and in many instances define, are very different from the original proposals, related as they are to the grand avenue to the Hoe. Despite its failings and inevitable opposition, the Plymouth plan has served as a substantive guide to the development of the city even though the unique regional planning opportunity was lost.

Kingston-upon-Hull

'Our stability is but balance,' quotes Abercrombie at the start of his report on the plan for Kingston-upon-Hull,[129] in a plea for a balanced logical scheme of reconstruction in the much bombed Yorkshire port. In any plan one must consider the national, regional and local setting and in the absence of any national guidance there would have to be an inward scrutiny, a searching of the civic conscience and a balancing of the whole structure.[130]

Like the other wartime plans, that for Hull had to be prepared in the absence of any reliable population figures, Abercrombie having to make do without even 'the surmise of the Registrar General, whose prophetic talents we must at times accept, though we do not altogether swallow his omniscience'.[131] In planning for a new town of about pre-war size a safety margin of about 10% and 20% was suggested,[132] and in the event the next quarter century was to see a reduction in population by about 10%.[133] Many of the Plymouth team worked on the Hull plan, where they were able to build on the Civic Diagnosis earlier completed by Max Lock,[134] thereby saving valuable time in plan preparation. Most importantly, the plan was begun in association with Sir Edwin Lutyens who contributed ideas and inspiration which after his death were translated into practicable form by his surviving colleagues. Lutyens was much impressed with the development prospects arising from the filling in of some of the docks, but was anxious to introduce some high land, a kind of Acropolis, to give topographical interest and symbolic significance,[135] a suggestion that was, perforce, abandoned as the plan developed. Whilst the plan included proposals intended to answer all the major town problems and was argued with Abercrombie's accustomed elegance, it is without doubt more difficult to discover in the report specific items of information that one might require. Had he taken on too much at one time? London, completed, still occupied his mind; the Clyde much of his time, and what then of the West Midlands and Edinburgh?[136] Whatever others might think, Sir

Patrick himself was unrepentant. He had enjoyed the stimulation of working with his young team of planners and with the erratic genius of Lutyens and he thought the plan was probably the best post-war report he had been connected with, though with its rather far-fetched shopping centre, not the most practicable. In the end, it was killed by the combined action of the shopping community, the city engineer, the Minister of Transport and the Minister of Town and Country Planning.[137]

The post-war years

With the completion of the great series of wartime plans and the passing of the Town and Country Planning Act of 1947, most of the planning work in Britain passed from the consultants, who had been its mainstay and provided its inspiration in earlier years, to the new statutory local planning authorities. These authorities, though each was concerned with a larger area than the districts formerly respons-ible for planning, displayed, no doubt quite properly, the narrow-minded concentration on the affairs of their own areas that Aber-crombie had criticised for so many years. Whilst this went on, imaginative proposals for the Clyde Valley and West Midlands, for Edinburgh, Warwick and elsewhere, when not abandoned, lay in the doldrums of the development scene.

The new towns, alone at first, later supplemented and in places rivalled by town expansion schemes, survived and prospered from the Abercrombie and other plans. In many instances the planners of the new towns were personal friends of Abercrombie and in almost every case they were people whom he respected. Yet there was perhaps a shade of disappointment in his almost complete divorce, officially, from the new town and regional planning scene, and especially from the London region. There was even greater disap-pointment that despite his long campaign over thirty years[138] there was still no national plan, nor even policy. In the absence of a vigorous *national* planning and housing policy, commented the *Town Planning Review*,[139] there was a danger that the building of the eight London new towns might become an unintended bonus to develop-ment in the south-east of the country. Yet as a result of the work of Abercrombie and his contemporaries, 'the Silkin machine [had] something to work upon, in place of perpetual improvisation or mere adjustment of claims on land use'[140] and as Abercrombie com-mented at the time, whilst the consultants might 'complain that their work is mutilated, that their bolder ideas are dropped, that their detailed treatment is condemned ... if the report is sound, its influence is, sooner or later inescapable'.[141]

In the post war years appearances as an expert witness at innumerable planning inquiries provided some interest for Sir Patrick, but not much inspiration. For that he looked to work abroad; first in Addis Ababa, then in Hong Kong and Cyprus – an island he loved dearly and where he was following in the footsteps of his mentor, Geddes – and finally to Ethiopia again in the years immediately before his death. Wherever he went there was still the outpouring of enthusiasm and experience and in no time at all, or so it seemed, the production of another plan shedding light on problems and suggesting solutions.

It was perhaps as an agent for and propagandist of planning that Abercrombie made his greatest contribution to planning in the post-war decade. In Britain he retained his association with the Town and Country Planning Association, stimulated by a lively correspondence with F. J. Osborn; with the Housing Centre, and especially with his creations, the Council for the Preservation of Rural England and that for Rural Wales, although increasingly worried lest they become too preservationist. As consultant for the Snowdonia National Park he worked in close association with his dear friend and near contemporary, Clough Williams-Ellis, a delightfully formidable partnership when in full flight together in common cause.

Abroad, Abercrombie assessed competitions and lectured, enjoying travel, particularly by flying boat, to many parts of the world, often in connection with the affairs of the Union Internationale des Architects with which he was intimately concerned for many years. His vast range of international contacts from his teaching days in Liverpool and London as well as from his practice, combined with his energy and enthusiasm and above all his tact and political awareness ideally fitted him for a highly successful term as President and, shortly before he died, President d'Honeur of the UIA.

Patrick Abercrombie came to epitomise planning and this seemed always to surprise him as well as to give him pleasure. He never had a large office, but always worked with a team drawn together for a particular task and usually consisting of people much younger than himself, perhaps his former pupils or his pupils' pupils, to whom he was a firm but kindly leader. So he was too for his profession, a leadership recognised by his election to the Presidency of the Town Planning Institute in 1925 and later by the award to him of a Knighthood and honorary degrees; of the Howard Memorial Medal; the Gold Medals of the American Institute of Architects and of the Town Planning Institute; and the Royal Gold Medal of the Royal Institute of British Architects.

When he died in 1957, still actively engaged on a detail of planning in Winchester and on his Addis Ababa Plan, he had probably done more for planning than anyone else of his time. If some of his small scale planning was conventional, perhaps even at times outmoded, though competently handled, at the large scale in town or region he was still in his old age boldly innovative in a practical way. It may be argued that he had advanced no new theories, brought no new order to the systemisation of planning. He was not primarily a theorist, though he had a clear understanding of the place of town and regional planning in society and government. For more than sixty years he had been at the forefront of advance in planning, developing ideas from any and every source (but especially from Geddes), working with people from as wide a range of disciplines as possible, introducing considerations of geology and landscape as well as economics, sociology, history and architecture to the development of town and regional planning – and whilst he saw and would argue for there to be a distinction between the form of town and country he was equally convinced about the indivisibility of the factors influencing that development.

Patrick Abercrombie had a remarkably wide range of expertise and ability. In his early days his wider interest complemented Adshead's competence as an estate planner, both being first class draughtsmen. In a different way he and George Pepler were also complementary in the development of regional planning; Pepler, the d'Artagnan of planning,[142] the great facilitator paving the way administratively and in Whitehall for Abercrombie to prepare the plans. Others were outstanding in different aspects of planning – Lanchester, the civic designer; Sharp, with his sensitivity to village and town design, but not to politicians; Lutyens, rogue elephant of the architectural profession and supreme planner in the grandest manner – but none had the breadth of professional versatility and competence that prompted Clough Williams-Ellis to describe Abercrombie as a 'genial wizard'.[143]

Abercrombie's role, or that he created for himself, was that of synthesiser and catalyst, a role for which he was admirably equipped; perceptive, sensitive, industrious; with a flair for exposition and an eye for detail.[144] He was optimistic, perhaps too optimistic, and he worked quickly, perhaps too quickly, but he had an amazing ability to learn from experience – something, too, that he had more of than anyone else in the profession – and to convey to others the results of it. He displayed an interesting combination of hard headedness and compassion in the application of his experience, combining it with the considerable intellectual range traditionally associated with academics of an earlier age. We could do with more of those characteristics today.

Acknowledgements

Some of this material has appeared previously in somewhat different form in the *Town Planning Review* and the *Architectural Review*: I am grateful to the respective editors for allowing me to incorporate it in this study. Final acknowledgements are due to Lois Dix and Susan Billington, without whose help this chapter could never have been completed.

Notes

1   See C. Williams-Ellis, 'A Genial Wizard: an appreciation of Sir Patrick Abercrombie', *Listener*, 8 August 1957, pp199–200
2   Abercrombie MSS Part 1, Chapter 2, p1
3   Abercrombie MSS, Note, *Chester*, written on Lloyd Triestino line letterhead, nd, probably July 1940
4   Abercrombie MSS, *op cit*, p32
5   Abercrombie MSS, Part V, Ch 1, p1
6   *Ibid*, p5
7   *Ibid*, p2
8   *Ibid*, p5
9   *Ibid*
10 C. Williams-Ellis, *Town and Country Planning*, Longmans, London, 1951, p7
11 L. P. Abercrombie, *Planning in Town and Country: difficulties and possibilities*, University of Liverpool Press and Hodder and Stoughton, London, 1937
12 L. P. Abercrombie, *Town and Country Planning*, OUP, London, 1933
13 *Ibid*, p27
14 R. Randal Phillips, *Small Country Houses of Today*, Vol 3, Country Life, London, 1925, pp129–132
15 J. Nolen, 'Greater Dublin: Competitive Designs for the Town Plan of Dublin, Ireland', *Landscape Architecture*, Vol VII, No 2, January 1917, p73
16 Geddes, writing to his daughter, 14 September 1922, quoted in H. E. Meller, 'Cities and Evolution: Patrick Geddes as an international prophet of town planning before 1914', paper to the Planning History Group Conference, London, September 1977, note 75
17 Abercrombie MSS, Part V, Chapter 1, pp9–10
18 See Barbara R. Penny, *Pilkington Brothers Garden Village Ventures: the end of the Garden City Suburb*, University of Liverpool Department of Civic Design, Working Paper 1, July 1976
19 Abercrombie MSS, Part V, Chapter 1, p14; G. L. (later Sir George) Pepler, 1882–1959, was Chief Technical Officer to various ministries of government, under a variety of titles, from 1914–1946

20   L. P. Abercrombie, and T. H. Johnson, *The Doncaster Regional Planning Scheme 1922*, University of Liverpool Press and Hodder and Stoughton, London, 1922, p9

21   *Ibid*, pvi

22   The South Wales Regional Survey Report, produced by a committee that included Abercrombie and Pepler amongst its members, was published in 1921, and made regional proposals but did not include a specific regional plan. For a brief discussion about this see *Architectural Review*, Vol CLXVI, No 992, October 1979, p203

23   L. P. Abercrombie, 'The Basis for Reconstruction: The Need for a Regional Survey of National Resources', *Town Planning Review*, Volume VII, Nos 3–4, March 1918, pp203–210

24   L. P. Abercrombie, 'A Comprehensive Plan for Development on a National, Regional and Local Scale', *Town Planning Review*, Volume VII, Nos 3–4, March 1918, pp211–222

25   L. P. Abercrombie, 'The Basis for Reconstruction', *op cit*, p205

26   This later committee issued its prospectus of requirements in 1937 (Abercrombie MSS, Part V, Chapter 9, footnote to p39). Among University of Liverpool Proposers were C. Douglas Campbell, Lecturer in Commerce; W. A. Eden, Leverhulme Research Fellow in Civic Design; P. M. Roxby, Professor of Geography; and T. S. Simey (later Baron Simey of Toxteth), Lecturer in Public Administration. The report proposal itself is undated.

27   Abercrombie and Johnson, *op cit*, p3

28   *Ibid*, p8

29   Royal Institute of British Architects, Town Planning Conference, London, 10–15 October 1910; *Transactions*, pp407–426. The ten cities are shown on the map between pp410–411

30   Abercrombie MSS, Part V, Chapter 5, p18

31   *Ibid*, p16

32   John Burns, letter to Abercrombie, 2 September 1924

33   Quoted in a list of books on Town Planning Regional Survey, published in March 1926 by Liverpool University Press

34   Abercrombie MSS, Part V, Chapter 5, p15

35   L. P. Abercrombie, in collaboration with R. H. Mattocks, *Sheffield: a Civic Survey and Suggestions towards a Development Plan*, University of Liverpool Press and Hodder and Stoughton, London, 1924

36   *Ibid*, piv

37   *Ibid*, pp44–45

38   *Ibid*, p42

39   Abercrombie MSS, Part V, Chapter 5, p20

40   *Ibid*

41   Doncaster, East Kent, Bath and Bristol, Sheffield and Barnsley, Middlesborough and Teesside, Chester and Deeside, North Wales 1, North Wales 2, Cumberland, Gloucestershire, Wye Valley, East Suffolk, Oxfordshire, Thames Valley, North Riding, Lincolnshire. In ten cases the dominant motive was rural development and countryside preservation. Abercrombie MSS, *ibid*, pp35–6

42 L. P. Abercrombie, and J. Archibald, *East Kent Regional Planning Scheme, Preliminary Survey*, University of Liverpool Press and Hodder and Stoughton, London, 1925

43 *Ibid*, Plate VI, facing p11

44 Abercrombie MSS, Part V, Chapter 5, p26

45 Abercrombie and Archibald, *op cit*, p83

46 L. P. Abercrombie, letters to his mother, 22 October 1900, 26 October 1900.

47 Private communication, H. A. Johnson, 7 February 1979.

48 C. Williams-Ellis, *England and the Octopus*, Bles, London, 1928, p66

49 L. P. Abercrombie, 'Epistola Epilogica', in Williams-Ellis, *ibid*, p181

50 L. P. Abercrombie, 'The Preservation of Rural England', *Town Planning Review*, Volume XII, No 1, May 1926, pp5–56

51 Council for the Preservation of Rural England, *Annual Report, 1956*, Volume XVI, No 5, pp1–5

52 L. P. Abercrombie, 'The Preservation of Rural England', *op cit*, p42

53 L. P. Abercrombie, *Country Planning and Landscape Design* (The Stevenson Lecture for 1933), University of Liverpool Press and Hodder and Stoughton, London, 1934, p33

54 L. P. Abercrombie, 'The Preservation of Rural England', *op cit*, p43

55 L. P. Abercrombie, and B. F. Brueton, *Bristol and Bath Regional Planning Scheme*, University of Liverpool Press and Hodder and Stoughton, London, 1930

56 L. P. Abercrombie, and S. A. Kelly, *Cumbrian Regional Planning Scheme*, University of Liverpool Press and Hodder and Stoughton, London, 1932

57 Gordon E. Cherry, *National Parks and Recreation in the Countryside* (Peacetime History, Environmental Planning, Volume 2) HMSO, London, 1975, p29

58 G. L. Pepler, letter to Abercrombie, 3 January 1939

59 L. P. Abercrombie and S. A. Kelly, *Gloucestershire: rural development*, unpublished, nd

60 Earl of Mayo, S. D. Adshead, and L. P. Abercrombie, with a preface by John Buchan, *The Thames Valley from Cricklade to Staines: A Survey of its Existing State and Some Suggestions for its Future Preservation*, University of London Press, 1929

61 L. P. Abercrombie, and S. A. Kelly, *East Suffolk Regional Planning Scheme*, University of Liverpool Press and Hodder and Stoughton, London, 1935

62 Abercrombie and Archibald, *op cit*, p108

63 Abercrombie MSS, Part V, Chapter 9, p47

64 *Ibid*

65 *Royal Commission on the Distribution of the Industrial Population: Report* (Barlow Report), Cmd 6153, HMSO, London, 1940

66 *Ibid*, 'A Dissentient Memorandum on Planning in Relation to the Location of Industry', by Professor Patrick Abercrombie, pp233–243

67 Abercrombie MSS, Part V, Chapter XI, pp83–4

68   Barlow Report, 'A Dissentient Memorandum', *op cit*, p233, para 3
69   *Ibid*, p239, para17
70   *Ibid*, p237, para13
71   Barlow Report, *op cit*, Report by Professor Abercrombie, Mr Herbert Elvin and Mrs Hichens, p229, para59
72   Planning Advisory Group, *The Future of Development Plans*, HMSO, London, 1965
73   J. H. Forshaw, and L. P. Abercrombie, *County of London Plan*, Mac-Millan, London, 1943, pv
74   *Ibid*
75   *Ibid*, p15
76   L. P. Abercrombie, *Greater London Plan 1944*, HMSO, London, 1945
77   L. P. Abercrombie, 'Town Planning in Greater London', *Town Planning Review*, Volume II, p262, *et seq*
78   Royal Academy Planning Committee Interim Report, *London Replanned*, London, Country Life, 1942
79   Abercrombie, autobiographical notes
80   Forshaw and Abercrombie, *op cit*, p52
81   C. D. Buchanan, *Traffic in Towns*, HMSO, London, 1963
82   Forshaw and Abercrombie, *op cit*, p3
83   Bressey, Charles (with Edwin Lutyens), *Highway Development Survey 1937 (Greater London)*, HMSO, London, 1938
84   Barlow Report, 'A Dissentient Memorandum', *op cit*, p237, para14
85   Forshaw and Abercrombie, *op cit*, Plate LIV, facing p139. See also S. E. Rasmussen, *London, the Unique City*, Cape, London, 1948, p417
86   *Ibid*, coloured Plate 1, Chapter 1, pp21–29
87   L. P. Abercrombie, 'Regional Comment', *Building*, October 1951, p412
88   L. P. Abercrombie, *Greater London Plan, op cit*, p5, para22
89   *Ibid*
90   *Ibid*, paras17–21, p5
91   *Royal Commission on the Distribution of the Industrial Population, Report* (Barlow Report), Cmd 6153, HMSO, London, 1940; *Committee on Land Utilisation in Rural Areas, Report* (Scott Report) Cmd 6378, HMSO, London 1942; *Committee on Compensation and Betterment, Report* (Uthwatt Report) Cmd 6291, HMSO, London, 1941
92   Abercrombie, *Greater London Plan, op cit*, p1
93   F. J. Osborn, 'A Great Future for a Great City', *Observer*, 17/December 1944
94   D. Foley, *Controlling London's Growth: Planning the Great Wen, 1940–60*, University of California Press, Berkeley and Los Angeles, 1963, p79
95   In fact he had sight in only one eye, having gone blind in the other in his youth.
96   P. Self, 'New Towns and the Urban Crisis', *TCP*, Volume 48, No 2, p60
97   Ruth Glass, 'The Mood of London' in D. Donnison, D. Eversley and

others, *London: Urban Patterns, Problems and Policies*, Heinemann, London, 1973, pp415–416

98 Osborn, *op cit*
99 Letter to Lewis Mumford, 7 December 1943, in *Letters of Lewis Mumford and Frederic J. Osborn*, Adams and Dart, Bath, 1971, p45
100 Osborn, *op cit*
101 *Ibid*
102 Comment, *New Statesman and Nation*, 23 December 1944, p414. Peter Hall (*London 2000*, 2nd pb edition, Faber, London, 1971, pp156–157) has pointed out that the 'C' and 'D' rings of the *London Traffic Survey* (GLC 1966) are inherited from the Abercrombie Plan of 1944
103 Mumford to Osborn, 11 December 1946, *Letters of Mumford and Osborn, op cit*, pp140–141
104 *Clyde Valley Regional Planning Advisory Committee Report* by Advisory Committee to the Constituent Local Authorities (as approved and adopted at a Meeting of the Advisory Committee, 30 January 1947), p2
105 Sir Patrick Abercrombie, and R. H. Matthew, *The Clyde Valley Regional Plan 1946*, HMSO, Edinburgh, 1949. By what *The Times*, 20 August 1949, described as an irony of coincidence the report was published on the very day when Government allowed a major break in the Greater London Plan
106 *Ibid*, para4, p2
107 *Ibid*, para7, p2
108 *Ibid*, para4, p2
109 L. P. Abercrombie, and R. H. Matthew, Interim Report, unpublished, November 1946, para8
110 *Ibid*, para62
111 *Ibid*, para75
112 *Ibid*, paras23 and 24
113 L. P. Abercrombie, MSS note on meetings of 5, 6, 7 January 1944
114 L. P. Abercrombie, MSS note on meeting of 13 October 1944
115 Abercrombie and Matthew, *Clyde Valley Regional Plan, op cit*, p1
116 *Ibid*, p11
117 West Midland Group, *Conurbation: a survey of Birmingham and the Black Country*, Architectural Press, London, 1948
118 *Ibid*, p63
119 L. P. Abercrombie, and H. Jackson, *West Midlands Plan*, London MoTCP mimeo, 1948
120 L. P. Abercrombie, Letter to Viscount Astor, 21 September 1941
121 L. P. Abercrombie, Draft Preliminary Analysis of the Programme for the Reconstruction of the City (of Plymouth) MS, 9 November 1941
122 L. P. Abercrombie, letter to Astor, *op cit*
123 *Ibid*
124 J. Paton Watson, and L. P. Abercrombie, *A Plan for Plymouth*, Underhill, Plymouth, 1943, pvii
125 *Ibid*
126 *Ibid*, Table 12, p73

127 *Ibid*, p308
128 L. P. Abercrombie, letter to Editor, *The Times*, 20 February 1957
129 E. Lutyens, and L. P. Abercrombie, *A Plan for the City and County of Kingston-upon-Hull*, Brown, Hull, 1945, p1
130 *Ibid*
131 L. P. Abercrombie, Regional Comment: The Smaller Towns, *Building*, January 1953, p33
132 Lutyens and Abercrombie, *op cit*, p1
133 *Annual Report of the Deputy Chief Executive Officer and Planning Officer for 1972/73*, Kingston-upon-Hull, 1973, Fig 1, p5
134 Max Lock, FRIBA, AADip, MTPI prepared a Civic Diagnosis of Hull on a Leverhulme Research Scholarship shortly after his appointment as Head of the School of Architecture there in 1939
135 L. P. Abercrombie, conversation with the author, Addis Ababa, September 1955
136 L. P. Abercrombie, and D. Plumstead, *A Civic Survey and Plan for the City and Royal Burgh of Edinburgh*, Oliver and Boyd, Edinburgh and London, 1949
137 L. P. Abercrombie, letter to the Editor, *TCP*, December 1955, p538
138 L. P. Abercrombie, 'The Basis for Reconstruction: The Need for a Regional Survey of National Resources', *Town Planning Review*, Volume VII, Nos 3 & 4, March 1918, pp203–210
139 Editorial Note (by Gordon Stephenson), *Town Planning Review*, Volume XXII, No 2, 1951, p100
140 L. P. Abercrombie, Regional Comment: 'Unofficial Reports', *Building*, October 1951, p416
141 *Ibid*
142 L. P. Abercrombie, *Twenty Years After*, sessional paper, RIBA, 4 March 1952, *RIBAJ*, March 1952, p186
143 C. Williams-Ellis, 'A Genial Wizard . . .', *op cit*, p199
144 Qualities especially valuable in his service as a member of the Royal Fine Art Commission

6

GEORGE PEPLER
1882–1959

Gordon Cherry

George Lionel Pepler was born at Croydon in 1882. His father, a brewer, died in 1884, and his mother remarried; his half-brother, F. Longstreth Thompson, became like Pepler himself a celebrated town planner. His son Richard (G. R. S. Pepler) became a Legal Member of the (Royal) Town Planning Institute and served as Hon. Secretary from 1968–79.

George Pepler was educated at a private school at Eastbourne, at Bootham School, York (1893–97) and the Leys School, Cambridge (1897–99). He served articles as a Surveyor with Walter Hooker and William Webb of Croydon, and in 1905 went into practice with a firm of architects and surveyors, which became known as Pepler and Allen. He was one of the founder members of the Town Planning Institute and in 1914 joined the Local Government Board, succeeding Thomas Adams as an Inspector. In 1919 he became Chief Town Planning Inspector in the Ministry of Health and in the same year was elected President of the Town Planning Institute. The pattern was set: his life was to revolve round an interest in and commitment to planning, both as a professional and a civil servant.

He became a Fellow of the Chartered Surveyors' Institute. He was also an honorary Member of the Institute of Municipal Engineers (1925), President of the International Federation for Housing and Town Planning (1938 and 1947–52), an honorary Associate of the Royal Institute of British Architects (1937) and Chairman of the Institution of Professional Civil Servants (1937–42). Within the Town Planning Institute he was Hon. Secretary and Hon. Treasurer (1914–59), and Chairman of the Joint Examination Board (1930–59), lecturer and external examiner, and President of the Town and Country Planning Summer School (1940–59). He was President of the TPI for a second term in 1949–50 and in 1953 was presented with the first Gold Medal of the Institute.

His successful years as a civil servant, marked by his CBE (1944) and his knighthood (1948) led to no idle years of retirement when he left his job as Principal Assistant Secretary in 1946. He became a consultant, preparing an Outline Plan and Report for North East England (with P. W. MacFarlane, 1946), advising Renfrewshire County Council and the Colony of Singapore. He was Chairman of the National Playing Fields Association Grounds and Layout Committee (1949–59); he became heavily involved in the work of the Council for the Preservation of Rural England, and served as a member of the Royal Commission on Common Land, 1956–58.

Pepler died in April 1959, the same year in which the TPI received the Royal Charter, for which he had done so much.

Prior to 1914

After serving his articles as a Surveyor, Pepler was in partnership with E. G. Allen, an architect and planner. The relationship was a successful one. In 1907 they won a silver medal for a £200 cottage in a competition run by the National Housing Reform Council. The next year they won two gold medals at the Wolverhampton Model Housing Exhibition, and in 1910 a further gold medal was awarded at a similar exhibition in South Wales.

In that year the firm took over the greater part of Thomas Adams' practice, when he was appointed to the Local Government Board as the first Town Planning Inspector; the firm also continued in various consultancies. The connection with Adams first began at Wolverhampton, where he was then advising Sir Richard Paget on the development of his Fallings Park estate. It led to a flourishing private practice, with the development of Fallings Park and other large estates as at Alkrington (Lancashire) and at Knebworth, for Lord Lytton.

The firm also organised co-partnerships and Tenants' Societies, at that time often influential in securing good layout and improved conditions for working class housing. Schemes at Knebworth, Cuffley, Southampton and Fforestfach were prepared. The latter was intended to be a model village for miners and was inaugurated by H. R. Aldridge of the National Housing and Town Planning Council; one hundred houses were proposed on the 8 acre site, with reservations for allotments, bowling greens and a playground, but the scheme had to be taken over by Swansea Corporation. However, at Knebworth, an example of a tenant's co-partnership housing scheme that survives in terms of organisation to this day, the houses that Pepler and Allen laid out and designed stand out in quality and style from the several later housing developments that surround them.

Pepler also became involved in Greater London affairs, particularly from a traffic point of view. A paper presented to the RIBA's Town Planning Conference[1] in 1910 outlined his proposal for a 'ringway' around London, approximately 10 miles in radius, picking up Croydon in the south, Barnet in the north, Ealing in the west and Woolwich on the east. The model of circular road schemes as parkways linking up outer open spaces had already appeared in America; perhaps the transference of the idea came with Lord Meath, a garden cities enthusiast, and Chairman of the Parks Committee of London County Council, who had visited the USA. But Pepler's imagination also embraced segregation of traffic by function; his 346 ft wide 'road' consisted of two footpaths (each 10 ft wide), two service roads (24 ft), three reservations for trees and grass (20, 50 and 40 ft respectively), a sunk railroad (96 ft), fast motor road (24 ft), tram reservation (24 ft) and slow motor road (24 ft).

As a civil servant

In 1914 Pepler joined the Local Government Board. In 1919 he became Chief Planning Inspector in the newly formed Ministry of Health, and with different titles he held this central planning position until his retirement in 1946.

His first work was in the organisation of the Greater London Arterial Roads Conference, but his years of influence really began with the period beginning in 1919. In June that year he reviewed the town planning position for Sir James Carmichael, Director General of Housing in the Local Government Board. Pepler was then the only Inspector engaged on planning work; the Department had been fully occupied on war work, Raymond Unwin had been engaged in carrying out building schemes for the Ministry of Munitions, and during the war years the Board had felt unable to stimulate local authorities to prepare schemes because of depleted staffs. But proposed legislation (the new Bill of the ultimate 1919 Act) promised much greater activity and Pepler summarised staffing and administrative needs as one general Town Planning Adviser and Inspector, eight other Inspectors with clerical assistants and six draughtsmen.

Pepler proceeded to act out the invaluable role of propagandist and teacher, persuading local authorities to prepare Planning Schemes under the Housing and Town Planning Act 1919, the Town Planning Act 1925 (a consolidating Act) and the Town and Country Planning Act 1932. Housing matters were still considered the more important, and Unwin remained the main general adviser, but this enabled Pepler to be an itinerant activist, enabler and promoter of town planning. History will judge him to have been remarkably successful over a 20-year period during which time the interpenetration of civil servant, advocate, entrepreneur and professional was almost complete. The detail of the work is imperfectly recorded but the ultimate achievements are clear. A steady programme of meetings with local authorities designed to stimulate Scheme preparation or to set up Regional Committees, speaking engagements with audiences of professional groups or of lay people, and promotional activity on behalf of the Town Planning Institute was conducted in a context of changing social and political attitudes towards planning. In 1939 the discipline and the profession were more influential than in 1919; Pepler was associated with a professional breaker coming up the beach of time. How much he created, how much was created for him is impossible to quantify, but his tireless advocacy and unquenchable enthusiasm impressed and encouraged others to his point of view. On balance we can say that not only did he live through, but he positively contributed to a remarkable period in town planning history.

The record of Scheme preparation by an increasing number of local authorities owed much to Pepler's exhortations. (See Table 1 for the situation in 1933.) Of particular significance was his success in establishing Regional Advisory Committees. (See pxix of plates for the 1931 Town Planning Regions.) A readiness to associate himself with Geddes' philosophy was securely grounded in statutory processes, and the establishment of joint committees of local authorities to prepare joint schemes constituted a remarkable achievement.[2] Even before the Local Government Act 1929, which allowed county councils to participate in planning, a wider geographical basis for planning had been established. He was himself a member of the South Wales Regional Survey team in 1920–21, and his earlier work on Greater London traffic indicated a capacity to conceptualise in wide territorial terms. Later, he could claim some responsibility for London's interest in the Green Belt in the 1930s. Following Unwin's report on open spaces issued by the Greater London Regional Planning Committee,[3] the LCC initiated its Green Belt scheme. Pepler claims to have converted Herbert Morrison, Labour leader of the LCC, to this programme by flying him over London on one occasion. Pepler's early appreciation of the regional scale of planning came also with his membership of the Unhealthy Areas Committee, 1920–21, chaired by Neville Chamberlain. Its reports[4] indicated that the slum question could not be dealt with in isolation; it required a general development plan dealing with housing, transport, reconstruction, distribution, and decentralisation into self-contained garden cities and satellite towns. For London, the establishment of new industries and the removal of existing factories to garden cities, with populations not exceeding 30–60,000, was advocated. Chamberlain himself claimed most credit for the Committee's

Table 1 Town planning schemes in England and Wales as at 31 March 1933

Position of scheme	No. of schemes	No. of LAs submitting schemes	Acreage covered by schemes
(1) Schemes finally approved	94	50	152 82
(2) Schemes submitted and under consideration	34	17	56 464
(3) Draft schemes adopted for local deposit but not yet submitted	33	20	67 758
(4) Preliminary statements approved	236	152	948 557
(5) Preliminary statements submitted and under consideration	113	97	829 658
(6) Schemes authorised under Act of 1909 to be prepared, but schemes or preliminary statements not yet submitted	43	29	85 741
(7) Special schemes authorised to be prepared for already developed areas under Act of 1925, but schemes or preliminary statements not yet submitted	4	4	878
(8) Resolutions under Acts of 1919 and 1925, deciding to prepare schemes, but schemes or preliminary statements not yet submitted:			
(i) Resolutions not requiring approval	627	502	6 536 293
(ii) Resolutions requiring approval, and approved	63	48	706 285
	1 235*	742 (net)	9 383 816

* Excluding amending schemes.
Source: Ministry of Health Annual Reports. Reproduced in Gordon E. Cherry, *The Evolution of British Town Planning*, Leonard Hill 1974.

Reports[5] but the philosophy was Pepler's too, throughout his working life.

The inter-war period saw a strengthening of the planning idea. Pepler was interwoven into that story. The compulsory legislation of 1919 was ignored in practice by many local authorities but yet by 1933 the idea of statutory Scheme preparation had become reasonably established (see Table 1 above). The 1932 Act was widely expected to be disastrous for planning fortunes in that it restored the permissive element in Scheme preparation. But it did not quite turn out that way. Greenwood's Bill of 1931 was reintroduced by Hilton Young in 1932; it was watered down in the context of sustained political hostility to the ideas of further State direction in environmental affairs, and in particular to the objections of the property lobby.[6] However, the increasing use of 'interim development control' measures and other developments by local authorities safeguarded planning's reputation. Moreover the dominant strategic impulses, decentralisation and suburbanisation, increasingly carried the day: the principles of lower density development on a wider territorial scale and land uses rationalised into neat parcels were considered the means to overcome the tight-knit chaos of the Victorian city. General sympathy with the objectives of the Garden City and Town Planning Association was carried forward by the Hundred New Towns Association, and the Marley Report[7] of 1935 espoused the idea of satellite towns. Furthermore, Regional Plans were an impressive feature of the inter-war period, although Lord Chelmer's report[8] in 1931 saw no need for administrative reform to accommodate regional government. However, the Barlow Commission,[9] established in 1937, to which Pepler as an official of the Ministry of Health gave detailed oral evidence, released a flood of evidence which led to policies of decentralisation and dispersal. In short, the inter-war period was one not only of planning consolidation but also of innovation, when an important new groundswell of ideas could be detected.

Some impressive regional planning schemes mark the inter-war period, products of vigorous consultancy minds, particularly that of Abercrombie, and a preparedness by local authorities to collaborate in new forms of institutional arrangements on a regional or sub-regional scale. Admittedly these voluntary arrangements failed to provide the framework for regional planning that emerged in later years, particularly during and after World War II, and certainly enthusiasm for plan making was not matched by a capacity to actually achieve very much (because of the lack of executive powers, something which frustrated Pepler a great deal). But nonetheless in the history of regional land use planning in this country the period of the 1920s and '30s represented an important experimental phase. In most of the developments that took place the enabling, guiding hand of the Ministry of Health can be seen, and that of Pepler in particular. The formation of Regional Advisory Committees was often stage-managed by Pepler at inaugural meetings of local authority representatives.

It is in this context that we should note such impressive examples as the Report for the Doncaster Coalfield (Abercrombie, 1922), the East Kent Regional Survey (Abercrombie, 1925), the Manchester and District Joint Committee's Report (1926) and the Report of the Bristol and Bath Joint Planning Committee (1930). It was in enterprises like these that the fundamentals of planning objectives in strategic terms were developed and tested. The principles for containing and shaping urban growth, the satellite settlement idea, and the inter-related concern for preservation and landscape planning were all examined. The proposals at Doncaster, for example, recommended building development in a series of villages related to each coal mine as satellites to the central town; the intervening countryside would be free from building, particularly important because of probable subsidence and flooding after coal extraction. A similar model was followed in East Kent; the zoning principle governed the Manchester and District scheme, and at Bristol and Bath requirements for landscape preservation were woven into the strategic consideration. It is important to note that Pepler was not the author of these reports; rather his role was to facilitate the arrangements whereby the reports were prepared at all. The consistent support and encouragement given from the Ministry must, with hindsight, be seen as most important in this phase of planning history.

The new Departmental arrangements which occurred in the early 1940s affected the pattern of work established over the previous two decades. Pepler joined the Ministry of Works and Buildings, though he may still have had some responsibilities in the Ministry of Health. These were confusing years.[10] In September 1940 the old Office of Works became the Ministry of Works and Buildings, with Sir John (later Lord) Reith at its head. Health retained the statutory town and country planning functions while Reith set up a Reconstruction Group to plan for the future. In 1943 the Ministry of Town and Country Planning was set up, and by that time proposals for post-war reconstruction were well advanced. In 1944 for example, Pepler was much occupied with provisional arrangements for future new towns, in the aftermath of Abercrombie's *Greater London Plan*.

Years of retirement
In 1946 Pepler resumed his career as a consultant planner. In his first commission, in association with P. W. MacFarlane, his long-standing interest in regional planning continued. (MacFarlane had worked with Abercrombie on Clydeside and Greater London and went on to work in private practice in New Towns and overseas.) Pepler and MacFarlane were appointed by Lewis Silkin, Minister of Town and Country Planning, to prepare an Outline Plan for the

'Physical Development and Conservation of the North Eastern Development Area'. Two part-time members (architect-planners) of the Clyde Valley Team, plus a geographer with draughtsmen, comprised the team which operated from an office in Newcastle. Pepler visited the group for three days each week, maintaining close liaison with the Ministry's Regional Office, where J. R. James was in charge of the Research Division.

Pepler and MacFarlane were not the only ones working on regional problems in the north east at this time. The North East Development Board, a voluntary body with Professor G. H. J. Daysh, a geographer of King's College, Newcastle as its research adviser, published *North East Coast: a survey of industrial facilities* (1949). Thomas Sharp also published his *Cathedral City* (Durham), in 1946. Thus Pepler and his associate were paralleled in at least part of their study, but more importantly they were overtaken by events during the conduct of their work. The New Towns Act, 1946, established the idea of Development Corporations with regard to the proper planning of new settlements, and the Town and Country Planning Act, 1947, radically revised the arrangements for statutory planning by local authorities. The number of local authorities with planning powers was almost literally decimated (from over 1,400 to 147) and Counties and County Boroughs became the powerful plan-making bodies.

The primary recommendation by Pepler and MacFarlane that a Development Corporation be set up for the North East Region therefore seemed contrary to the events engineered by the Ministry of Town and Country Planning in 1946 and 1947; the provisions of legislation could not be reversed. However, the various parts of the broad ranging recommendations found their way into the Development Plans and the planning thinking of the local authorities. There were 95 principal recommendations, covering every aspect of the region's problems and potential: industry, derelict land, services, housing, transport, open space and the coast, all matters to be co-ordinated through the Development Corporation, a Regional Planning Authority. Certain strategic proposals have been followed. For example, a new spine 'motor road', north–south through the region with a Jarrow Tunnel under the Tyne, has been implemented well enough in the form of A1(M). On the other hand a proposal for one regional airport at Boldon on South Tyneside adjoining the motor road has been superseded by two regional airports at Newcastle and Teeside. A proposal for a 'quasi new town' (mainly dormitory but with some industry) at Holywell north of the Tyne has been achieved in part by the development of Killingworth and Cramlington, both near Holywell. On the other hand neither a similar quasi new town at Barlow, south west of Tyneside, nor a new town at Brandon proposed for County Durham found favour. However, analysis of the needs for the renewal of the regional industrial base was well founded, and so too were the observations on the need for coastal improvement and development. But perhaps the most widely reported of the proposals which entered into the Development Plans, particularly of Durham but also of Northumberland, related to the classification of mining villages according to their future employment prospects. Thus developed the categorisation of mining villages, with their life geared to the life of their pits. Coalfield villages with unsatisfactory future prospects were not to be extended, but groups of villages were to be relocated where revitalised village life could be recreated in relation to improved employment.

The issue of 'dead villages' became controversial. The instance of the settlement of Tow Law in County Durham may be offered as an example. Pepler and MacFarlane observed: 'Tow Law stands 1,000 ft above sea level upon an exposed site. It owes its existence to local mining, and that mining is now a thing of the past. Also, its buildings have inadequately served their purpose and have more than outlived their useful life. It is therefore time for a new start in more comfortable surroundings, with opportunities for employment at hand and where the grand local patriotism that exists can find new expansion. Consequently we recommend that the industrial population which comprises the great majority should be given the opportunity to migrate to Aycliffe and the rural portion to nearby Wolsingham. When this process has been sympathetically completed the site should be cleared up and be merged again with the moorland on which it was planted'. Tow Law was placed in Category C of settlements in the County Durham Development Plan, where 'only sufficient capital should be invested to cater for the needs of a reduced population'.

Pepler and MacFarlane's report was not published. Hugh Dalton became Minister after Silkin; his constituency was Bishop Auckland in South West Durham and he was opposed to a policy of letting old villages die. In spite of civil service support, Pepler did not push opposition to the Minister's views, and the Report was denied the wider readership for which the authors must have hoped. However, as has been observed, many of the recommendations found their way into official policy; failure to publish could not stop that.

Pepler's retirement years were marked by other consultancies. For example, in 1948 he was asked by the Ministry of Town and Country Planning to preside at certain enquiries regarding the use of land held by Service Departments, including that at Fylingdales (to come into prominence later when the amenities of the North Yorkshire Moors National Park were held to be threatened by the installation of an early warning, anti-ballistic missile station). Further, he was retained as a consultant to Renfrewshire County Council between 1948 and 1956.

However, his appointment as Town Planning Adviser to the Colony of Singapore, 1950–54, must have seemed rather more exciting. The background to the appointment was that of the Singapore Improvement Trust, formed in 1927, the main duty of which was to prepare a General Improvement Plan; it had built a small number of public authority dwellings before 1942, constructed roads and carried out certain Improvement Schemes. After the war rehabilitation and the building of public housing were the first tasks; the squatter problem was intensifying, further public housing was called for and the proper planning of the whole island was demanded. A visit of Abercrombie to Singapore in 1948 stimulated interest in the idea of a survey and Master Plan. After negotiations, Pepler was appointed Planning Adviser; he arrived in December 1950, charged with a concern for the planning of the colony and the preparation of a Master Plan.

The Plan was presented to the Government in November 1955. After a statutory enquiry in 1956 the Master Plan, with a number of amendments, was approved by the Governor, in August 1958. The time scale is reminiscent of the submission and approval of plans in Britain at the same time; the planning philosophy exported was also typical of the British situation, mirroring the exercises in colonial planning which we might now criticise as the imposition of alien values on other cultures. City redevelopment schemes were outlined to overcome existing densities of more than 1,000 persons per acre; three new towns beyond a city Green Belt to accommodate an overspill of 200,000 persons were proposed, together with new and expanding villages for a further 47,000 persons; open space targets raised an existing 0.84 acres to 2.71 acres per thousand population; improved road communications, new industrial estates and new school provision completed the picture.

At home, Pepler's concern for the countryside was met in a number of ways. His years after 1946, when he was an expert witness in planning appeals, embraced many aspects of planning, but the biggest single group of enquiries was concerned with the extraction of sand and gravel, when he was able to marry his commitment to such things as the Green Belt and countryside preservation with a pragmatism towards acceptable forms of development. The most substantial engagement, however, was as a member of the Royal Commission on Common Land, appointed in December 1955, under the chairmanship of Sir Ivor Jennings. The report was published in July 1958. Seven years later the Commons Registration Act, 1965, applicable to 4% of the land surface of England and Wales (there are no commons in Scotland), took up one of its major recommendations, namely to establish and register 'rights of common' and other land variously known as town or village green and manorial wastes.

Professional and related activities

Pepler's commitment to planning – conscious forms of control over community activity and individual preferences in relation to land and environment – inevitably brought him into contact with the agencies and institutions through which the planning movement was to prosper, or not at all. As a civil servant and as a private consultant he saw the institutional arrangements of planning prosper in his life time: changes in political philosophy, developments in social attitudes and the consequences of two World Wars led to an enlargement of the public sector's responsibilities in matters formerly little or no concern of the State. The idea of planning grew to almost characterise the 20th century, and particularly those years in which Pepler was at his prime; advanced and sophisticated land planning, town planning and forms of environmental planning developed in consequence.

British planning practice came to adopt a number of important features. One of these was the nature of the central-local government relationship which has given great strength to planning at local authority level. The other derives from the professional base to planning in this country and its relationship to a variety of propagandist, pressure or special interest groups in the same field. Pepler's life interpenetrated the spheres of official employment, professional service and association with related interests to which he was deeply attached. The degree of interpenetration was remarkable and sustained throughout half a century.

His own professional Institute was the cornerstone. It became the medium through which he committed his skills and energies to a developing field of technical knowledge and competence, while at the same time acting out the role of an advocate to a wider community in keeping with the dominant ideology. The Town Planning Institute was formed in 1914 with Pepler as its Hon. Secretary and Hon. Treasurer, positions he retained until his death. From the start, therefore, he was involved in the hard work of establishing a new professional body: codes of conduct, Institute organisation and structure, relationships with other bodies, rules and regulations for competitions, and educational syllabi.[11]

He was regularly elected to the Institute's Education Committee
and was an examiner in town planning practice when the TPI first
held its own examinations in 1920; he became an external examiner
to most Planning Schools; and when the Town Planning Joint
Examination Board was established in 1930 he was appointed
Chairman, and he held this post until his death. He was a dedicated
supporter of the Town and Country Planning Summer School,
succeeding Thomas Adams as President in 1940 and remaining in
that office until 1959. As a guiding hand in education his influence
must have been profound, steering between the Scylla of professional
aggrandisement and the Charibdys of intellectual arrogance
towards the smoother, surer waters of pragmatism beyond. His
views were succinctly summarised in 1938: 'we do not want to
produce either pretenders to omniscience or persons who are into-
lerant of people or circumstances which do not go according to plan.
The object of the planner is to provide a fair field for life – not to
dictate how life shall be lived'.[12]

During the 1930s planning education was established separately
from the other professions to which it had been formerly bound, and
although these were years of slow growth, nonetheless some effective
base had been prepared for the post-war boom to come. Even during
the war the floodgates had been opened; 1,600 persons enrolled on a
War Office conducted correspondence course run by Jacqueline
Tyrwhitt for members of HM Forces, the arrangements fully backed
by Pepler. This developed later into the School of Planning and
Regional Reconstruction, in London. Later that decade the
Departmental Committee set up by Silkin, chaired by Sir George
Schuster,[13] to consider the qualifications appropriate for those
engaged in town planning, presented the TPI with an opportunity to
state its case; the Institute's Memorandum for the Committee was
prepared by Pepler. His commitment to education continued well
after his retirement from Government service. Pepler gave lectures
to students in the Department of Estate Management, Cambridge
(1948–53); from 1956 up to his death he was concerned with the
education of planners for overseas territories, now rapidly becoming
self governing, and he was a member of the Housing and Town
Planning Advisory Panel to the Colonial Office.

This wealth of personal contribution can be mirrored in many other
aspects of the Institute's work. Indeed, together with Alfred Potter,
Secretary to 1960 (who gave notice of his retirement in 1959 shortly
after Pepler's death), it might even be remarked that he *was* the
Institute, providing it with continuity, an enhanced reputation and
an ever-widening scope of influence before the public mind and in
corridors of Government power. He successfully contributed to care-

ful manipulation of tiny budgets and slender manpower, nourishing the tender plant of an emergent Institute to gain its charter (1959), its royal prefix (1970), its branch organisation and its overseas connections. His prodding and persuasive tactics sought out new opportunities for the planning ideal to be established. In virtually every initiative Pepler was involved. Every major paper had his hand. The Institute's rewards were no more than his due: President twice and the first recipient of the Institute's Gold Medal in 1953. But if he received, he gave in equal measure, and even after his death the Institute proceeded to benefit from the gift by Lady Pepler of the annual International Award which bears his name, enabling people to travel abroad to study particular aspects of planning, and of the Memorial Library.

As we have observed, an essential character of British town planning has stemmed from the professional organisation of its membership. The Town Planning Institute became a qualifying association, rather than a society of like-minded individuals. In short, its membership was to be on the basis of competence in knowledge and skill, proven through examination; in due time the 'Associate' class of member, linked to the Institute by sympathy with broad aims or work association, withered, leaving the membership characterised by technical expertise alone. However, in the wider spectrum of the planning movement as a whole there were (and are) many organisations concerned with planning. The Town Planning Institute set itself apart by its preference for professional status, and this, on occasion, has caused no little difficulty in its relationship with other bodies which rely on an activist, propagandist role, where membership depends not on examination entry but on subscription to an ideal. The early years of the TPI were marked by some cautious, defensive postures whereby its performance could be seen unambiguously as 'professional' (apolitical, serving the interests of public and private clients alike, giving technical advice where required) rather than propagandist (following single mindedly a particular cause or sectional interest). Undoubtedly there were stresses and strains in institutional relationships over particular issues, but many individuals belonged to a variety of professional and non-professional organisations, and in many ways the strength of the emergent planning movement derives from this catholicity of allegiance. Pepler was a person who maintained this varied approach.

It was difficult, if not impossible, for a planner in the early decades of this century at least not to be drawn to the ideas of Ebenezer Howard[14] and the Garden Cities Association, founded in 1901 to uphold his teaching. (In 1907 it became the Garden Cities and Town

Planning Association, as if to demonstrate the inevitably close relationship, and in 1941 the Town and Country Planning Association.) Pepler was closely associated with the garden cities movement throughout his life: prior to government service he was chairman of the Association's Executive Committee, and a member of Council from 1919 till his death. He subscribed to a belief in low density development and the attributes of garden, fresh air, outdoor space and accessibility to a farmed countryside, all features which permeated his planning philosophy.

Garden cities soon assumed an international importance, and in 1913 the International Garden Cities and Town Planning Association was founded. A new development took place in 1937 when the International Housing Association (as it had then become) merged with the Federation of Town Planning to form the International Federation for Housing and Town Planning. Pepler became its first President. This international work was soon shattered by World War II: in 1939 both the President and the Secretary were German and the Headquarters were in Brussels, and up to 1944 the Federation was carried on under German auspices. Meanwhile, however, a Free Section of the Federation was formed in England in 1941, and Pepler chaired an Inter-Allied Committee working on future European housing and planning under the auspices of the Ministry of Town and Country Planning. After the war the International Federation was resuscitated, and the Hastings Congress in October 1946 was attended by over 1,250 delegates from 29 countries. Pepler's involvement led to him becoming President in 1947, an office which he held until 1952.

Housing and planning questions in Britain were seldom far removed from matters relating to the countryside. The National Trust, founded in 1895, and particularly the Council for the Preservation of Rural England, formed in 1926, embodied ideals to which planners have naturally responded. The CPRE indeed originated as an initiative by the then President of TPI (Patrick Abercrombie) in association with the President of RIBA. It soon established itself as an informed and influential body, and a popular pressure group for countryside preservation and the development of rural amenities, including National Parks. Before (and indeed since) the scope of town planning assumed a rural dimension the CPRE has identified particular problems and pressed measures for their solution. After his retirement from the Ministry Pepler served as Vice Chairman of CPRE from 1952–57 and as Chairman of its Central Panels Committee from 1957 to his death. During these years he worked on such matters as advertisement control, downland ploughing, preservation of agricultural land, green belts and various countryside developments which raised amenity questions, all illustrating his capacity to harness his professional training and public experience to the interests of a particular organisation.

Another example was in his work for the National Playing Fields Association. During his years as a civil servant and in planning practice his philosophy led him to urge the adoption of improved open space standards in local authority Schemes. After his retirement a more formal position could develop, and Pepler was chairman of the Association's Grounds and Layout Committee from 1949–59. This was an influential position and its importance may be seen in Technical Memorandum No. 6, *Open Spaces*, published by the Ministry of Housing and Local Government in 1956, which contained as an Appendix a Memorandum of the NPFA, under Pepler's signature.

Finally, we may instance Pepler's longstanding interest in traffic and road planning. On the death of William Rees Jeffreys, a Trust Fund, administered by the TPI, was established in 1950 to promote lectures, studies and scholarships, to promote schemes for roadside parks and open spaces and related ventures to encourage improvements in highway planning to secure safety and beauty. The fund had been set up by Rees Jeffreys himself by deed in 1947. Jeffreys had been a fanatical and life-long roads lobbyist, organiser of the Motor Union (1903–10), Secretary of the Road Board (1910–18) and Secretary (and later Chairman) of the Roads Improvement Association from 1901. Pepler was President of the Trustees until his death, yet another example of his profound capacity to stimulate, support and encourage on a broad planning front, using those institutional opportunities which came his way.

Evaluation

It is sometimes difficult for biographers to exercise a sufficiently critical faculty over their chosen subject. Faults may be overlooked, limitations relegated, errors forgotten; instead, glowing praise may pervade. But Pepler's work has to be measured both in its own terms and in relation to others, as well as in the context of his time. Moreover the longer term consequences of his endeavours, 20 years and more after his death, have to be appraised.

Carefully weighed obituaries give us a lead. Pepler died in 1959 at the age of 77. *The Times'* obituary suggested that 'his contribution to the eventual acceptance of Planning as obviously necessary may well outweigh that of any other single individual'. It is clear that this contribution came from his personality and exercise of personal skills in encouragement and persuasion, rather than in any regard gained from scholarship, his output in planning practice, as an administrator or as a leader of a cult or single minded objective. He was no Abercrombie or Geddes, no Unwin, no Osborn or Howard; his reputation comes from elsewhere. *The Times* again: 'between the Wars, with little official support, he showed great skill in coaxing local authorities into forming regional groupings and preparing regional advisory plans to constitute an orderly framework for local planning decision. Here it was his negotiating tact and awareness of psychological factors as much as his technical competence which made him so valuable an agent in his Department'. *The Builder* wrote succinctly that he 'preferred persuasion and negotiation to compulsion, and had a deep love of humanity'. F. J. Osborn's entry of Pepler in the *Dictionary of National Biography*, 1931–60, confirms this: 'Pepler's qualities proved admirably suited to the task of inducing local authorities to adopt town planning powers and guiding them in putting these into practice. Having a passionate belief in the necessity of planning, as well as persuasiveness, patience, and tact, he was allowed by successive Ministers, or perhaps quietly assumed, exceptional freedom and scope in what was essentially propaganda. He was a major influence in the conversion of public and official opinion to acceptance of a new, contentious, and difficult government process'.

Pepler, then, had unique gifts of personality and temperament which were harnessed to planning – the subject field, the movement and the profession. His life, enormously varied, nonetheless had this unity of purpose and commitment to an ideal which must leave many people today perhaps disturbed and bemused but not a little humble and awed. As William Holford remarked at the Memorial Service at St Lawrence Jewry, Guildhall: 'It will be a long time before we stop listening, subconsciously, for that loyal "Hear! Hear!" that was not only the invariable signal of George Pepler's presence at a meeting but also the key to the message which he was calling on the world to listen to. It was the note of his tuning fork, sounded so as to keep in pitch his errant and sometimes wavering choir. It was the rallying call of his faith which held – in the words which he was fond of quoting – that the earth was the ultimate and God-given platform for all our human activities, that its use was something of supreme importance, transcending selfish interests and local feuds, that all land was held in trust for posterity, to be exploited with care, and preserved wherever possible with skill and patience.'

This was the philosophy to which he was deeply committed. It penetrated the planning profession with its work dedicated to 'the right use of land', and it supported the related interest groups to which he subscribed – garden cities, housing improvement, countryside preservation and playing fields. It offered a frame for his life and work. He used it (and in turn he was used by others) in such ways that 20th century planning benefitted enormously. This explains how a person without any literary work of importance to his name, with no outstanding reputation as a practitioner and with his one important Plan in this country (for the North East) refused publication, achieved the results he did.

The evidence is tangential and circumstantial, because on his retirement Pepler's personal office files were destroyed. But his great gifts as an enabler, stimulator, friend and advocate gave to planning a much-needed base and sense of security when it needed these things most. His determination to follow certain lines was accompanied by no dogmatism; a 'pragmatic incrementalist' would have described him well. No conservative, he was always striving for the next step – not for self-glory, but for the wider interests of which he was part. His personality and temperament favoured commitment touched with compromise; he lived at a time when these attributes had the greatest chance of success.

Perhaps we might identify the following as the key factors that influenced his make-up. In the first instance the family's roots lay for generations in the Wiltshire countryside. Pepler's grandfather went to London to seek his fortune; he did indeed prosper in the city as a Common Council man. To his son and grandson were communicated a love for and sympathy with cities. Domestically there was the happiness and repose of Pepler's first marriage. Professionally, there was the admiration for the work of Patrick Geddes. Spiritually there was his Quaker upbringing; probably this was pre-eminent, as in Quaker meetings he learned how to listen to others and to wait for guidance.

A conclusion must be that his reputation above all may rest securely on at least two matters: his years as a civil servant between the wars, and his life-long work for the Town Planning Institute. Success in both these fields has helped to shape the course of 20th century planning. On the first matter there was the careful cultivation of central-local relationships which saw a significant take-up of planning activity by local authorities. Pepler made it his job to know personally all town and district clerks throughout the country (it was even said he claimed to have played golf with most of them). The planning legislation of 1919 and 1932 offered an insecure base for statutory planning; that the Acts succeeded at all was due in some measure to Pepler's own exhortations and encouragement expressed both as a civil servant and a professional. But the exhortations were never strident or even intense. He retained the approach of a common sense amateur in his dealings with people – town clerks, fellow professionals, students or a lay audience. Not only wisdom and understanding, but geniality and kindness make for progress and solutions to problems. Pepler had that gift.

The second matter was interrelated – his nurturing of the TPI. The profession could have been stillborn. After Adams's early departure, the disruption of war, and the relative dominance of sister professions in planning affairs, the TPI could have run into the sand. Pepler's was a wise guiding hand; he was at once Home Secretary and Foreign Minister, and if in the end he became an elder statesman his was no restraining influence. He may have been seen as a benevolent godfather, but he directed no Mafia.

In his working life Pepler successfully managed the twin careers of public servant and professional spokesman. The fact that he was able to do this had clear benefits for both Government and profession, and we may now regret that the days of unconventional civil servants are over. Indeed, it may be unlikely ever again for a person to successfully devote a lifetime to planning in the way that Pepler was able to do. Professionally, long service on RTPI Council may not be possible or desirable; for a public employee service to a professional Institute may have to be discounted; and late 20th century society is today sceptical of enthusiasms for altruism, high standards and a seeming rejection of private interest for wider public concerns. We should be thankful that these things have not always been so, and that planning in this country has been successfully pioneered because of them.

Pepler died at his country cottage near Lulworth. East Point at Lulworth Cove was renamed Pepler's Point at a ceremony performed by Dame Evelyn Sharp, Permanent Secretary to the Ministry of Housing and Local Government, in October 1960. A stone commemorates the occasion; it carries a small bronze plate in memory of Pepler '. . . who loved the land of England; worked to the end that it be used for the benefit and enjoyment of its people'. British planning owes much to this simple but enduring philosophy, and the ways in which he expressed it.

Acknowledgements

Mrs Heather Mc Crae was a Research Assistant in the Department of Urban and Regional Planning in the University of Strathclyde when I first met her in 1975 as one of the founding members of the Planning History Group. She was working on the Pepler papers, which had been deposited at Strathclyde, and her Research Monograph *George Pepler, Knight of the*

Planners was published by her Department in December of that year. It represents a first attempt to sort a mass of documentation; it needed revision, but Heather McCrae died in April 1977.

In her Monograph her references are sometimes difficult to track down, and there is much duplication in the text, but researchers will be grateful for her interim sifting. I wish to acknowledge her research; this chapter is largely drawn from her work. I have reworked her chronological story, tightly condensing 226 pages into a short biographical sketch; I have interwoven my own knowledge of planning history from the Pepler years, and the evaluation of his work is entirely mine.

I am also grateful for the help and advice of Lady Elizabeth Pepler and Richard Pepler. Most kindly, they supplied photographs and corrected a number of points of detail in my text.

Notes

1 *Transactions of the Town Planning Conference*, RIBA, London, 1910
2 Gordon E. Cherry, *The Evolution of British Town Planning*, Heath and Reach, Leonard Hill, London, 1974
3 *Second Report of the Greater London Regional Planning Committee*, LCC, 1933
4 *Interim Report* of the Committee appointed by the Minister of Health to consider and advise on the principles to be followed in dealing with unhealthy areas, HMSO, London, 1920. *Second and Final Report*, 1921
5 Gordon E. Cherry, 'The Place of Neville Chamberlain in British Town Planning', in *Shaping an Urban World: Planning in the Twentieth Century*, Mansell, London, 1980
6 Stephen Ward, 'The Town and Country Planning Act, 1932', *The Planner*, Vol 60, May 1974
7 *Garden Cities and Satellite Towns*, Report of Departmental Committee, Ministry of Health, HMSO, London, 1935
8 *Interim Report of Departmental Committee on Regional Development*, Cmd 3915, 1931
9 *Report of the Royal Commission on the Distribution of the Industrial Population*, Cmd 6153, 1940
10 J. B. Cullingworth, *Environmental Planning, Vol I, Reconstruction and Land Use Planning, 1939–1947*, HMSO, London, 1975
11 Gordon E. Cherry, 1974, *op cit*
12 G. L. Pepler, 'Education for Planning. 1. Introduction', *JTPI*, Vol XXV, No 1, November, 1938
13 *Report of the Committee on the Qualifications of Planners*, Cmd 8059, 1950
14 Ebenezer Howard, *Garden Cities of Tomorrow*, Sonnenschein, London, 1902

7

THOMAS SHARP
1901–1978

Kathy Stansfield

Thomas Sharp's entry into the young profession of town planning was not premeditated. He drifted into the movement as an untrained surveyor's apprentice in the 1920s from an undistinguished educational background in the mining towns of the south-west Durham coalfield. The environment of his childhood and youth had a strong effect on him, moulding his character. Like his native landscape he was never insipid; pessimistic and melancholy at times, but inspiring and dramatic at others; he was challenging, stubborn and uncompromising to a fault. As a planner he reacted violently against established contemporary practice in town building, attacking garden cities and suburbia and expressing through his writing his love of beauty and order, of the formal and informal qualities of street architecture, and of the village and the countryside. It was as if the sordid environment of his early years enhanced his receptiveness to urban and rural beauty.

He was born in Bishop Auckland, a small mining and market town, in 1901, and lived in the same locality until he was nineteen. His family were mostly miners, though his father was an insurance agent, and the women of his family had been domestic servants. Sharp was influenced as a child by his mother, from whom he inherited an intuitive feeling for poetry and landscape. It was thanks to her that he did not become a miner himself, but was apprenticed to a surveyor in Spennymoor. After three years there, he made the break with home and moved south to Margate which opened up a new world to him and effectively set him on the road to becoming a qualified planner, as this town was one of the first in the country to undertake a town plan. By 1924 he had become a Planning Assistant to the City Surveyor of Canterbury and for the first time lived in an historic town – an experience which was to be important to him in later life.

From Canterbury, Sharp moved to London where he joined the

150

small office run by Thomas Adams and Longstreth Thompson and worked on advisory regional plans for areas around London. Whilst there he took and passed the professional examinations and became a member of the Town Planning Institute. He was one of the first to achieve this distinction without having previously obtained any other qualifications.

Planner as writer

Between 1932 and 1968 Sharp wrote a number of important books about planning in addition to all the reports he prepared for specific towns. Taken together they form a permanent record of the development of his ideas and his skills as a writer, and they reflect the ways in which the planning profession itself grew and changed, and how Sharp himself became isolated after the 1947 legislation.

His first book, an angry polemic, was written during two and a half years of unemployment following a dispute over the authorship of a mammoth report on South-West Lancashire which he had prepared in his capacity as Regional Planning Assistant to the South-West Lancashire Regional Advisory Group.[1] Full credit for the report went, as was traditional, to the Honorary Surveyor who had nominal responsibility. Sharp set a precedent he was to follow many times in his career when he refused to bow to bureaucratic tradition and protested. He resigned in anger and earned himself an unfavourable reputation within the profession which made it difficult for him to find work.

Town and Countryside, published in 1932,[2] was thus written in the isolation of unemployment and Sharp was influenced more strongly by his knowledge of 18th century literature and poetry and the achievements of that age in architecture and landscape than by his own contemporaries. It formed an outlet for all his feelings and bitterness, possibly coloured by the environment in which it was written, among the cotton mills and mean terraces of Preston, and later in the mining town of Ashington. It was to establish his reputation as a writer of controversial books, stirring up both enthusiasm and animosity among its readers. It formed the foundation for his subsequent work; his ideas would undergo modification with maturity, but in principle would not change radically over the next forty years – and this in a world which was to change almost beyond recognition. Much of what he advocated in the book has since been absorbed into planning thought and practice. But when he wrote it, there was no leadership from the movements which could have been expected to take the initiative for improvement. There were few articulate voices to be heard among the many, and even fewer capable of expressing what they believed in readable form. Thomas

Sharp was one of these few; it was his gift to be able to communicate his ideas in original and eloquent prose.

The main theme of the book was that the separate, individual qualities of town and country should be maintained: 'the only way to save the country is to make the town fit to live in', he wrote. He regarded the man-made lowland English landscape as one of the loveliest in the world, and the English village as a perfection of the village idea, themes to which he was to return in later books. But by far the most controversial ideas were those which challenged the garden city movement founded by Ebenezer Howard and given practical expression at Letchworth in 1903 and Welwyn in 1919. The ideal of the garden city as a self-contained settlement with its own industry, agriculture and lavish gardens, surrounded by open country, had been corrupted in the suburb. But Sharp challenged the ideal as well as the results. Howard, he wrote, was not interested in the town as a 'thing of beauty, a work of art, an expression of man's dignity and civilisation'. He had ignored the example of the country towns which had, despite the industrial revolution, retained their 'separate, urbane and civilised' character. Instead he had sought to bring town and country together creating 'a hermaphrodite; sterile, imbecile, a monster; abhorrent and loathsome to the Nature which he worships'. Hitherto the garden city had remained largely unchallenged as an ideal, even if the practical results had failed to live up to expectations. The savagery of Sharp's attack brought down upon his head the outraged astonishment of garden city enthusiasts. It was primarily low density housing development, characteristic of garden cities and suburbs, that he disliked so intensely. His plea was for a return to the street:

Let us again have *streets* of houses grouped closely together, clear in their symbolism of social order, pure strong, and independent in their material beauty. Let us again build TOWNS . . . Let us return after a century-long interval of barbarism and romanticism, to reality and the true and dignified expression of civilisation.

The irony, as Sharp saw it, was that England, through her statutory laws, had more control over building than any enlightened autocrat on the Continent had ever had when Renaissance building took place. Yet all that had been produced was a mass of suburbs. The years that have passed since this reflection have given us little evidence of the effectiveness of such statutory laws in improving the design of towns, and Sharp was to be a constant critic of the major legislative changes which followed the Second World War.

Sharp's conclusions at the end of his first book were pessimistic – the more disconcerting because no reader could doubt his sincerity or

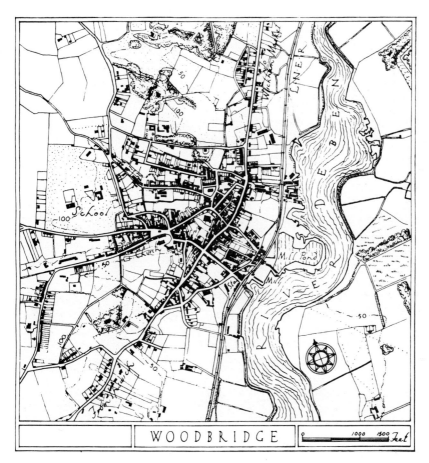

WOODBRIDGE

0   1000   1500   Feet

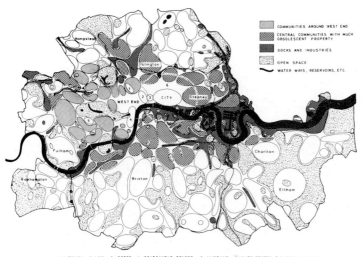

COMMUNITIES AROUND WEST END
CENTRAL COMMUNITIES WITH MUCH OBSOLESCENT PROPERTY
DOCKS AND INDUSTRIES
OPEN SPACE
WATER WAYS, RESERVOIRS, ETC.

1. UNIVERSITY   2. LAW   3. PRESS   4. GOVERNMENT CENTRE   5. MUSEUMS   6. MIXED GENERAL BUSINESS & INDUSTRY.

(xvii)

Sir George Lionel Pepler, 1950, as President of the Town Planning Institute for the second time. (Royal Town Planning Institute)

The Opening Day at Knebworth, one of Pepler's pre-war housing projects. Cecil Harmsworth is on the platform. Lord Robert Cecil on the extreme left, Pepler third from left, and Lord Lytton in front of him wearing a white hat

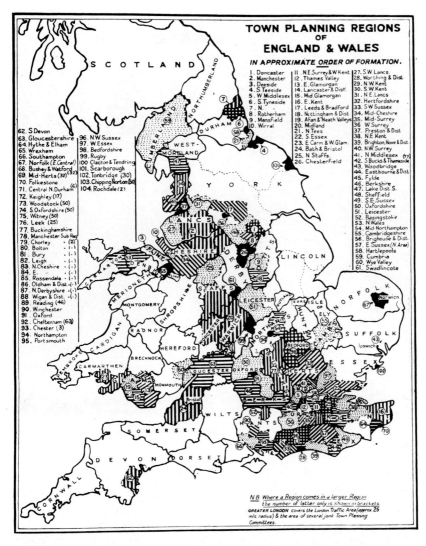

Town planning regions of England and Wales. (G. L. Pepler, 'Twenty-One Years of Town Planning in England and Wales', Journal of the Town Planning Institute, *Vol XVII, No 3, 1931)*

Leaving the hall after the inauguration of the New Delhi S.E. Asia Regional Conference of the IFHTP, New Delhi, 1–5 February 1954. Pepler, Honorary President, is second from the left, with Pandit Nehru, then Prime Minister of India, on his left. (Punjab Photo Service)

Lewis Silkin and George Pepler at the International Federation of Housing and Town Planning meeting in Zurich, 1948

Thomas Sharp, as President of the Town Planning Institute, 1945–6. (Royal Town Planning Institute)

(xxi)

1930s road and ribbon suburbia typical of that which Sharp vehemently criticised in English Panorama *in 1936. (Architectural Press)*

Durham Cathedral as Sharp saw it in 1945 in Cathedral City, *rising like a 'great grey ship' above the jumbled rooftops of the town. (Architectural Press)*

(Right) Sharp's plan for Kielder Village, Butteryhaugh, 1949. The black terraces were built. (Thomas Sharp)

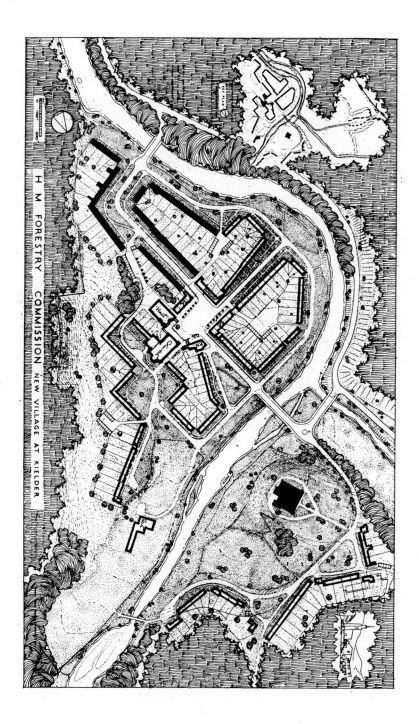

H.M. FORESTRY COMMISSION NEW VILLAGE AT KIELDER

(xxiii)

Kielder Forest Village, Butteryhaugh, to the east, near the road bridge (see plan). (Thomas Sharp)

Road proposals for Durham from Britain and the Beast, *1938. (a) The County Council's route (b) Sharp's alternative proposals. (Thomas Sharp)*

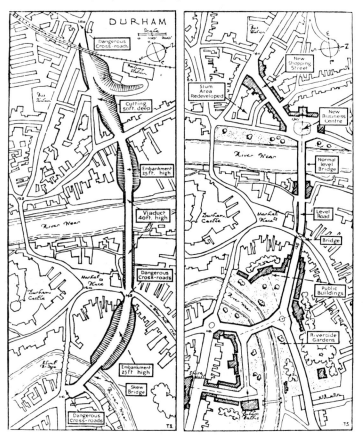

Sir Frederic Osborn as President of the Town and Country Planning Association, 1971–78. (Town and Country Planning Association)

(xxv)

Cockneys' excursion: the young Frederic with his father and uncle, from a tintype in the family album. (Osborn Papers)

The Forest Gate Fabian Society goes rambling (about 1911). Osborn (middle row on right) was its secretary. He was later to bring many Fabian propaganda and research techniques into the town planning movement. (Osborn Papers)

A rally in 1914, Osborn appearing as chairman of the Letchworth Trades and Labour Council. He was an active trades unionist and socialist and often regretted in later life the failure to mobilise working class support behind the housing and planning movements. (Osborn Papers)

When Osborn first met Herbert Morrison at the Brixton Discussion Forum they were office boy and errand boy respectively: fifty years later Morrison meets the newly-knighted Sir Frederic with Lady Margaret at the celebration dinner in the Royal Festival Hall, 1956. (Osborn Papers)

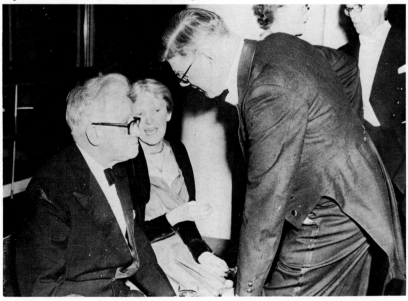

Lewis Mumford with Osborn on his visit to Welwyn in 1946; the two maintained an affectionate and mutually respectful correspondence for almost forty years. (Town and Country Planning Association)

Some of the garden city's earliest completed houses, in Brockswood Lane, which was Osborn's first Welwyn address. Note the unfenced front gardens. Osborn's very strict views on this and other matters of housing management can be studied in chapter 5 of Green Belt Cities, *written in 1946. (Central Library, Welwyn Garden City)*

During the war the TCPA held well-attended fortnightly lunchtime meetings in central London. This was in May 1944. The audience is clearly middle-class. (Osborn Papers)

Sir Colin Buchanan, 1964. (Author's collection)

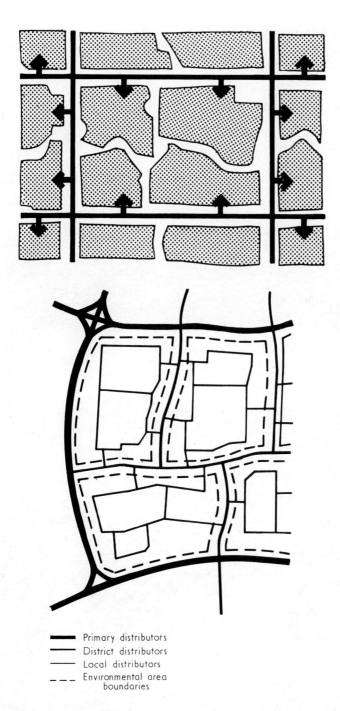

Primary distributors
District distributors
Local distributors
Environmental area
boundaries

The basic principles underlying the Traffic in Towns *ideas. (*Traffic in Towns, 1963)

(xxxi)

The popularised view of the implications of the Traffic in Towns *proposals.*
*(*Traffic in Towns, *1963)*

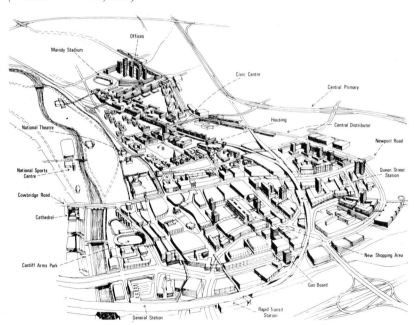

Sketch of the implications arising out of the application of Traffic in Towns *ideas*
*to the redevelopment of central Cardiff. (*Cardiff Development and
Transportation Study, *1968)*

lack of complacency as reviews of the book showed. Five years after its publication in 1932, the *RIBA Journal* reassessed the importance of the book:

Town and Countryside marked the end of an epoch, the first epoch in English official planning in which one school could dominate practice without effective interference. Mr. Sharp was not the first to argue that all was not well, nor even the first to propound an ideal halfway between the garden city of Howard, and the Ville Radieuse of Le Corbusier, but his arguments were so downright and closely reasoned . . . that they immediately attracted attention . . . Pessimistic or not, the book remains now, five years after its first publication, one of the best written, most sincere, and most fundamentally important works that have appeared within the field of architecture and planning literature.

After the publication of *Town and Countryside* Sharp became Regional Planning Assistant to the North East Durham Joint Planning Committee – a miserable, uninspiring job in a depressed, depressing area, but one which gave him time to get to know the city of Durham which was to be so great an influence later on. It also gave him the opportunity to consolidate his views and establish himself more firmly in the world of planning literature. He was commissioned by the *Architectural Review* to write a series of articles on the historic development of the English town, and these formed the basis of his second book, *English Panorama*, which was published in 1936.[3] In it he delved further into the past than he had done in his first book, and looked more searchingly at the development of the urban and rural environment. His style of writing matured. It was more measured and eloquent, more controlled. Most important was his view of Renaissance and medieval towns, which in the first issue of the book concentrated on the qualities of formal street architecture, the order brought by Renaissance man to his environment, recognising 'that conformity to certain rules of conduct is as necessary to the harmonious association of buildings as it is to men's'. The supreme example was the English country town – 'lively yet harmonious, varied yet ordered, urbane yet unmannered, rich yet unostentatious, disciplined yet free'. But by the time the second edition of *English Panorama* was published in 1950, Sharp had changed the emphasis from the formal qualities of urban architecture to the informal beauty of the medieval town, which in the intervening years of planning historic towns he had grown to love. Pure Renaissance towns, he said in the second edition, were mere monuments. 'They gave an immediate, perhaps breathtaking sensation; and then they had no more to give . . . there was nothing to learn, and nothing, by learning, to love.' The medieval town was by contrast 'a living town' and one which should provide inspiration for the future. He drew upon his own experience of life in Canterbury, a town in which he had discovered

the quintessence of all the pictorial subtleties that characterise the medieval street – variety, incident, surprise, intimacy, intricacy, enclosure, drama, contrast, subsidiary climax, delayed climax and more . . .

Although his attitude to towns had changed, he had found nothing to compare with the landscape achievements of the 18th century which formed a constant source of inspiration for him. But he had to admit in the second edition that the 'old balance between town and country has gone and will never return'. The war had marked the change, and the town had become dominant. He had put forward the case for satellite towns in both books, and by 1950 these had become reality in the shape of the New Towns, which Sharp criticised as being 'still clouded with garden-city suburbanism'. *English Panorama* was one of the first books to popularise the idea of neighbourhood planning in Britain and it found favour in the post-war years – by no means an ideal solution to the development of communities as was quickly realised, but it was evidence of the growing social concern of planners.

Reviewers of the second edition recognised the continuing importance of the book, noting the changes for the worse which had taken place in developments, particularly in the countryside. But on the whole, they looked to a future in which, following the 1947 legislation, there was hope that effective controls had been established. The 'time of indignation' was over. It was, however, a complacent view.

A further commission, this time by Penguin publishers, during the final countdown to war, while Thomas Sharp was teaching at Durham University, resulted in a Pelican paperback entitled *Town Planning* published in 1940.[4] It was to be his most popular book, selling a quarter of a million copies in 10 years and being translated into German and Spanish. Between the covers of an inexpensive paperback Sharp reached a far wider audience than he would otherwise have done, and possibly influenced young men serving in the armed forces to think about planning as a career when they returned to peace-time activity. It was, unlike his earlier works, an appropriate time to reach a wide public with such a book. There was an unparalleled desire to 'build a better Britain' when the war was over and a general dissatisfaction with the urban environment permeated all levels of society.

Sharp emphatically restated his case against suburbanism and the garden city and went on to discuss popular ideals concerning the forms of settlements and how best to contain the outward spread of towns. But in practice there was still little readiness to accept his ideas. Sharp was becoming acutely sensitive to the three-dimensional aspects of planning, and to the view of the man walking in the street. It was his aim, through his writing and later in his plans, to teach people to see things around them in a more critical way, in the hope of improving their appreciation of the qualities and possibilities of the every-day urban environment.

Town Planning was written during a war which was to mark the end of an era. The years that followed were to bring great changes to the urban environment. In general the book reflected the problems and ideals of its own time, but some of the changes were beginning to be apparent when Leo Desyllas, writing in the *Architectural Review* in October 1940 said:

[Planning] is concerned with the problem of a way of living . . . In reading this book we must decide whether it is still possible to tackle each separate problem of this way of living one at a time: the physical: the spiritual: the economic background, each with a separate solution: or whether the structure of human civilisation is so inter-dependent that the solution of one must be the solution of all. Thomas Sharp, in his simple but accurate statement on man's physical background rather precariously sits on the fence.

Possibly Sharp's most well known book today, *Anatomy of the Village* was published in 1946 by Penguin.[5] It was written as a handbook for the Ministry of Works and Buildings where Sharp had joined the Planning Section and worked as Joint Secretary with Dudley Stamp on the Scott Report on Land Utilisation in Rural Areas. This report laid the foundation for post-war legislation to protect the countryside, stressing the importance of agricultural land and recommending the creation of national parks and access to the countryside – many of the ideas about which Sharp had written earlier. His report on villages was almost supressed by the Ministry who refused to publish it, and it took 18 months of pressure to allow Sharp to publish it in a form in which it would not be associated with the department. Ironically the book, which sold 50,000 copies, became a classic on the subject of villages.

He stressed in particular the form of the village, the importance of the feeling of enclosure where houses were grouped closely together along the road or around a central space, and where views out were blocked by buildings. There were, he recognised, problems in planning new villages, some of which he was to face in practice in the man-made forests of Northumberland, when he designed villages for the Forestry Commission. There was no way of creating the informal, irregular village of the past in a planned settlement to be built in a few years or months. The existing planned villages of the 18th and early 19th century had been created at a time when more formal planning was popular, and were all 'built under the directing force of one man or one body of men'. Nevertheless they achieved a pleasing simplicity of design which was 'well within the main stream of the English village tradition'. Blanchland in Northumberland, was one especially successful example, others he looked at were Tremadoc in Caernarvonshire and Harewood in Yorkshire.

Sharp's preference for urban streets extended to the village, where he preferred houses designed in continuous terraces. He wrote 'the street or block contains the essence of the sense of neighbourliness and community'. These blocks were for him most successful when they enclosed a space, and provided the same sense of security and enclosure that was common in established villages.

Anatomy of the Village was published at the peak of Sharp's professional career, when he had become President of the Town Planning Institute and was preparing plans for Durham, Oxford and Exeter. The reviews it received reflect the continued recognition of Sharp as one of the few good writers on town planning. For Sharp himself it was the first time he consciously developed the concept of 'townscape' which he described as a 'kind of counterpart to landscape', analysing the quality of space as a kinetic experience. It was a novel idea, at root inspired by urban design, which may have owed something to Sharp's contact with the Architectural Press, where the theme of townscape was publicised from the early 1940s under the direction of Hubert de Cronin Hastings with whom Sharp worked on his plan for Exeter. Or it may have been that Sharp developed his own idea of townscape at about the same time. In any event Sharp wrote townscape analyses into most of his plans for historic towns and made familiar places come alive to his readers in a new way. And Gordon Cullen's lively series in the *Architectural Review*, presented through his exceptional skills as an artist, explored townscape graphically. Unfortunately the sketches which appeared in Sharp's plans failed to convey his ideas on townscape and his proposals for enriching the quality of urban surroundings. Likewise his ideas sometimes were lost in practice. Exeter in particular was a disaster; the new buildings were insipid boxes which had no townscape qualities. And in Durham a new road which Sharp saw as an exciting visual element designed to integrate sympathetically with the form of the historic town had no such qualities when it was built. There were reasons for these failures which were beyond Sharp's control, and these are explored more fully later.

After his book on villages Sharp wrote only one full length book on planning, and that not until 1968, though he produced many reports, a *Shell Guide to Northumberland*[6] and wrote a volume of poetry and several unpublished novels,[7,8] some of which took their themes from his work. In 1968 *Town and Townscape* was published which restated his ideas on kinetic townscape, attacked tower building and promoted conservation.[9] By this time Cullen's book *Townscape*, a collection of his *Architectural Review* series, had become the accepted reference book on the subject.[10] Sharp had done little to promote his own interest in townscape after the publication of his plans for historic towns, having barely survived as a planning consultant during the 1950s and 1960s. Although the idea of townscape has come into common usage among planners, it is often merely used to describe the static urban scene, and as understood by Sharp, Cullen and Kenneth Browne, who took over the series in the *Architectural Review*, has not received the attention it deserves. Trends in planning moved away from the environmental concern which inspired much of the early movement. It may be that the stage is set for a return to a greater awareness of both the intricacy and the beauty of the urban scene.

Cathedral City

One of Thomas Sharp's most important plans was that for Durham,[11] a city with which he was associated professionally for twenty years, long after he had left County Durham, to live in Oxford. His commission, in 1943, from the City Council, paralleled that of Patrick Abercrombie for blitzed London and Plymouth, and Sharp's own reconstruction plan for Exeter.

Durham was rather different. It had survived the war without destruction, and the problem was, according to the *Architects' Journal* (February 1945), concerned with 'the understanding of a place as a scene and a symbol'. It was the kind of study for which Thomas Sharp was to become famous, and a landmark in Sharp's work, in which the seeds of ideas sown in his books began to germinate. He wrote of Durham:

The city has a situation as romantic and spectacular as any city in Western Europe . . . The backward loop of the river is so swift that it makes almost an island, the bottleneck at the head of the peninsula, before the river swings away again, being little more than 250 yards wide. Here, round the thin loop of the peninsula the river is in a valley so steep and narrow that it might be termed a gorge whose precipitous sides are now hung thick with great banks of trees and whose summits are majestically crowned with the buildings of the old city.

His plan was aimed primarily at protecting what he called the 'sovereign architectural rights on the Peninsula', both from within and without. The character of the city as a whole derived from the domination of the rock and its buildings over the jumbled rooftops of the town and Sharp's attempts to protect it involved him in a protracted battle with the County Planning Authority over the siting of a new road through the city centre which would have ruined the town; with the university, which wanted new buildings on the peninsula, and with proposals to build a power station on the outskirts of Durham which would have disastrously affected the skyline.

Most important of all was the approach to the cathedral along Owengate. In his analysis of the townscape of this street Sharp described the relationship between buildings and spaces – now witholding the view, now allowing a glimpse, and finally the contrast of an explosion of space as the sequence builds up to a climax. In a memorable passage describing the sequence along Owengate, he wrote:

The curving narrow street climbs slowly, with a glimpse of the Cathedral at the head. Then at the top of the rise, at the head of the curve, the enclosed street suddenly opens out into Palace Green, broad, spacious, with a wide expanse of sky. And there, dramatically, the whole length of the Cathedral is displayed to the immediate view.

Throughout his time as planning consultant to Durham he acted as guardian and protector of the peninsula. His plan proposed its protection, and the control of building height, roofline and the colour of building materials. But in new building he disliked imitation of past styles; 'new buildings should be true to their own times and their own functions' he wrote.

There can be no doubt that the lasting importance of Sharp's plan for Durham lay in his perception of the spirit of place, on which his main planning proposals were based. It was the deep impression made on him by the groups of buildings on the rock which carried his appreciation of urban scenery into a world of moving sequences, changing views, enclosures, surprises – a personal involvement with space which was to be perfected in his plan for Oxford.

Perhaps the most important assessment of *Cathedral City* came from the *Architectural Review* which saw it as a plan with a lesson, declaring that

in those places which possess aesthetic and symbolic value, whether for the whole nation or only for the immediate inhabitants, (planners) should assess the significance of these qualities truly in relation to other factors; the machinery they devise for safe-guarding and improving should be designed not to a stereotyped pattern, but with the particular conditions and resources of each place in mind and . . . by their own understanding and enthusiasm they should heighten people's awareness of their surroundings, and consequently their sense of responsibility towards them.

But as the plan was published aesthetic concerns were over-shadowed by the controversies concerning the power station and the new road. In his plan Sharp had condemned the proposals of the North East Durham Electricity Company to build a giant power station at Kepier, a flat site close to the city centre. 'Michelangelo himself', he said, 'could not fit them into this setting,' speaking of the cooling towers and the cathedral rock. 'To build this power station at Durham would be an act of blind and brutal philistinism.'

A month before *Cathedral City* was published, a public inquiry was held in which Sharp gave evidence against the proposals as a private individual. Against the handful of objectors were all the powerful local bodies, including the electricity companies, trade unions, the County and City Councils and even the University, all of whom appeared to be completely insensitive to the crucial question of the scale of such a development in Durham. Sharp illustrated the visual effects by using photomontages which showed how the power station would intrude and dominate the city. 'The soaring chimneys and elephantine cooling towers will be seen from Palace Green itself', and they would destroy the 'nobility of the outline of the Cathedral', he wrote. His objection was the single most influential factor in the Minister's decision not to allow the power station to be built.

He was not so lucky with the road proposals. A new road through the city centre had been approved in 1931. Sharp had criticised the plan and published an alternative route in his contribution to *Britain and the Beast*, a series of angry essays edited by Clough Williams Ellis.[12] In it he described the road as one which ran 'for half a mile through the ancient city with as much regard for its features as a railway track'. The outbreak of war held up construction and the road had not been started when Sharp prepared his plan – with a different design for the road. It followed a similar alignment to the County Council's route, but with different levels which took it under Claypath rather than along an embankment, thus introducing a new and visually spectacular hillside road from the east, looking out across to the Cathedral. The two roads were totally different in concept, one an engineer's solution, the other, Sharp's, taking into account the special qualities of Durham. A quarrel ensued, despite acceptance of Sharp's proposals by the Ministry of Transport after a public inquiry in 1946.[13] The dispute went on for the next twelve years, during which the County Council consistently refused to accept the plan. In the end the road that was constructed bore little resemblance to the one he had proposed.

Conflict between Sharp and the County Council was a feature of his association with Durham where he was retained by the City Council as planning consultant until he resigned in 1963. During these years he was in a unique position to protect the city from a number of disastrous proposals. In 1959 he successfully preserved a key building along Owengate, the approach to the Cathedral, from demolition proposed by the University and the planning authorities. It took a campaign in the *Architectural Review* and a good deal of persistence and pressure before the building was instead restored, and the interior redesigned. Owengate today remains outwardly unchanged, and the magnificent approach to the Cathedral can still be enjoyed to the full.

In 1960 he blocked proposals to build a sixteen storey tower as part of a new General Post Office complex on the opposite bank of the river to the Cathedral, again supported by the planning authority. When he resigned in 1963, mainly as a result of County Council resentment at his interference, he could claim a long list of successes in Durham, most of which will not be remembered because they were successes which prevented disasters. In July 1969 the editor of *Northern Architect*, in a special Durham issue, looked back to Sharp's plan and wrote:

this was not so much a plan as an intervention by an individual who identified himself with his problem in a highly personalised way . . . Thomas Sharp came and went regretting the impossibility of achieving his personal aspirations . . .

In the hands of his successors (the planning authority, since Sharp was not replaced by a consultant), the editor wrote, the future of Durham was a 'more impersonal concept capable of being manipulated by remote control'. This is the method of planning today, but it was not a way which Thomas Sharp followed. Both may have their merits and much depends upon the personality of individuals in powerful positions. But our cities are the poorer when an impersonal concept ignores the special qualities of a place.

Oxford Replanned

Sharp's plan for Oxford was a turning point in his career. His commission in 1945 coincided with a period of deep dissatisfaction with his prospects as a college lecturer when, having devised what was to be the first undergraduate course in town planning in Britain, he saw little chance of its being established in the near future. He abandoned his hopes for a chair in the new course and left County Durham for good. It was in Oxford that he made his home and he was to remain there for the rest of his life. It was a welcome change, as he wrote in a bitter poem, *Farewell to County Durham*.[14] He had come

> . . . from the extremes
> Of greyness to this brightness, from a landscape
> Where the monuments are slag heaps, a pit's headstocks,
> To where these historied spires look down and dream . . .
> . . . the early memories and squalor
> Sharpened, not blurred the vision; made me see
> Beauty more clear since unaccustomed; keep
> the mind free of the glamour to see only
> Reality unfalsified by myth.

Sharp was not the first to recognise that planning in Oxford had become a question of conserving the identity and spirit of the historic city in face of both the growth of a new, industrially oriented centre at Cowley, and of the traffic problem of the town.[15] Where his plan was unique was in his method of analysing the visual quality and spirit of Oxford, and in his boldness in suggesting solutions to the problems of industrial location and traffic.[16]

His understanding of townscape came close to perfection in his study of Oxford. He wrote:

Today we are attending the rebirth of an art which is of significance to the whole community. It has the virtue that it can be practised by anyone who has a weakness for architecture or a personal interest in a given town.

For Sharp, Oxford was the supreme example of his idea of townscape, with its 'casual splendour' and 'dignity without formality'. It was to be seen at its best in the High Street and in Catte Street, examples to which he was to return often in later writing. He wrote of the High Street:

. . . this miracle of harmony-in-conflict is sustained in a series of well-punctuated instalments for three-quarters of a mile on one side of a street curving broadly like a great river.

His special feel for the qualities of the High Street later became part of a long poem which was broadcast on radio.[17] It can be seen as the consummation of his professional life with his more private 'love affair with literature', and puts into words a concern for Oxford which went far beyond the mere preparation of a planning document.

... From the long balustraded bridge
Beyond the tower, which on May morning
Welcomes the Spring's first daybreak chime,
The quiet civil frontages flow down,
Flow smoothly for a space, until,
Out from the shadowed curve's opposing crown,
Bright to the sun, move in
Queen's twin pavilions and her cupolaed screen;
While, base-obscured beyond them, Radcliffe's dome
Rises in Roman grandeur. Now
The townly buildings, and the green
Bosoming of that marvellous tree
Foil the predominant store a space,
Till straightly, suddenly,
From the receding southern face
Comes out St Mary's tower and fretted spire
Powerfully urgent, hesitates, moves free,
Resolves about the central sky, to ride
Topping All Souls: a few yards more and then,
Beyond long pinnacled nave and twisting porch,
Out from the curve again, by Brasenose gables,
Straightly leaps in,
Ordered with a cunning difference,
The storeyed tower of Aldrich's own church –
Two splendoured heights, as though for the street's pride
Merely the one insistent incident
Were too poor riches. And then to point again
The principle, as Mary's steeple backs,
Recedes, is left behind,
And mitred inn and ashlared stores extend
Down to Carfax,
Yet one more tower stands out to make an end.

Sharp believed that the human scale and pedestrian movement were guiding principles in the appreciation of kinetic townscape, and this was probably best illustrated in his analysis of the approach to the Radcliffe Camera along Catte Street. Sharp called it 'the greatest architectural sequence in England'. Each building was in its own right a superb piece of architecture, but the total experience was brought about by the changing relationships between the buildings, and between the buildings and their environment as the observer moved from one to the other.

... the experience is elemental, beyond the power of words or photographs to describe. Cube, cylinder and cone are suddenly juxtaposed, or rather suddenly deploy the one from the other, with a result that is, architecturally speaking, sensational.

These were the most obvious elements of his townscape analysis which also took in the special qualities of the Backs, the river banks, the details of materials and street furniture and the importance of trees.

Oxford Replanned elicited a good deal of praise and became a classic of its kind. William Holford wrote in *The Listener* (11 March 1948):

this book finally sets the seal on its author's pre-eminence in that school of planning that regards all towns and cities as having a life and personality of their own that must be preserved, cleared of alien accretions, and allowed to develop freely as modern conditions demand. He sees a city as a physical thing not merely as a social utility.

The townscape theme in the report was of sufficient importance for Sharp to write a separate book concentrating on it, which was published as *Oxford Observed* in 1952.[18] Aimed at a wider readership it was reviewed in *Country Life* as:

the most influential contribution to the appreciation of scenery since Sir Avedale Price on the Picturesque a hundred and fifty years ago – the principles of which it brings up to date.

Sharp's deep personal commitment to the preservation and creation of beauty in the environment gave him the tenacity to pursue his ideals relentlessly in Oxford. But not for nothing is it labelled 'the home of lost causes' and not for nothing was he to conclude despondently in his poem

> . . . The time
> Is heavy with disaster. Who
> Can hopefully pray should do so now;
> That still this centuried townscape, this
> Zenith of cities, may endure;
> May yet survive its threatening doom.
> By hazardous years and present men;
> May keep for citizens still to come,
> Its character whole, its beauty sure,
> Till worthiness shall come again.

Oxford was a city, he wrote, 'whose apparent destiny which has been followed over a period of seven hundred years has been thwarted – thwarted largely by a bicycle in a backyard'. He identified the growth of the Cowley works as the major problem within the city, and believed that removal of the industry was the only positive, long-term way of ensuring that Oxford survived as an historic centre of great beauty. Unrealistic as the idea may seem, there were in fact precedents. His suggestion was a piece of planning surgery inspired not only by the wholesale removal of Short's armaments from Rochester to Belfast as a security measure during the war, but Ford's peacetime removal twelve years earlier from Manchester to Dagenham for purely personal reasons, not social or national ones. Sharp's own recommendation was made in the light of indications from the events of the previous few years that the firms might have to move of their own accord if they were not allowed to expand in Oxford. But it was a futile hope, and although many people agreed with his diagnosis, the cure he proposed was unacceptable. The Development Plan for Oxford accepted only the need to prevent a large population increase in the city and speculated that a reduction in the heavy industries might allow diversification.

Sharp did, however, eventually succeed in removing the Gas Works from its site close to the city centre and Christ Church College, which he considered entirely inappropriate. He wrote that plans to expand the works would 'knock the dreams out of Oxford's spires forever', and fought against the Private Bill introduced into Parliament early in 1946 to allow the extension. The matter was debated for three years at various levels, until it reached the House of Lords. After hearing Sharp present the main case for the opposition on behalf of the City Council, the Lords rejected the proposals to build the retort house and new gas holder without recourse to further evidence and chose to disagree with the Ministry of Fuel and Power which had supported the gas company. Over the next twenty years the gas works were removed and supplies piped from Reading and stored at Cowley.

The Meadow road

Of all the battles Sharp fought in historic towns, that of the Oxford Roads was the most protracted and frustrating, a telling illustration of the weaknesses in the planning system. He fought for twenty-five years and through five public inquiries to convince the authorities that the best solution to the acute traffic congestion in the city centre was to drive a new road across Christ Church Meadow. Whilst he fully appreciated the value of quiet riverside open space penetrating the heart of the city, he believed that:

If it is a matter of losing the peace of Broad Walk and Christ Church Meadow to gain quietness in High Street it cannot be unreasonable to argue that the comfort and safety of thousands of university people and the tens of thousands of citizens and others who daily use that street outweigh in importance the calm afforded to the handful of people who frequent the two paths between the city walks and the river.

In *Oxford Replanned* he had identified the need for a relief road to remove congestion from the High Street, Carfax and Cornmarket, the main shopping area. The route had, he said, to be close enough to the city centre to be an attractive alternative, and yet had to avoid too much destruction of property. Thus he came to the conclusion that

the only possible line, and one which is nearly perfect *so far as traffic considerations are concerned* stands out as plain as a hundred pikestaffs . . . a direct line running alongside the Broad Walk between the Plain and the middle of St. Aldate's and thence Northwards; a road with all the quality of inevitability about it.

The road was an integral part of Sharp's traffic plan for the centre of Oxford, linked to new routes to the north and west designed to relieve Carfax. He later refined his proposals for the road and they were printed in the *Oxford Times* on 10 March 1950, two years after his plan was completed. Magdalen Bridge would be closed and a largely enclosed precinct would be created in the historic town centre. Unlike Durham, he had had no contact with the City Council since *Oxford Replanned*, and though he sent them a copy of his ideas, they chose to side step the issue when the Development Plan was published in 1953. Despite the fact that 80 per cent of the town's traffic was generated within the city, they declared that the outer bypasses must be completed before any other changes could be considered.

Sharp objected at the subsequent planning inquiry, and at those which were to follow, as a private citizen. Duncan Sandys, Minister of Housing and Local Government, even produced his own solution, known as the Lamb and Flag route, although it was never a serious contender. The main alternative was a much longer route which went well to the south of the Meadow, taking the name of Eastwyke Farm by which it passed.

Sharp's evidence of the inquiry was published in the *Town Planning Review* of October 1956. His proposals were based on the second of the alternatives originally published in his plan, his route following the line of the Broad Walk. His proposals did not change substantially in the following years, though they were improved and adjusted in detail. In 1956 Sandys decided in favour of the Meadow road which for a time became known as Sandys Boulevard.[19] The matter had even been referred to the Cabinet. The University's reaction was to issue a writ against Sandys on the grounds that it was unconstitutional of him to make proposals on a matter in which he was the final arbiter. This coincided with the Suez crisis which diverted public attention. There was little reaction when Sandys stated that his decision was not a direction under the Act and therefore was not mandatory to the City Council. The writ was withdrawn.

Sharp was commissioned by the City Council to prepare a detailed plan for the new road, but, characteristically, he resigned after a dispute with the City Architect and Planning Officer who had produced his own plans without reference to Sharp. The Council eventually gave up and in 1957 announced that it could neither accept the Meadow road nor produce any new plans for the Minister. The subject provided scope for debate, but no action was taken for the next two years, until in 1960 the Minister declared an 'inquiry-at-large' – a free for all in which any suggestions could be proffered. Several variations on the Eastwyke Farm route were presented; Sharp stuck to his Meadow road and was the only person to present fully worked out drawings at the inquiry. The City Council offered a variation on the Meadow route. Sir Frederick Armour was the Inspector and in his report declared 'if peace and quiet is to be restored in the central university area a road across the Meadow is inescapable' and he recommended adoption of the City Council's scheme.[20] In 1962 the Minister agreed and was of the opinion that 'it is doubtful whether the construction of the Eastwyke Farm [route] would be justified, and it . . . should be excluded from the submissions'.[21]

A further two years passed before the City Council's plan was produced, and to be different, it proposed a *sunken* road across the Meadow. It pleased no-one. Inevitably it meant yet another inquiry, held in 1966, after which the Minister declared the City Council's plan unsatisfactory and decided that a comprehensive plan for a traffic system for Oxford should be produced. Two years later, and a fee of 160,000 guineas later, a massive document typical of the sixties style appeared. The *Oxford Central Area Study* was produced by the engineers Scott, Wilson and Kirkpatrick and Partners, and architects Hugh Wilson and Lewis Womersley, with the Ministry footing part of the bill. The main recommendation was that the Eastwyke Farm route should be built and the report rejected any plan based on the Meadow road.

The fifth and final public inquiry lasted from June to December 1970. Sharp again objected, but this time in alliance with others. Funds for legal fees were raised by jumble sales and appeals. Sharp was in the witness box for three days, giving evidence and being cross examined on his scheme, improved to take advantage of the cleared slums at St Ebbe's. He estimated that the road would cost £3 million as against the £13 million estimate for the Eastwyke Farm route, and take three years to construct set against 20 years for the latter.[22]

Sharp was critical of the consultants' document and, refusing to be intimidated by it, dissected it in his proof of evidence to the inquiry. He found errors in the figures, maps and tables and pointed out that there were 140 inaccuracies that could be checked. The consultants had favoured private transport at the expense of public, instead of suggesting 'park and ride' or other similar solutions. It was a document which 'should never have been published in this form . . . as it has been presented it is most gravely unsatisfactory as a basis for the formulation of the plan,' he declared. The scheme gave 'no evidence whatever . . . of any attempt to give ordered shape and design to spaces, to bring buildings into a balanced relationship with their setting' and it was 'mechanistic and brutal', and totally out of place in Oxford. Of the Meadow he commented:

it is hard to believe, too ironical not to wonder at; but the defenders of that one open space, the miasma-bound unused meadow, have smashed into and wrecked no less than twenty three other spaces of various kinds by the roads they have at such expense devised supposedly for the protection of the environment.[23]

The Inspector suffered a mental collapse during the course of the inquiry and had to be replaced. In October 1971 the Inspector's Report decided in favour of the Meadow road, but the Minister chose to disagree, declaring that there was 'little to choose between the two routes' and that the Eastwyke Farm road should be built. His modifications to this route, however, proved unacceptable to all but the University.

It later came to light when Sharp appealed unsuccessfully to the Ombudsman that the Minister had not even seen the Traffic Assessor's substantial report which favoured the Meadow road. The controversy had raged for twenty years and each attempt at a solution had been blocked either locally or at the national level, with strong political overtones in the action. The final irony within Sharp's lifetime came when the Conservatives were defeated by the Labour Party in the local Oxford elections of 1972, whereupon the Council refused to carry out the Minister's plan and resorted instead to a policy of traffic management to solve Oxford's problems.

Thus Sharp's efforts had come to nothing over a period of time in which it had become a characteristic of the planning profession to produce ever more complex and costly studies and solutions, mystifying the public they were intended to serve, and leading to expensive public inquiries and disillusionment with the planning process. The planning system was and still is incapable of even solving the traffic problems of Oxford in face of determined politically oriented opposition, and this saga shows the impossibility of even producing a solution without clear objectives. Sharp's own objectives were crystal clear and this made it easy for him to confidently prepare and defend planning solutions to this and other similar problems. Today's planners on the whole lack such confidence because the field in which they operate has become so wide and so complex that an individual's skills and perception can no longer embrace it.

Exeter, Salisbury and Chichester

Most notable amongst Sharp's plans for historic towns, apart from Durham and Oxford, were his studies of Exeter, Salisbury and Chichester. Exeter alone had been bombed during the war and lost the famous crescent, Bedford Circus. In his plan *Exeter Phoenix*,[24] Sharp insisted that it would be utterly wrong to try to re-create what had been destroyed, as in fact was successfully done in Germany. Thus instead of rebuilding Bedford Circus, he proposed a new pedestrian precinct on the site, aligned to provide a new view of the Cathedral. The sketch provided in the plan, however, does little to inspire the reader with his idea. Princesshay was one of the first post-war shopping streets; although it did indeed provide a new view of the Cathedral, as a street it is totally undistinguished. Perhaps Sharp's confidence in the ability of the local authority to produce a satisfactory replacement for Bedford Circus using an attractive idea with a Cathedral as its focus, was misplaced. Exeter is certainly no success story. The rebuilding of the main shopping street along a road too wide for the scale of the new shops has blown open the former intricacy and illustrates only too well Sharp's comment that 'even the most perfect ground plan will be barren of all good except mere convenience if the buildings along it are mean, bad or disordered'. Major road proposals and attempts to open up other views of the Cathedral and city walls came to nothing, though some of the bomb damaged buildings were preserved and landscaped as memorial gardens, as Sharp suggested. The enforced austerity and post-war shortages were partly responsible, but as in Durham and Oxford, the local authority was reluctant to act in keeping with the spirit of Sharp's plans and the interpretation of his ideas devalued them.

His plan for Salisbury, *Newer Sarum*,[25] though an excellent study, lacks the appreciative warmth of his other studies. It was a town with which he did not so readily identify, perhaps because it had been newly built in medieval times to a grid iron plan and, for him, lacked the superb townscapes of Durham and Oxford. He commented 'there is no other city in the kingdom which, while possessing such great architectural distinction from the past, offers such wide architectural freedom to the future.' There did not seem to be so much at stake in Salisbury: there were no major environmental battles to be fought and no precious townscapes in danger. Even the Cathedral Close did not inspire him as much as others he knew.

Chichester, by contrast, held a special charm for Sharp. He was particularly attracted to the small scale Georgian architecture which characterised the place and called his plan *Georgian City*.[26] He analysed the qualities of the dignified streets and back lanes with a sympathetic eye, and fought successfully against a proposal by the County Council to widen the main shopping streets which met at the old Market Cross and divided the city into four quarters. Proposals for small car parks on back land behind the shops, using existing walls to subdivide the spaces, were carried out. But when the lavish Conservation Study of Chichester[27] was produced by the Ministry of Housing and Local Government in 1969, it made no reference to Sharp's plan for the city, and despite all the studies, there has been much evidence of insensitivity and outright mutilation in Chichester since. In 1972 Sharp was called in by individual citizens when the County Council, following the planning fashion of the day, proposed to pedestrianise the four main streets. Sharp pointed out that this would force traffic into the narrower, quiet residential back streets which held such charm.

The forest villages

One of Thomas Sharp's greatest disappointments resulted from a commission which promised satisfaction of a personal desire to design villages as well as write about them. The Forestry Commission appointed him to design new forest villages to house their workers in the Kielder Forest, Northumberland, in 1946. He proposed eight villages some of the plans for which appeared in the Journal of the Town Planning Institute in May 1949, but work was abandoned by 1952 when only three had been started. Post-war shortages in materials and manpower, changes in forestry practice requiring fewer people, and increased mobility allowing workers to commute from existing towns, meant that the idea was doomed to failure. The plans and parts of the villages built at Kielder, Stonehaugh and Byrness show some of Sharp's ideas in practice, though somewhat mutilated and unfinished. His designs were for strongly nucleated villages focussing on the church or community centre which broke the horizontal emphasis of long terraces of white washed cottages facing onto open greens, with private gardens behind. As built they are austere, obviously incomplete and lack even the tree planting which Sharp proposed to give shelter and soften the built forms. The long terraces are overemphasised because the communal buildings with which they were to contrast were never built. Sharp's desire to build villages, backed initially by the Forestry Commission, had been unpopular from the outset with the local planning authorities. In the event they were proved right in preferring transport of workers to the forest to the isolation of new villages in such remote parts.[28]

The post-war years

The period just after the war proved to be the height of Sharp's career, with public, academic and professional recognition for his work. But it was followed by an almost total eclipse and nearly thirty years of disillusionment, partly due to his rejection of opportunities which presented themselves and partly to changes in the nature of the planning profession. An unfortunate but persistent streak of bad luck seems to have dogged Sharp's working life and this was not helped by his impatience and inability to compromise – a characteristic which was a strength as well as a weakness.

Sharp had worked at the Ministry during the war and as we have seen was appointed one of the two secretaries of the Scott report on Land Utilisation in Rural Areas which reported in 1942. There were opportunities to develop this work but he chose not to pursue his career at the Ministry. The experience with his manuscript for *Anatomy of the Village* and the general difficulty he found in working with a group of civil servants, together with ill health and an emotional upheaval, took him back to academic life in Durham in 1943. In his absence he had been given a personal Readership in the School of Architecture, with the distinct possibility of a Professorship after the war. He also started his own consultancy with offices in Newcastle. During the next two years he designed what was to become the first undergraduate course in Town and Country Planning in the country, eventually approved with a department of its own. He was informed, however, by the university administrators, that in the short term there was little likelihood of the course being started. Disillusioned, he left the university, and Durham, driven by his own impatience, and attracted to Oxford by the work he had obtained there. He found out indirectly only a few months later that the course had been established and a professor appointed. It was a bitter blow to Sharp, and he saw it as a deliberate snub. Had he had the freedom of a Professorial Chair, it is possible that he might have led his own particular field from that position. Planning as a profession has suffered from a dearth of people who are able and prepared to speak their minds freely – partly because of their responsibilities as civil servants in local or central government. Sharp always refused to be intimidated by bureaucracy. He needed the professional independence which a Chair could have given him, and the security it would have brought during the difficult times after the 1947 Act. Possibly as a result he would have kept in closer touch with the profession during the 1950s and '60s, instead of which he turned inwards for creative satisfaction in his work.

For a few years Sharp's consultancy in Oxford attracted a large number of commissions. In addition to the plans for Durham, Exeter, Oxford, Salisbury and Chichester, there were smaller schemes for St Andrews, King's Lynn and Taunton in 1948; plans for Todmorden (1946), Stockport (1950) and Minehead (1951) and other small schemes. He was commissioned to define the designation area and make the first plan for Crawley new town, but, characteristically, he resigned after a row with the chairman.

These were years of academic and professional distinction as well. In 1948 the university awarded him a Doctor of Letters for his planning books. In 1945–46 he was President of the Town Planning Institute and he held the same post in the Institute of Landscape Architects in 1949–50. He was awarded a CBE in 1951.

But the brevity of this period of achievement was ensured by the changes in the profession brought about by the post-war planning reforms embodied in the 1947 legislation and Sharp's inability to adjust to them. The new Act strengthened the planning function of the local authority and the position of the planning officer, which Sharp himself had fought for as a member of the Town Planning Institute working in local government in the 1930s. He had edited the quarterly journal of the Planning Officers' Section of the TPI and had written passionately about the downtrodden position of planning officers, compared with consultants who dominated the Institute at the time.[29] Significantly, the Section was wound up in 1950, by which time most of the Institute's members were planning officers.

As a result of the changes there was very little work for planning consultants. Sharp suffered particularly badly in this respect because he chose to keep his office small and did not diversify the skills of the practice. It was characteristic of him to want to continue to work in a situation in which he dominated, among people sympathetic to his ideals. Other planners, to survive, formed partnerships with architects and looked abroad for work. The price Sharp paid was a heavy one. He was forced to close his office in Oxford in 1950 and work from home.

He was critical of the 1947 Act in a pessimistic paper given to the TPI in 1957, 'Planning Now',[30] in which he expressed concern about public disillusionment with planning which he attributed partly to the nature of plans produced under the Act 'plans which provided too little, too few hopes, to reconcile people to the control that is exercised over their activities'. The paper caused a storm of protest. Lord Silkin described it as 'outspoken, courageous, sincere, stimulating, unorthodox, controversial . . . and gloomy' and criticised Sharp for being too rigid in his views.

The nature and scope of town and country planning became the subject of debate both within the profession and among those experts in other fields who contributed their skills to an ever greater degree, throughout the period following the 1947 Act. Silkin had set up the Schuster Committee in 1948[31] to look at these problems and at the professional qualifications necessary to become a planner. Sharp's evidence to the committee[32] provides us with a statement of his own views, views which had been the basis upon which the undergraduate course which he devised in Durham were founded. He believed that the planner needed to draw upon the specialised knowledge of a team of people, applying his own special design skills to the subject. As far as he was concerned, design was one man's responsibility. He cited the main technical qualifications as:

1. Complete equipment within his specialised technique of design.
2. Working knowledge of specialised techniques upon which his own impinges (ie, architecture, civil engineering, landscape design).
3. A broad understanding of related fields of knowledge (eg, geography, economics, public administration, law).

His views formed one end of the spectrum of ideas about the nature of planning, and the trend was increasingly towards that opposite school of thought which saw planning as 'determining the right use of land, which is fundamentally an economic and social activity, and . . . the technique of the designer . . . is ancillary'.[33] The emphasis was on the synthesis of all the related activities and knowledge necessary to produce a plan, rather than planning as design. Matters came to a head in 1964 when the TPI's special committee on membership policy suggested that both trained planners and specialists with an interest in planning be admitted 'on level terms of corporate membership'. Many planners, including Sharp, felt threatened by this proposal and objected to the way in which the matter had been handled by the Council. They forced an Extraordinary General Meeting in January 1965, at which Sharp and Lewis Keeble led the debate;[34] a month later most of the former Council of the TPI was deposed, Keeble became President and Sharp sat on the Council for a year. It was Sharp's last stand, and one which allowed the Institute to continue to resist for a while changes which were to prove irresistible and which were to isolate Sharp still further.

The debate within was reinforced by uncertainty and dissatisfaction in the world of planning in practice. By 1968 another sweeping set of reforms in statutory planning were replacing the 1947 system which had become more and more unpopular. Following the proposals of the Planning Advisory Group in 1965, *The Future of Development Plans*, the new system brought into being Structure Plans and Local Plans to distinguish strategy from tactics. Once again, as he had in 1957, Sharp attacked the changes, this time at the TPI conference in Hastings in 1966, when he emerged briefly into controversial limelight. In his paper 'Planning Planning' he savagely attacked the idea of planning as teamwork, but in so doing revealed his isolated position rather than rallying support.[35] He was particularly concerned that Structure Plans would not be understood by the public who could only object at the local level. He declared:

I have come to wish that we would consider objectively what our reactions would be, as private citizens, against the restriction we place on the use of private property that might perhaps be our own.

This proved to be a just criticism.

He was speaking at a time when the planning consultant had returned to favour in the 1960s building boom, commanding higher fees than ever before and producing mammoth reports such as that on the Oxford Roads, incorporating a variety of new planning techniques borrowed from other disciplines in an effort to objectively quantify future needs. Sharp did not even try to fit into such a professional world, but remained as he had been in the '50s, a bystander, occasionally emerging from relative seclusion in Oxford to make his views known, as we have seen. His planning work was reduced to a trickle, and his need to be creatively active found an outlet in writing novels and poetry, most of which have not been published. He took on planning inquiries concerning proposed development in Piccadilly Circus and Parliament Square, as well as continuing to fight the Oxford roads inquiries, and gained a reputation for being as intimidating in the witness box as many of the legal representatives who faced him. He produced a planning report for Cambridge in 1962, *Dreaming Spires and Teeming Towers*,[36] where, ten years earlier he had redesigned and replanted the grounds of St John's College.[37] This report together with his final book on planning, *Town and Townscape*, published in 1968, stressed his continued preoccupation with physical form and the quality of urban space at a time in which, ironically, some of the greatest environmental disasters were being perpetrated in the name of town and country planning, by the allegiance between planners who no longer seemed to have a feel for place and space, and developers whose prime concern was with profit.

The poetry of planning
Thomas Sharp once wrote of his own, personal aspirations:

I felt that what would most satisfy me in life, what would most justify my ever having lived, what would crown my whole life's work, would be to build a good new village and to write a good . . . lyrical poem.

The village, that microcosm of society which in its physical form embodies so clearly the feeling for townscape as Sharp understood it, was thus fused with his passion for literature and poetry, which formed the foundation of his planning career. It is the poetic insight which glimmers through Sharp's writing combined with his intuitive awareness of the qualities of three-dimensional space, of townscape, which form his greatest and most lasting contribution to the planning profession. Where most of his creative efforts went into his planning work, his desire throughout his life was to give an appropriate form to what he described as 'an intensity of feeling' which only poetry could express. This 'love affair with literature' was so important to him that it overrode his need for people with whom to share his life, although ironically much of his creative literary effort was concentrated into the years following his marriage in the early 1960s. And despite his desire to achieve distinction in the world of literature, it is as a planner that he will be remembered for his writing.

Perhaps the fact that Sharp's inspiration was drawn from the writers and poets of the past, particularly those of the 18th century, isolated him within his profession. Ours is an age which in spirit is far removed from the 18th century. In contrast, the industrial revolution accomplished a great deal in the destruction of our nation's environmental consciousness, and the planning movement which grew in response has in recent years placed scientific method in its narrowest sense above intuition and artistry. The poetic instinct has an important part to play in restoring the balance of the arts and sciences in planning. We need, as John Burchard wrote in *The New Landscape*, to 'assimilate with the scientist's brain, the poet's heart, the painter's eyes'.[38]

At a time when there is no longer any reassuring image of the future, when there are no absolute ideals, and when the way ahead is more complex, fraught and uncertain than ever before, Sharp's convictions can help us restore faith in ourselves. His belief that the town can be a beautiful place to live in needs firm assertion, for our faith in towns lies in ruins. His hatred of waste and sprawl, and his love for lowland England should be defended, for our countryside is threatened as never before. His courage and tenacity in face of the worst aspects of the planning system and his ability to question it should serve as an example. Some things are worth fighting for. No matter what misfortunes and difficulties Thomas Sharp experienced, he could still write, from the comparative contentment of retirement in Oxford before his death in 1978,

> So still I stay here; still I walk these streets;
> Plans, aspirations, hopes, myself forgot,
> Unknown, unknowing, while urgent time permits
> A few more years till my short lease runs out.
> Still do I grateful stay, for once to have come
> Midway from that fouled field I once called home
> Into this richness was itself as much
> Fortune, maybe, as I had right to. Here
> At last is recompense, reward most dear,
> For a life's groping after beauty; such
> Wealth as sometimes a lone prospector found
> When after barren years he came on golden ground.[39]

Notes

1 *The Future Development of South-West Lancashire*, Liverpool University Press, Liverpool, 1930
2 T. W. Sharp, *Town and Countryside*, Some aspects of Urban and Rural Development, OUP, London, 1932
3 T. W. Sharp, *English Panorama*, Dent, London, 1950 (revised edition). First published in 1936 from a series of essays in the *Architectural Review*.
4 T. W. Sharp, *Town Planning*, Penguin, Harmondsworth, 1940
5 T. W. Sharp, *Anatomy of the Village*, Penguin, Harmondsworth, 1946
6 T. W. Sharp, *A Guide to Northumberland and Durham*, A Shell Guide, Faber, London, 1937 (reissued as *Northumberland* 1969)
7 T. W. Sharp, Unpublished novels – *The Way to the Cathedral, A Dying Fire, Memoirs of Eden, Happy Returns*
8 T. W. Sharp, *Selected Poems* 1960–75, Holywell Press, Oxford, 1977
9 T. W. Sharp, *Town and Townscape*, John Murray, London, 1968
10 G. Cullen, *Townscape*, Architectural Press, London, 1961
11 T. W. Sharp, *Cathedral City – A plan for Durham*, Architectural Press, London, 1945
12 Clough Williams Ellis, (ed), *Britain and the Beast*, Dent, London, 1937
13 T. W. Sharp, Evidence to the inquiry by Ministry of Transport into proposed central road and bridges, City of Durham, 2–3 May 1946
14 *Op cit, Selected Poems*, 'Farewell to County Durham', first published in *Durham University Journal*, 1962
15 See R. Newman, 'Town Planning in Oxford', Oxford, 1948
16 T. W. Sharp, *Oxford Replanned*, Architectural Press, London, 1948
17 *Op cit, Selected Poems*, 'A City', retitled 'A Townscape'

18   T. W. Sharp, *Oxford Observed*, Country Life, London, 1952
19   F. Allen, (Deputy Sec. MHLG) 'Oxford Road Decision' letter to Oxford City Council conveying decision of Mr Duncan Sandys, MHLG on the Oxford Road Problems, 21 September 1956
20   Frederick Armour, 'Report on the Oxford Roads Inquiry', March 1961
21   The Inspectors Report; Official Announcement, Armour Inquiry, 15 March 1962
22   T. W. Sharp, Proof of Evidence to the Public Inquiry: City of Oxford Development Plan, 16 June 1970, Amendment No 2, Objection No 96
23   *Ibid*
24   T. W. Sharp, *Exeter Phoenix – A plan for rebuilding*, Architectural Press, London, 1946
25   T. W. Sharp, *Newer Sarum – A plan for Salisbury*, Architectural Press, London, 1948
26   T.W. Sharp, *Georgian City – A plan for the preservation and improvement of Chichester*, Southern Publishing Co Ltd, 1949
27   *Chichester – Study in Conservation*, Report by Chichester County Council to MHLG, HMSO, London, 1968
28   Further information can be found in
     a) Ironside, 'A Summary of the New Forest Settlements', Chapter XIII, PhD Thesis on 'Rural Depopulation in Northumberland', Department of Geography, Newcastle University, December 1960
     b) V. Smith, 'A Sociological Survey of the Border Forest Settlements 1973', Department of Psychology, Durham University
29   T. W. Sharp, as Jeremiah Barebones, 'Pity the Poor Planner', *The Planning Officer*, January 1936
30   T. W. Sharp, 'Planning Now', *JTPI*, Vol XLIV, May 1957, pp133–141
31   *Report of the Committee on Qualifications of Planners*, (The Schuster Report), HMSO, London, 1950
32   T. W. Sharp, 'Notes in Evidence' to Schuster Committee, 1948
33   *Ibid*
34   Discussed more fully in G. E. Cherry, *The Evolution of British Town Planning*, Leonard Hill, London, 1974
35   T. W. Sharp, 'Planning Planning' *JTPI*, Vol XLII, June 1966, p233
36   T. W. Sharp, 'Dreaming Spires and Teeming Towers – the character of Cambridge', *Town Planning Review*, Vol XXXIII, No 4, January 1963
37   T. W. Sharp, 'The Replanning and Replanting of the College Grounds', *The Eagle*, 1951, pp314–19
38   Georgy Kepes, (ed), *The New Landscape in Art and Science*, Theobald, Chicago, 1951, p14
39   *Op cit, Selected Poems*, 'A City'

8

FREDERIC OSBORN
1885–1978

Michael Hebbert

The man whom Sir Montague Barlow presented to a conference in 1944 as 'that high priest, or shall I say prince of planners' was not himself a planner, indeed had no technical qualification of any kind. Throughout his active career in the town planning movement, for which he was knighted in 1956, he characterised himself like his mentor (Sir) Ebenezer Howard as an ordinary chap, 'a representative man, sharing the common feeling'; we find the same theme in all the tributes paid to him towards the end of this career and after his death.[1] Osborn's status as, in his own words, 'perhaps the only surviving entire layman who continuously thinks, writes and talks on planning' must be central to any assessment of his contribution to British town planning.

His formal education ended in 1900 when he left the Hackford Road Board School, Brixton, at the age of 15.[2] There had been a brief spell at a private school some years earlier, but the family's fortunes had declined with the illness of his father, a mercantile clerk, and Osborn was now sent off in a bowler hat and stiff collar to work for five shillings a week as an office boy in Mincing Lane, first of a series of clerical positions in city firms. But his education continued. At evening classes – his 'university' – he learnt music, languages and economics. Under the inspiration of H. G. Wells, purchased in 4½d editions, he became a freethinker and joined the Brixton branch of the Independent Labour Party (ILP). He discovered a talent for organisation as Chairman of the Clapham Common Cricket Association and secretary to the South London Cricket League. And most important of all, he developed his confidence as speaker and writer through two media which have no contemporary equivalent, the debating society and the circulating manuscript magazine. From 1904 he was secretary of the Minerva Debating Society, which met fortnightly to discuss a wide range of cultural, philosophical and political issues, and he could also be heard at the Sunday morning meetings of the Brixton Discussion Forum. Herbert Morrison, then an errand boy, was another member[3] and later recalled Osborn's style of debate in the following terms: 'he was very argumentative with them and with me and would give you no peace until you agreed with him'.[4] Osborn's skill as a journalist was developed as founder and editor of *Genii*, a manuscript magazine of book reviews, essays, poems and waggish comment which circulated around a small group of subscribers.

In 1903 he moved across London to East Ham: ILP activities, *Genii* and the debates continued, but he added a new dimension by joining the Fabian Society. He was particularly active in its junior arm, the Fabian Nursery, for which he edited a duplicated magazine called *The Nursling* from 1910–12.[5] But while he was the mainstay of the political and social activities of his local branch, the Forest Gate Fabian Society, he felt himself excluded from full participation at the centre. Most of the other Nurslings were just down from university, and it was these that the Webbs singled out for preferment rather than Osborn – 'dowdy, spotty-faced and pathologically diffident; obviously lower middle class and council school'. From everything which he later wrote about progressive metropolitan intellectuals we may infer that this rankled deeply.[6]

In the meantime Osborn had become acquainted with a very different London in his working hours, having taken employment as a rent collector for a housing trust with tenement blocks in the East End and terraced properties in the southern and eastern working class suburbs. Much of his propagandist inspiration during the next half century was to revolve around the perceived polarity between two worlds; on the one hand, 'ordinary workaday London life . . . these vast areas of drab dwellings and the cramped lives of the millions of people therein', on the other, 'the infinitely smaller and entirely different London once summed up in the word "Bloomsbury"' with its 'Post-Impressionist exhibitions, first nights of Shaw and Strindberg, political theorising, emotional experimentation and social irresponsibility'.[7]

Although Osborn had no special interest in the garden cities movement, his experience and his social interests made him a good candidate for the new post of Secretary-Manager, at £150 per annum, to the Howard Cottage Society in Letchworth Garden City. He moved from London in 1912 at the age of twenty-seven, returning with decreasing frequency to Nursery meetings[8] as he became active in local Labour politics and trades-unionism and in the new community's intense programme of folk-dancing, home recitals, rambling and lectures. He loved Letchworth and became an eager disciple of Ebenezer Howard. The idyll continued after 1914 when Letchworth provided a sympathetic haven for pacifists and for the reviled and isolated opponents of the war. Osborn followed Phillip Snowden's and Ramsay MacDonald's position, which is to say that he was anti-war without subscribing to the complete pacificism of the ILP. Though he married in 1916[9] he could not avoid call-up under the universal conscription introduced in the same year. A paradox resulted: while his old Brixton ILP friend Herbert Morrison, now Secretary to the London Labour Party, was sent as a conscientious objector to work on the land and spent two very happy years in Letchworth as a market gardener's assistant, Osborn refused service, absconded and was forced to return to London for the final year of the war as a fugitive from the police.[10]

Supported in hiding by his wife and by Ebenezer Howard, himself a pacifist, he initially resumed his socialist contacts.[11] For the winter of 1917–18, however, his daytime residence became the Reading Room of the British Museum where, with the encouragement of Howard and C. B. Purdom, he worked on the history of community projects and, more importantly, on propaganda for the role of garden cities in post-war reconstruction. Purdom, the former accountant of Letchworth, had returned from the army eager to pursue the argument of his 1913 book *The Garden City*, that the garden city movement should cut itself clean away from suburban planning; he now campaigned for the post-war housing drive to be concentrated on fifty or more government-financed new towns, enlisting Osborn as fellow propagandist in the National Garden Cities Committee, a fundamentalist splinter group from the Garden Cities and Town Planning Association (GCTPA).[12] Osborn showed himself to be an able publicist. In January 1918 he obtained a unanimous resolution at the Labour Party Conference in Nottingham that the bulk of future building ought to be diverted to new towns of limited size and in permanent contact with country life.[13] He prepared at Purdom's commission the persuasive little book called *New Towns After the War* which was published under the pseudonym 'New Townsmen'.[14] He travelled the country canvassing municipal authorities, many of whom were now corporate members of the GCTPA, and giving public lectures. An interesting indication of the arguments he advanced in the mayoral parlours is given in the article contributed under the pseudonym Edward Ormiston to the *Economic Journal* in December 1919, on 'The Public Control of the Location of Towns'. Here he argued that economists had neglected the real costs of urban expansion in terms of transport inefficiencies, public health, and inflated site values. These costs were aggravated by state intervention which facilitated the further growth of towns beyond their optimum size. 'Theoretically the best situation for industry is a relatively small town with a good technical equipment and a varied population, and above all with industrial areas planned in relation to means of transportation.' Since such towns could not arise through spontaneous market forces there was, he argued, a case for the state to take on a coordinating role to redistribute industrial and urban activity on a scientific basis, instead of continuing to subsidise congestion at increasing cost. Throughout this article, seemingly his first publication in a major journal, he was at pains to establish the case for decentralisation as against suburban expansion on a scientific rather than a utopian and perfectionist basis.

The imminence of a major post-war housing drive gave a new edge to the campaign, not least within the GCTPA, where a vigorous argument continued between suburban and new town ideals.[15] No sooner had Purdom won the Association round to advocacy of a general decentralisation to new industrial centres under the supervision of a National Town Planning Commission,[16] than Howard forced him and Osborn, to their pique, to turn back from general propaganda and work on a second demonstration project. His purchase of 1,458 acres at Welwyn in May 1919 was a brilliant entrepreneurial stroke. The site was positioned at just the right distance out of London, far enough to have the advantages of rural land values and freedom from other development, yet near enough to reduce to some extent the difficulties of colonisation in the early stages. Within months the scheme had obtained the necessary establishment patronage, including the acceptance by Sir Theodore Chambers, KBE, of the Chairmanship of Second Garden City Limited, and the reluctant blessing of Lord Salisbury of Hatfield House.[17] Osborn had participated in the venture from the outset, but was excluded from the provisional board of the company and given the role of temporary secretary. When Welwyn Garden City Ltd was registered in April, 1920, he was appointed company secretary, again without a place on the board of directors. Development of the new town began in the same year, and he moved out of London for the second and last time. The other leading propagandists of the GCTPA – Howard, Reiss and Purdom – also moved to work full-time on the development, a diversion of energies which Purdom and Osborn both questioned but one which could be justified in the long term by the success of Welwyn as a demonstration project for the British new towns.

Osborn had come to Letchworth too late for the pioneering stage, but he relished it to the full at Welwyn. Though he was to live in the town for more than half a century, his best time was when everyone wore gumboots, cooking and lighting were by oil lamp and social life was concentrated in one army hut. Whatever other arguments he was later to adduce for the development of new towns, his conception of them was always warmly coloured by the experience of himself and his young family in early Welwyn. As he wrote in 1946, 'A wider circle of friends and companions, a sense of partnership in a great enterprise with permanent results, a deepened consciousness of community, a share in another kind of culture springing from voluntary activity and personal creativeness – these are among the dividends of investing one's life in community building'.[18] As the town's population grew, so the range of activities broadened, with musical evenings, political discussions, literary excursions, flower rambles, woodland concerts, sports, and (of course) amateur theatricals confirming the idyllic promise of its publicity leaflets.[19]

While the majority of his neighbours travelled up to their London offices each morning, Osborn had only to stroll across the Parkway. He served as Company Secretary from 1920 to 1936, doubling this from 1921 to 1930 with the part-time position of Clerk to the Urban District Council. He also held the post of Estate Manager. In the earliest years he had responsibility for all properties but as the size of the housing stock grew it was placed under a separate housing management department and Osborn concentrated on the development and letting of industrial and commercial premises. Without doubt he should have much of the credit for the successful building up of the town's manufacturing base, which ensured that it would become more than merely – as Lewis Silkin later disparagingly said – 'a dormitory town that was started for the middle classes'.[20]

Welwyn Garden City Ltd was indeed a quite remarkable enterprise. The company, with its various subsidiaries, not only owned and managed the stock of housing and factories and had a monopoly on retailing, but also did its own building, gravel extraction and brickmaking, as well as farming its green belt through a cooperative guild. To manage such varied undertakings was inherently difficult and the difficulty was exacerbated by chronic shortage of capital. 1920 had been a bad year for a launch: less than half the first issue of shares were subscribed, and additional capital had to be borrowed, on the directors' sureties, at high interest rates. On at least three occasions the organisation was restructured and since nearly all the officers and several of the directors lived in the town, and were participants in its intense social life, the accompanying struggles for status and control had a bitter personal aspect. In a particularly acrimonious episode C. B. Purdom was ejected from his position of Finance Director in 1928 when all seven principal officers informed the board that they would resign if he did not.[21] Subsequently the company accountant, Sir Harry Peat of Peat Marwick Mitchell, advised further changes including the abandonment of the agricultural

experiment which had been Purdom's special pride. He introduced John Eccles, a qualified accountant, who became Financial
Secretary in 1930 and after writing off some half a million pounds
supervised a series of reforms in the interests of sound commercial
practice. As the organisation grew more professionalised, not for the
last time in his life, Osborn found himself relegated by men with the
technical qualifications which he lacked. In 1936, when Eccles
became General Manager, the company was reconstructed once
again and Osborn was dismissed.

However it may have appeared at the time, the release from full-time
employment came at a fortunate moment in his career. His interest
in national propaganda for decentralisation had revived. Though he
still maintained his contacts with the Fabian Society – lecturing on
'National Control of Town Development' at the 1930 summer school
and appearing as a co-speaker with Sir Ernest Simon at a New
Fabian Research Bureau conference in 1933[22] – he was becoming
known more generally in professional planning circles through his
letters to the press, his lectures, and his involvement as Treasurer of
the Town and Country Planning Summer School, which he founded
(on the Fabian model) with Dr Thomas Adams in 1933. He had
three hobby-horses. First, as the influence of the modern flat began
to be felt in British housing circles, bringing with it a new perception
of the prospects of high density development within towns, Osborn
reasserted the Tudor Walters principles of low density building. He
attacked flats as un-English and inimical to family life, a fad which
was being foisted on the public by an arrogant élite of young
architects, and he had an acute perception of the ridiculousness of
the utopian visions of high density collective living then in vogue.[23]
Secondly, he continued the anti-metropolitan argument of his 1918
Economic Journal paper, concentrating his attack particularly on the
suburban estates of the big city housing authorities, and on the
activities of London Transport, which did so much to open up new
peripheral areas for development in this period. The ameliorative
activities of both housing and transport agencies, he argued, made
big cities less efficient, not more.[24] Thirdly, Osborn continued to
maintain the need for a *public* programme of planned decentralisation into new towns. His experience with factory development in
Welwyn deepened his conviction that although industrial location –
or as he called it, localisation – was now elastic and industry was
actively desirous of decentralising to more convenient sites, this
could not be achieved without a state programme, both to provide
bridging finance for factory building at the early stages of new town
development[25] and to ensure a coordinated movement of population
and jobs from existing cities.[26] In his Fabian conference paper of

1933 he had already identified the *ad hoc* body on the lines of a public utility company – a 'developing corporation' – as the most appropriate local agency for building new towns, while at the national level he expressed a preference for an autonomous Industrial and Commercial Siting Board rather than an extension of the territorial planning powers of the unenlightened Ministry of Health.[27] Within the GCTPA he continued to play the part of fundamentalist, rejecting statutory town planning as an irrelevance on account of its compromise with the existing settlement pattern.[28]

Already the distinctive character of Osborn's contribution to the planning movement was clear. He was not an innovative thinker. His arguments for low density development echoed Raymond Unwin on the practical aspect, G. K. Chesterton on the ideological.[29] Green belt containment combined with planned decentralisation to satellite towns had become, under the influence of the New York Regional Plan, a tacit GCTPA objective,[30] and had been consistently promoted within the London Labour Party since 1918 by Herbert Morrison.[31] As to the question of state control of industrial location, Osborn seems to have greatly overestimated the significance of his own writings[32] not least as these showed, both then and later, a curious blindness to what was happening to industry outside the home counties, and to the implications of mass unemployment in the old industrial areas, emphasising rather the politically less significant issues of metropolitan traffic jams and 'straphanging'.[33] On the other hand, it was his Welwyn-based experience, together with his great organising ability and stamina and his clear head for figures, which already marked him out as the most effective lobbyist for the Association's predominately London-centred objectives.

On losing his position in 1936 Osborn was offered (by his Welwyn friend, Frank Murphy) the post of financial director in the fast-growing Murphy radio business, with the understanding that he would be free to devote a substantial proportion of his time to town planning work. At the same time, he became Honorary Secretary to the GCTPA, being joined in the following year by Gilbert McAllister as Organising Secretary.[34] The previous Honorary Secretary had been staid and unadventurous and Osborn's arrival at the Association's premises, where he was to be the central figure for the next three decades, was palpably revitalising. His first task was to draft, at the Executive Committee's request, a memorandum to update its policies and outline a plan of campaign. This stated that while the GCTPA's essential principles needed no amendment, private initiative new towns could no longer be regarded as the only or even the prime means to decentralisation. 'We have tacitly added to our original method the alternative methods of (a) the municipal or State promotion of satellite towns or garden cities and (b) the control of the size and development of towns by statutory planning machinery, local, regional and national. It may be said, therefore, that the truly essential idea of the Association is a particular physical arrangement of towns in relation to countryside, in order to secure certain social or sociological ends.'[35] To these affirmative objectives, which were accepted by the Association, Osborn in the next year added an explicit statement of opposition to high flats and tenements that accentuated urban congestion and were inimical to family life. Having got his policies in black and white he restricted membership to people in express agreement with them[36] and transformed the GCTPA into a combative, modern pressure group, launching a new series of propaganda pamphlets, installing Miss Jacqueline Tyrwhitt as a full-time research assistant on a grant from the Joseph Rowntree Village Trust, and setting up study groups to work on specific issues. 'This stage of controversy', he wrote ten years later, 'was entirely different from the fundamentalist-argumentative-idealist stage of 1918–20'.[37]

The first great challenge came within a year, when Chamberlain established the Royal Commission on the Geographical Distribution of the Industrial Population under the chairmanship of Sir Montague Barlow. It is commonly noted that the GCTPA evidence against London's size, prepared by Osborn and presented jointly on the 20th and 23rd days by himself and Cecil Harmsworth,[38] weighed more heavily with the Commission than the contrary arguments from London Transport, the London County Council and government departments,[39] and that Osborn's influence was also at work behind the scenes in private correspondence with Patrick Abercrombie (a member of the GCTPA Executive) over the drafting of the final reports.[40] We should naturally be wary of accepting at face value any pressure group's estimate of its own influence on policy, and even without Osborn the Commission might well have reached similar conclusions, given the prevalence of New Deal notions of national planning as a remedy for social ills and the shock of seeing gas masks issued and London parks dug up for air raid precautions. If Barlow's report in 1940 mentioned garden cities and satellite towns as a means to population dispersal, so had Chamberlain's Unhealthy Areas Committee in 1920 and Lord Marley's Departmental Committee of the Office of Works in 1934, and there was every possibility that it would have as little effect as its forerunners. Osborn's real achievement was not to obtain the favourable report but to exploit it relentlessly as a basis for Government action. Barlow became 'the next great document in the case after *Garden*

Cities of Tomorrow', because Osborn resolved to make it so. It had no popular impact, unlike the later reconstruction white papers[41] and reaction in the specialist press was lukewarm. The newly renamed Town and Country Planning Association (TCPA) might, like the Town Planning Institute, have expressed regret at the failure to reach unanimous recommendations and at the majority reports finding that no changes were required in the machinery of government. Instead it was decided 'that if the Barlow Report were interpreted as a triumphant vindication of the Association's own policy, it would be made so in fact. And this bold judgement turned out to be correct'.[42] Barlow himself joined the Association shortly afterwards, and played an active part in the campaign which Osborn now set about orchestrating to get his recommendations implemented.

Osborn's wartime activity in the planning field had to be sandwiched between civil defence duty and full-time work as finance director at Murphy, its order book filled with munitions contracts.[43] Nevertheless, this was also his most active period as a propagandist, and he contributed with great energy and flair to what Churchill sardonically called 'the continual buzz of ardent discussion' about reconstruction. In 1941 he published *Overture for Planning*, a reiteration of the Barlow orthodoxy and the first of the highly successful 'Rebuilding Britain' series of booklets which he edited for Faber. He subsequently wrote *The Land and Planning* (1941) and *Planning and the Countryside* (1942) for the same series.[44] Having participated in a sequence of weekly talks on reconstruction with the Home Service of the BBC he edited these too for publication in booklet form under the title *Making Plans* (1943).[45] In 1942 he reissued – under his own name – the 'New Townsmen's' essay of 1918, *New Towns After the War*. His articles appeared everywhere from *Country Life* to the *Daily Herald*, from *The Political Quarterly* to *Woman's Journal*.

These literary activities occupied his evenings and weekends. By day, he coordinated as best he could the TCPA's increasingly successful propaganda. The Association's full-time staff increased from one in 1940 to three in 1942 to meet the demands of a growing membership (with an increasing proportion of local authorities) and to sustain such extensive activities as publishing *Town and Country Planning* and *Reconstruction Leaflets* (generally off-prints of the former), preparing and presenting evidence and memoranda, corresponding with politicians and administrators, and organising exhibitions and lectures.[46]

Osborn contributed not only managerial skill but a canny sense of pressure group politics. In October 1940 the TCPA submitted a well publicised memorandum to the Prime Minister and Cabinet on

'Town Planning in Relation to the Present Emergency and After-War Reconstruction': five days later Attlee announced that the new Minister of Works and Buildings (Lord Reith) had been asked to report on this. In 1941 Osborn drafted with McAllister a succinct statement of TCPA policy with the heading 'A National Planning Basis': within a year it had been adopted by such leading groups as the Royal Institute of British Architects, the National Council for Social Science, the National Playing Fields Association and the Council for the Preservation of Rural England. At a time of proliferating interest in town planning – the range of groups and interests can be seen in the *Planning and Reconstruction Yearbooks* which Osborn edited for the Todd Publishing company – the TCPA gained status not only by promulgating its own philosophy but by providing a forum for the discussion of planning in general. At its annual conferences Osborn brought together major speakers on major issues. The proceedings, well edited and published as a series of books by Faber, formed then as they do now a definitive source.

His vision, or perhaps we should say illusion, was that all this activity was building up a common front for national planning. It was an illusion in two senses. Firstly, the planning movement was much more deeply divided on policy than Osborn cared to acknowledge. The TCPA annual conferences show this very well. The discussion at the Oxford conference of 1941, which Osborn intended 'to crystallise and if possible to carry a stage further the National Planning policy outlined in the Nine Agreed Points of the Royal Commission on the Distribution of the Industrial Population' instead revealed fundamental divergences between the TCPA line and the LCC's fears (voiced by Lewis Silkin) on loss of population and jobs, and Dudley Stamp's on release of farmland.[47] The difficulty of winning the rural lobby to decentralist thinking was also apparent at the 1942 Cambridge conference, on industry and rural life, though Osborn had the satisfaction of noting the publication of the favourable Scott Committee report, as he was correcting the final proofs of his introduction to the Cambridge proceedings.[48] The 1943 London conference, on the relation between economic and physical planning and housing policy, again revealed the doubts of the big cities at the proposed haemorrage, despite Osborn's attempt to persuade those present of the economic and administrative viability of low density redevelopment.[49] The density issue, which he regarded as 'the one strong card in the hands of the thorough-going city planners'[50] was indeed a rock on which agreement between planning enthusiasts was always liable to founder. Many of those who shared the TCPA's views on the need for effective urban containment and industrial location policies, found themselves at variance with Osborn because he rejected not only the high density fantasies of the MARS group but also the medium-density concepts associated with the names of Trystan Edwards, Geoffrey Boumphrey, Professor Adshead and Thomas Sharp.[51]

A second and more fundamental flaw, common to all factions within the movement, was its naive conception of the politics and administration of planning. It was one thing to demand a Central Planning Authority but quite another to resolve how it might operate within the system of sectoral ministerial responsibilities and conflicting political interests. Osborn wished away the problem by assuming a natural harmony of interest in dispersal policy. Taking it as axiomatic that there was a latent if unmobilised popular consensus for TCPA policy[52] he looked to a strong central agency working through regional councils to cut through political obstructionism.[53] After years of association with the Fabian Society and his local labour party he had abandoned socialism for the TCPA's all-party position – he would later question the wisdom of this – and from his vantage point in an organisation whose council embraced the conservative Lord Balfour of Burleigh and the communist Dean of Canterbury, Hewlett Johnson, as well as the liberal B. Seebohm Rowntree and several local labour politicians, it was easy to suppose that politicians at large needed only persuasion to fall in behind an agreed programme for national reconstruction. The illusion was most intense in 1941 when Lord Reith, under the aforementioned clause in his terms of reference as Minister of Works and Building, called together a Consultative Panel on Physical Reconstruction. Members were recruited from representative groups, Osborn taking his place as honorary secretary of the TCPA. It proved to be a cumbersome and formal organisation ill-suited even to providing expert advice.[54] But Osborn shared Reith's initial hope that he was participating in an embryo organisation for a national planning agency with wide directive powers over executive ministries.[55] Even had Churchill not removed Reith from Ministerial office, it is inconceivable that this direct assault upon the departmental principle could have proceeded very far in enforcing TCPA policies onto a reluctant Board of Trade and Ministry of Health.[56] In the words of Sir Gwilym Gibbon, a senior civil servant in the latter ministry and a shrewd commentator on the wartime planning movement, such schemes betrayed 'the simple innocence of inexperience'.[57]

It was perhaps inevitable that Osborn should have been disappointed when, towards the end of the war, the first firm reconstruction proposals began to emerge from government departments and local authorities, and were found to assume a distribution of urban population far divergent from the standard of 85 persons per acre which he regarded as the maximum.[58] Thus, while Abercrombie and Forshaw's *County of London Plan* (1943) was popularly acclaimed as a triumph of the town planner's art, Osborn led the TCPA Executive in a hopelessly doctrinaire attack on its proposal for zoning areas of inner London at 136 and 200 persons per acre.[59] Abercrombie would himself have preferred lower densities, but had carefully sought a standard which would not entirely disrupt the employment base of the capital. Osborn, however, could only see it as a supine concession to the housing and transport lobbies. He was fortunate that Abercrombie, always an understanding friend, did not resign his Vice-Presidency of the TCPA, and when the *Greater London Plan* was published in the following year, with the same densities, Osborn had the opportunity to make amends. As he wrote to Mumford, 'it is so important that the principle of dispersal is now fully accepted by the LCC, and the difficulties are so great and genuine, that it would clearly be a mistake to make a song about the inadequate quantitive scale of the dispersal'.[60]

By the end of the war it began to seem that the momentum for a planned reconstruction was being lost. In a particularly ominous parallel with 1918, vast suburban sites were being acquired for municipal housing developments. 'Nearly all the discredited inter-war tendencies are being resumed', he wrote. 'A more elaborate organisation is doing the wrong things at greater speed than after the last war'.[61] In the meantime progress in town and country planning awaited the arrival of a post-war government and the passage of fresh legislation. Osborn had naturally submitted evidence to both Conservative and Liberal reconstruction committees, and he was himself a member during 1942–4 of the Labour party reconstruction committee's subcommittee on planning and housing which was chaired by Lewis Silkin. Here he had come face to face with the unwillingness of big city labour politicians to plan for population loss, his only ally in the decentralist cause being the Rev. Charles Jenkinson of Leeds. When the Attlee government was returned in 1945 Osborn was initially pessimistic. He predicted to Mumford that cities would now be allowed to proceed with high density building while he would be dismissed as a wrong-headed idealist.

But he was wrong. Even before the election, Lewis Silkin had made steps towards setting up a joint LCC/TCPA committee to investigate the implementation of Greater London Plan satellite town proposals[62] and when a few months later he was appointed Minister of Town Planning he at once obtained for new towns a position of priority in the legislative programme.[63] Since 1942 George Pepler had been pressing quietly forward with interdepartmental liaison on overspill and satellite town development; the groundwork, known to

Osborn only through hints dropped by Abercrombie and Pepler over lunch in London clubs, was now well advanced. A draft New Towns Bill existed, and the job of Lord Reith's committee was to finalise technical and administrative arrangements in time for its insertion into the 1946 Parliamentary session.

Osborn was delighted by the invitation to serve on the committee. He had at last given up daily work in industry and taken the chairmanship of the TCPA executive in order to devote himself full-time to planning. When the membership and terms of reference of the committee were announced he was just completing the proofs of *Green Belt Cities*, much of which had been written at Pepler's request as an unofficial report for the Ministry of Town Planning in 1944.[64] With characteristic sense of timing he had also just published a new edition of Ebenezer Howard's *Garden Cities of Tomorrow* with introductory pieces by himself and Mumford to draw the present lessons. 'The long period of debate seems to be drawing to its close', he wrote, 'and the period of action to be setting in'.[65]

The Reith Committee worked rapidly and purposively. Osborn relished his collaboration in this 'able body of successful industrialists and professional men'. He left his imprint most clearly on the report's recommendations about the optimum size for new towns,[66] manfully swallowing the necessity for compromise on other issues.[67] But the Government's commitment to a programme of planned decentralisation, and the pace at which it was being launched, were evident tributes to the success of his personal campaign since 1918. This was recognised by the TCPA at a public dinner organised by Patrick Abercrombie in February 1946, where the Association's galaxy of peers, baronets, bishops and ministers gathered at the Savoy Hotel to celebrate the ordinary man, a contrast which he relished.

There followed around his sixtieth birthday a period in which Osborn was – quite mistakenly – preoccupied with a sense of old age. When he went to the United States in 1947 on a tour arranged by the National Housing Agency and the American Institute of Planners his itinerary had to be adjusted because of ill health – an American immigration doctor diagnosed 'senility' – and in the following year he underwent a stomach operation. He was also depressed by continuing indications of the low priority for environmental planning within the Labour government: 'our campaign to stop the big cities expanding and increasing their density has so far failed', he wrote to Mumford in March 1949. The first experiences with development control under the 1947 Act had not enhanced town planning's popularity with the public at large. The new towns programme was proceeding slowly and he was playing no part in it.[68] 'My friends are as puzzled as I am that I was not brought into this work somehow', he wrote to Mumford in 1951.[69] But defeatism was quite foreign to Osborn's nature. The fact that the TCPA could no longer be perceived to ride the crest of a wave of general enthusiasm made it all the more necessary that he should sustain its campaign. This he was to do for a further two decades. Being now a wealthy man by virtue of his shareholding in Murphy Radio (in which he had invested his severance pay in 1936) and the state purchase of his shares in Welwyn Garden City Ltd in 1948, he could devote himself to unpaid public work, or as he put it, to being 'a full-time freelance nuisance in the planning world'.

The TCPA had a paid staff of four at this time: a Director – Desmond Donnelly – and three assistants. Osborn spent several days a week in its office in King Street, Covent Garden, working particularly on the magazine *Town and Country Planning* which he edited from 1949 to 1965, in the leaner months writing much of the contents as well. From 1950, when Desmond Donnelly obtained a seat in Parliament, until the appointment of Wyndham Thomas in 1958, the TCPA could no longer afford the services of a full-time Director; credit for its continued activity and influence in the fifties lies squarely with Osborn who attended the office daily. He often expressed frustration with this administrative burden, but as he observed to Mumford, 'the trouble is that I know what I am in fact doing is not quite useless'.

What was he doing? First, the new town cause had still to be promoted, and he was its one tireless publicist.[70] In the pages of *Town and Country Planning* we find a traditional advocacy of the fulfilments of family life and voluntary activity in a planned community; a typical cover photograph showed amateur theatricals or a public sculpture, or plump children in the sunshine of a large garden with their puppy and birdtable. These had to be defended against many kinds of attack. The programme would have been terminated by the Conservatives were it not for lively resistance within the Ministry and for the impetus of Macmillan's drive for 300,000 house-completions a year, no matter where. Then the housing which had been built was criticised in the architectural press for its wasteful layout, and connections were popularly made with sociological reports of discontent and neurosis among new town tenants.[71] Wherever these criticisms were made, Osborn would energetically respond with counter-evidence,[72] and he took the initiative wherever possible to bring the towns' achievements before the public eye. Thus it was he who initiated the celebrations of the 50th anniversary of Letchworth in 1953 (against local uninterest), and the New Towns Exhibition mounted jointly by the TCPA and the fifteen

Development Corporations in 1959. He was also active as a Parliamentary lobbyist, not least in 1962 when Letchworth council sought by private bill to buy out the property company which had taken over – again, despite Osborn's energetic lobbying of shareholders – First Garden City Ltd.[73]

The attack on the new towns was part of a more general movement against the TCPA's decentralist philosophy. As in the 1930s, and again in the 1940s,[74] Osborn observed a rival convergence of the powerful farming lobby, landscape protectionists, urbanist architects and municipal interests. Its one saving feature was a new seriousness about containment, best expressed in Duncan Sandy's green belt circular of 1955. Where suburban growth was prohibited, some measure of dispersal became inevitable, whether to new towns or to the smaller expansions of existing towns which had – thanks largely to the influence of the TCPA Country Towns Committee – been made possible by the Act of 1952. Sandys was not unsympathetic to TCPA thinking – indeed, he nominated Osborn for a knighthood in 1956 – but he conceived overspill provision and green belt restraints as complements to intensive urban redevelopment, best epitomised in his Barbican project. Aesthetic fashion pointed this way, and so did the interests of the municipal authorities and of the building industry. Osborn, for whom 'high density was the main disease against which planning was to be the great prophylactic', now saw flats rise from the planned redevelopments first of London and then of the provincial cities. While other journals, closer to local government, emphasised housing completion rates, *Town and Country Planning* documented the decline in housing standards, and repeatedly exposed the irrational expense of high rise construction. Osborn could not have been more active in his propaganda and lobbying, both at central and local levels, but there was little to show for it beyond the retrospective satisfaction of a Cassandra. Besides, these were old issues. 'I suppose' he wrote to Mumford in March 1957, 'I am a bit bored just now with the necessity of saying the same things again and again, which I have done for twenty-one years, and not being able to interest myself by thinking of a new way to say it'. He perhaps weakened the force of his argument against flats by his inflexible attachment to the other extreme of low density. Lewis Mumford believed so, but was entirely unsuccessful in his attempts to win his friend round to the middle ground, which would have made it less easy for bright young architects to dismiss him as an isolated old utopian.

Osborn recognised this danger, and was particularly gratified by two reassuring trends in this period. First was the growing international interest in the British new towns and dispersal programme.[75]

The TCPA focussed much of this interest, not least because of the international study tours which it regularly offered to foreign visitors, with Osborn as guide. He also acted as organiser and leader for the Association's overseas Study-Holiday Tours which from 1946 onwards visited European countries on an annual basis. And together with Sir George and Lady Pepler he revived the International Federation of Housing and Planning after the war, becoming its first Honorary Member in 1974. Meeting and corresponding in the most senior circles of international town planning, including the Soviet Ministry of Construction, he was well aware of the global reputation of the new towns. The book which he wrote with Arnold Whittick in the late fifties rightly displayed the British experiment in planned decentralisation as a prototype of international significance.[76]

A second source of satisfaction was the support he began to receive from social scientific research, a reward for his long campaign to stimulate academic interest in planning issues.[77] At the Building Research Station, the work of Weston and Stone confirmed Osborn's argument[78] that the additional costs of multi-storey building could not be justified on land economy grounds.[79] At Wye College, Robin Best and J. T. Ward revived his long-standing and intuitively improbable contention – which the Scott Committee had dismissed[80] – that the produce from well-cultivated gardens in a low-density development was greater in value than that from the whole area of farmland taken for such a development.[81] When the American Donald Foley looked at the TCPA in the course of his research into the London planning system, he characterised it as an amateurist group in the utopian reform tradition, in need of the modernising influence of applied social science.[82] This was a misjudgement, given the correspondence between the Association's line, as presented unchangingly by Osborn throughout the decade, and the work now coming from social scientists of the calibre of Colin Clark, J. B. Cullingworth and Gerald Wibberley.[83] What is more, he had always recognised the importance of a first-class intelligence service for a pressure group such as the TCPA, and in the fifties he enlisted into active participation some of the best young minds in the planning movement, particularly Derek Senior of *The Guardian*, David Eversley of Birmingham University and Peter Self of the London School of Economics, the latter's *Cities in Flood* (1961) being a particularly persuasive restatement of TCPA philosophy for post-war circumstances.

In 1959 the Association's policies were redrafted – for the first time in twenty-four years – by someone other than Osborn. Two years later he resigned the chairmanship of the executive to Peter Self and in

1965 Hazel Evans took over the editorship of *Town and Country Planning*. Despite eye trouble he was an active octogenarian, and continued to visit the TCPA offices regularly. The last annual general meeting of the Association which he attended and spoke at was in 1978, some ten months before his death at the age of ninety-three. He lived to see the rejection of high residential densities and the development of a further generation of new towns, republishing his *Green Belt Cities* to coincide with the latter. He enjoyed a dignified and honorific old age, complete with knighthood, honorary fellowship of the RIBA and gold medal of the TPI, holding court to doctoral students and to an American sabbatical scholar, and keeping up a copious international correspondence to the end.

Any attempt at a concluding assessment of Osborn must start from the fact that – unlike all the other figures in this book – he was an old-fashioned social reformer and apologist. His best medium was the ephemeral one of the editorial, the letter to the newspaper, the public address. He had a sharp ear for the apt simile, comparing for instance big cities to ladies boasting of the biggest waistline at the lunch club, or the role of the Ministry of Agriculture in post-war planning to supercharging one cylinder of an internal combustion engine. Three quotations may indicate the vigorous quality of his prose. On 'the comedy of transport':

Transport has come to be looked on as an end in itself, instead of an instrument for a purpose. A fire engine is an instrument, and one capable of elaboration; but because with the progress of technique we can make more powerful fire engines, we do not insist on having larger and larger fires in order to put them out. Yet no one thinks it odd, even if anyone realises it at all that rapid transport creates larger towns so as to have further to take people to and from the places between which they divide their lives.

From an address to the London Society at the Royal Society of Arts:

I do not need to tell the London Society that Londoners are the sweetest-natured people that ever walked between earth and sky. In fact, of course, they never walk in that position.

Reviewing Mumford's *The Highway and the City*:

Some readers of Mumford's big books, while fascinated and delighted by his historical and cosmographical flights, have wondered whether his orbit at perigee only avoids a crash by not quite landing.

Ever since his Brixton days he had the habit of writing light verse, and neat little rhymes on planning and housing topics continued to appear in *Town and Country Planning*.[84] A frequent theme of his letters to Mumford was his wish to write a large-scale book, a more solid and permanent contribution instead of a stream of minor pieces. 'But', he observed in 1944, 'I haven't the apparatus or the capacity for things like *The Condition of Man* or *The Culture of Cities*'. He published just three books, two in joint authorship: *New Towns After the War* (1918, 1943), *Green Belt Cities* (1946, 1969) and *The New Towns: the Answer to Megalopolis* (1963, 1969). To read them is to be reminded of the simplicity and continuity of his world-view. He himself was well aware, in later years, of his failure to assimilate the new ideas in the growing quasi-scientific literature of urbanism;[85] but then, he also remained proud of his status as an old original.

Though Osborn's ordinary-man style was unsuited to extended argument it did make him a most effective debater. It also accounted for both the strengths and the limitations of his permanent contribution to the debate about the methods and purposes of town planning. As we have suggested, the limitation was a profound political innocence. With the warrant of his rent-collecting experience, he took it as axiomatic that there existed a latent popular consensus for decentralist and low density ideals, and as a Welwyn industrialist he could conceive no conflict between locational planning and business interest.[86] In a sense he was right: he correctly foresaw that dispersal would occur spontaneously after the Second World War, whatever planners did to promote or check it.[87] On the other hand he was wrong to suppose that consensus could be mobilised into a mass social movement transcending all political differences[88] and naive in hoping to overcome administrative obstacles through the agency of a strongly centralised Ministry staffed by enlightened generalists.[89] He belittled all opposition to his convictions into merest partisanship. On the question of the very low densities of the first generation new towns – which, it should be noted, were the product not of generous garden sizes but of the inflexible engineering standards specified in the final report of the Reith Committee, whereby all mains were laid side by side under eleven foot grass verges – Osborn's obstinacy was undoubtedly counter-productive. As Mumford chided him: 'The position you have taken, dear FJ, seems to you an impregnable one because you simply can't imagine any reasonable man having another point of view than your own, or proceeding from a different set of axioms than those which seem to you self-evident'.[90]

But this same Chestertonian conviction of the rightness and Englishness of a particular planning philosophy also gave Osborn's work its enduring interest. He was always an untypical and isolated figure in the movement, a Rotary Club member happiest in the company of

businessmen, allergic in equal measure to simple-life and back-to-
nature ideals, to the romantic modernism of architectural progressives and to what he called 'the chilling "objectivity" of the sub-
human social scientist'. However illusory his concept of the common
man may have been, it fortified him against much ridicule and
indifference; and his stand on two issues was an important one.

First, Osborn was one of the only writers who consistently exposed
the more ludicrous pretensions of the modern movement in architecture. Though his attack on the progressives was bilious and at times
a shade xenophobic, his arguments were quite to the point. He
showed how, in its fashionable attachment to flat-blocks which were
expensive to build and unpleasant to inhabit, the modern movement
was false to its own functionalist ideals: 'it is the vice of façade-
fancying taking them off the straight and narrow path of function'.[91]
He particularly deprecated – again with reason – the tendency to
dress up the new aesthetic in pseudo-sociology, whether the thirties'
theory 'that we are passing into an age when buildings express the
communal life which is to replace, rather than supplement, the
family life' or the fifties' concept of the vertical community. Whatever the economic and political factors behind the catastrophic
episode of local-authority high density building,[92] it would not have
been possible without the persuasion in educated circles that flats
were inevitable and that working class people would in time come to
enjoy living in them,[93] a view which Osborn characterised as 'the
saddest of all examples of the betrayal of mankind by the intelligent-
sia – la trahison des clercs – and no more respectable because it is held
by many who are themselves delightfully housed in country parks or
spacious suburbs'.[94] Though Osborn's voice was an isolated one, he
spoke for a genuinely national tradition,[95] and all current social
research into working class housing preferences has borne him out.[96]
The fact that architectural fashion now acknowledges the tradition,
as he predicted it would, only enhances our respect for his stand.

Secondly, Osborn was a redoubtable anti-technocrat. Many of his
best perceptions flowed from his status as an exponent of the
common-sense approach in a professionalising and technicising
milieu. Any Fabian faith which he might once have had in the
reforming potential of expertise was destroyed by his experience in
the planning movement, which he felt to be weakened both by the
jealous concern of professional town planners for their career opportunities,[97] and by the social scientists' tendency to substitute elaborate varieties of research for action.[98] Criticising the neglect of
Ebenezer Howard's book by economists and sociologists – as often,
we can substitute his own name here – he concluded: 'It is not read in
those circles because it is too easy to read. Because no one needs a

wet towel around his head to grapple with it, it does not seem a serious contribution to thought'.[99] This line of criticism was often aired in *Town and Country Planning*, and acquired fresh vitality with the expansion of the so-called planning sciences in the sixties, when it was no longer Osborn who sustained the generalist argument but Peter Self and David Eversley.[100]

Being an activist rather than an academic, Osborn worked largely through personal influence, and this influence is still strongly felt by many in the planning movement. Our chapter has been assembled from books and papers: the last words should be from someone who knew Osborn as a colleague and friend.

He enjoyed his causes, but he enjoyed also the company and friendship of many whom he met in their pursuit. He had an infectious vitality and enthusiasm for life, which seemed to be born afresh daily or even hourly. He was an interesting talker on many subjects besides planning, as his letters to Lewis Mumford make clear. He was a romantic; and he had a lot of curiosity. I suppose he was basically a Victorian or Edwardian idealist or progressive, little tainted by the pessimism of much modern life.[101]

Acknowledgements

For the preparation of this chapter I was given access to the papers of the late Sir Frederic Osborn by his son and daughter, Dr Tom Osborn and Mrs Margaret Fenton. I am most grateful for their kindness to me on my two visits to Welwyn Garden City. Many thanks too to Mr Michael Hughes of Welwyn Garden City Central Library and to the cheerful staff at the TCPA where Osborn's spirit still lives.

Notes

1 For instance Sir Desmond Heap: 'FJO is a simple man in the best meaning of that expression' *TCP*, April 1966, or Wyndham Thomas on 'The Quintessential Amateur' *TCP*, May 1975

2 Osborn broadcast some of these early biographical reminiscences on the Home Service in September 1967. Transcripts of the five talks, titled *Escaped Londoner*, are in the Welwyn Garden City Central Library.

3 B. Donoughue and G. W. Jones, *Herbert Morrison, Portrait of a Politician*, Weidenfeld, London, 1973, p18. Morrison became the Forum's Press Secretary in December 1908, *his* first public position.

4   Speech at the dinner for Sir Frederic Osborn, Royal Festival Hall 1956; MS in Osborn papers.

5   Fabian Nursery Executive Committee Minute Book, 13 July 1910

6   For his resentful view of 'Bloomsbury' see for example Michael R. Hughes (ed) *The Letters of Lewis Mumford and Frederic J. Osborn*, Adams and Dart, Bath, 1971, pp56, 348

7   F. J. Osborn, *Green Belt Cities*, revised edition, Evelyn, Adams & Mackay, London, 1969, p19

8   From the Minute Book of the Fabian Nursery we find that the last meeting chaired by Osborn was in May 1913, the guest speaker being G. B. Shaw, who arrived with no paper prepared, offering instead a solo reading of his new and as yet unpublished *Androcles and the Lion*

9   To Margaret Robb, a middle-class Glasgow girl whom he met at a Fabian summer school in Keswick. The marriage was a long and happy one; she died in 1970.

10 For Morrison at Letchworth, where Ebenezer Howard converted him with important future consequences for British town planning, see Donoughue and Jones (1973) Ch 4. For Osborn's position see Hughes (ed), *The Letters of Lewis Mumford and Frederic J. Osborn, op cit*, p447

11 C. B. Purdom found Osborn working for the Fabians in Holborn: see his 'Account of the Trouble at Welwyn Garden City' (1952), typescript, Welwyn Garden City Central Library

12 C. B. Purdom, *The Garden City*, Dent, London, 1913, pp201–2; *The Building of Satellite Towns*, revised edition, Dent, London, 1949, p182; *Life Over Again*, Dent, London, 1951, pp60ff. For a more detailed discussion of these controversies see S. Buder 'Ebenezer Howard, the genesis of a Town Planning Movement', *Journal of the American Institute of Planners*, November 1979, pp390–8

13 The resolution was: 'that overcrowding in the large towns shall be relieved by the establishment of new towns and the reconstruction of the smaller existing towns, on garden city principles (including the reservation of a stretch of open country all around, the wide spacing out of houses and factories, the provision of gardens, allotments and small holdings, and the installation of the most modern power-plants and labour-saving industrial facilities); land for this purpose to be compulsorily acquired and development financed by the State, and the whole enterprise in each case to be administered by a municipal authority or non-profiteering democratic body in the interest of the local community.' As Osborn later admitted, the resolution was of little significance; Hughes (ed), *The Letters of Lewis Mumford and Frederic J. Osborn, op cit*, p162

14 Purdom paid for the book and inspired its argument, Osborn wrote it up. Hughes (ed), *ibid*, p447; Purdom, *op cit*, p60

15 The GCTPA had now reabsorbed the National Garden Cities Committee and taken C. B. Purdom as full-time secretary. The sources for the internal controversies noted by Buder (1969) p398 have since vanished

16 See the Association's Memorandum to Dr Addison, President of the Local Government Board, February 1919, in Purdom, *op cit*, pp183–4; and editorial reaction in *The Times*, 24 February 1919

17 Chambers was a surveyor known for his advocacy of dispersal of the industrial workforce into rural areas: eg, 'The Repopulation of our Rural Districts', *Transactions of the Surveyors' Institution*, xlix, 57

18 *Green Belt Cities, op cit*, p20. Osborn was a good amateur pianist and a keen actor. In 1929 he chaired the committee for the first Welwyn Garden Drama Festival, the stage director being Flora Robson. Purdom, *op cit*, pp72ff gives a good account of the early days

19 *Welwyn – Where Town and Country Meet* emphasises altitude (400 ft), social activities, clean atmosphere, low rates, rapid access to King's Cross, and high standards of amenity and design

20 For the development of Welwyn Garden City, Osborn's brief *Genesis of Welwyn Garden City: Some Jubilee Memories*, Town and Country Planning Association, London, 1970, complements Purdom's detail in *The Building of Satellite Towns*

21 See Purdom, *op cit*, pp74ff, and the typescript account referred to in Note 11 above, which carries comments by Osborn

22 F. J. Osborn, *Transport, Town Development and the Territorial Planning of Industry*, New Fabian Research Bureau Publication No 20, 1934

23 *Green Belt Cities, op cit*, pp40–46, describes 'The Period of Confusion'

24 See note 22 above.

25 *Memorandum on Welwyn Garden City and Industrial Decentralisation*, 1928, manuscript in Welwyn Garden City Central Library. Osborn submitted this to Raymond Unwin's Decentralisation Subcommittee of the London Regional Town Planning Committee

26 *Evidence on Behalf of Welwyn Garden City Ltd*, 1932, submitted by F. J. Osborn and R. L. Reiss to the Office of Works Departmental Committee on Garden Cities, Chairman Lord Marley. The same points are made in Osborn's 'Industry and Planning', *Town Planning Institute Journal*, July 1932

27 *Transport, Town Development and the Territorial Planning of Industry, op cit*, p32. This developed Purdom's notion of a statutory Garden Cities Commission, expounded in the first edition of *The Building of Satellite Towns*, 1929

28 In Ebenezer Howard, *Garden Cities of Tomorrow*, Faber, London, 1946, 3rd edition, p17, Osborn lists those within the Association who 'upheld the essential idea when fashion was against it'

29 G. K. Chesterton, *What's Wrong with the World*, London, 1910

30 See especially Thomas Adams on the nature and origins of the idea in Chapter 10 of H. Warren and W. R. Davidge, *Decentralisation of Population and Industry– A New Principle in Planning*, P. S. King, London, 1930, referred to as 'our textbook' in GCTPA Leaflet No 15, *Garden City Principles and Policy*, 1934

31 Donoughue and Jones, *Herbert Morrison, op cit*, pp48, 86, 89, 203

32 He believed his paper on 'Industry and Planning' to have had a seminal influence (Hughes (ed), *op cit*, p5), but credit should lie

rather with J. M. Keynes (see *Regional Studies*, 1979, 13, pp497–500) or according to Colin Clark, with R. H. Tawney (*TCP*, December 1953, p680). We must remember that propagandists are not the best judges of their own efficacy.

33 *London's Dilemma: the only way out*, GCTPA, London, 1935?

34 Gilbert McAllister 1906–1964: a Glaswegian journalist and subsequently Labour MP for Rutherglen

35 *38th Annual Report, GCTPA* 1936

36 Hughes (ed), *op cit*, p126

37 *Ibid* p163

38 Royal Commission on the Geographical Distribution of the Industrial Population *Minutes of Evidence, Twentieth and Twenty-third Days*, HMSO, London, 1938

39 F. J. Osborn, 'The Problem of the Great City: a Royal Commission at Work', *Political Quarterly* IX, 3 (1938) 408–420, discusses the evidence submitted. The best analyses are still Peter Hall's in *London 2000*, Faber, London, 1969 (second edition), Ch 2, and *The Containment of Urban England*, Routledge, London, 1973, Vol I pp106–108, Vol II pp46–71

40 Hughes (ed), *op cit*, pp17, 271

41 As Osborn said in *Green Belt Cities, op cit*, p47, the Barlow report might as well have been written in Sanskrit; 'what made this country planning-conscious was the bombing of our cities in 1940–1'.

42 F. J. Osborn and A. Whittick, *The New Towns: the answer to Megalopolis*, Leonard Hill, London, 1969, p88

43 In 1940–1 the TCPA decentralised temporarily to Welwyn, which was convenient for Osborn's daily routine but not for access to the centres of influence.

44 Popular presentations of the TCPA evidence to the Scott and Uthwatt committees. Gladys Keable, *Tomorrow Slowly Comes*, TCPA, London, 1963, p25 states that 50–60,000 of the Rebuilding Britain booklets were sold.

45 *Making Plans*, Foreword by Lord Balfour; Todd Publishing Co, London, 1943

46 See 42nd, 43rd and 44th Annual Reports of the TCPA

47 See his introduction to F. E. Towndrow (ed), *Replanning Britain*, Faber, London, 1941

48 H. B. Newbold (ed), *Industry and Rural Life*, Faber, London, 1942

49 D. Tyerman (ed), *Ways and Means of Rebuilding*, Faber, London, 1944

50 Hughes (ed), *op cit*, p13

51 G. D. H. Cole, for example, chided Osborn privately for pressing his density thesis too far. (Letter of 10 December 1943 in Osborn papers.)

52 He constantly cited survey evidence on housing preferences, eg *Houses versus Flats*, TCPA Reconstruction Leaflet (1943).

53 Memorandum from Osborn to Reith on Regional and Local Organisation for Reconstruction, 17 September 1940. Public Records Office, HLG 86, 16

54 Osborn's chief contribution seems to have been on the unlikely topic of architectural considerations in development control.

55 Hughes (ed), *op cit*, p15; Lord Reith's intentions were indicated in his welcoming words at the first meeting of the Panel – 'he wished to reconcile all in a constitutional scheme of national planning'. (Public Records Office, HLG 86, 8.) A room was reserved for members of the Panel on the second floor of the ministry. Osborn used later to recall, mistakenly it seems, that this had been his room and that he had been an 'unpaid under-secretary' by virtue of it

56 J. B. Cullingworth, *Reconstruction and Land Use Planning 1939–1947*, HMSO, London, 1975, Ch 2

57 G. Gibbon, 'Reconstruction and Town and Country Planning', *Architect & Building News*, 1943, p142

58 For Osborn's line, see 'Space Standards in Planning' in G. and E. G. McAllister, *Homes Towns and Countryside*, Batsford, London, 1945

59 T. C. P. Summer 1943; the *Architects' Journal* of 21 October 1943 observed that the TCPA line on density was 'fanatical to the verge of irresponsibility'.

60 Hughes (ed), *op cit*, pp65, 87. See Osborn's review of these controversies in 'Which Way London' *TCP* (1945) XIII, 126–131

61 TCPA 47th Annual Report (1945). See also Hughes (ed), *op cit*, p51

62 Osborn and Whittick, *The New Towns*, *op cit*, p99

63 Herbert Morrison was coordinating the government's massive legislative programme as Lord President: Osborn's old acquaintanceship may have been of some value here – and it is clear from his personal correspondence that he did his best to exploit it.

64 In 1943 Osborn wrote to W. S. Morrison to ask if he would set up a small expert committee on new town development. He was instead invited to submit an informal report, which he then discussed with Pepler who, like Abercrombie, knew Osborn well enough to deal with him on a friendly basis. Public Record Office, HLG 90, 336

65 *Green Belt Cities*, *op cit*, p22

66 He circulated some 'Notes on Size of Towns' to members of the Committee. Public Records Office HLG 84, 8

67 He wrote to Mumford (Hughes (ed), *op cit*, p113), 'No one else on the Committee combines experience in town-building with experience in the philosophic and political warfare on the subject – so you can imagine the torments I have gone through and the restraint I have had to exercise'.

68 In 1949 he declined the chairmanship of Bracknell Development Corporation, explaining subsequently to Herbert Morrison that he sought to serve in some central advisory capacity.

69 Hughes (ed), *op cit*, p197

70 He wrote of himself in 1953 as 'the one person in England who knows the importance of the garden city movement and will take any initiative to keep it in evidence', Hughes (ed), *op cit*, p212

71 He lists the standard 'antagonisms' in Chapter 10 of *The New Towns*, *op cit*

72 For instance, *TCP*, January 1954
73 The story is told in C. B. Purdom, *The Letchworth Achievement*, Dent, London, 1963
74 *Green Belt Cities, op cit*, p41; Hughes (ed), *op cit*, p188
75 See for instance the international comments which he collected in *TCP*, January 1956
76 Osborn and Whittick, *The New Towns, op cit*
77 See for instance the series of booklets published jointly by the TCPA and the University of London Press under his editorship in the early fifties, including Lord Beveridge's *New Towns and the Case for Them*, London, 1951
78 eg, 'How subsidies distort housing development', *Lloyds Bank Review*, April 1955
79 The BRS work was summarised in P. A. Stone, *Housing, Town Development, Land and Costs*, Estates Gazette, London, 1963. See also N. Lichfield, *Economics of Planned Development*, Estates Gazette, London, 1957, and Colin Clark, 'The Economics of High Building, *TCP* February 1958, pp73–75
80 Cmd 6378, p72
81 R. H. Best and J. T. Ward, *The Garden Controversy*, Wye College, Ashford, 1956
82 'Idea and Influence: The Town and Country Planning Association', *Journal of the American Institute of Planners*, 1962, vol 28, pp10–17
83 Colin Clark, *Population Growth and Land Use*, Macmillan, London, 1967; J. B. Cullingworth, *Housing Needs and Planning Policy*, Routledge, London, 1960; G. P. Wibberley, *Agriculture and Urban Growth*, Faber, London, 1959
84 He published a selection under the title *Can Man Plan?* Harrap, London, 1959
85 Hughes (ed), *op cit*, p337
86 A frequent theme of his writing was that enlightened industrialists should support town planning as they had helped to create it. In 1953 he organised a meeting of the TCPA with the Federation of British Industry in a vain attempt to revive the alliance.
87 In D. Tyerman, *Ways and Means of Rebuilding*, Faber, London, 1944, p52
88 He expressed this hope most clearly in *Overture to Planning*, Faber, London, 1941, pp26–28
89 eg, 'Planning Commentary' in *TCP*, XXI, 1953, p514
90 Hughes (ed), *op cit*, p275. See also Mumford's comments on pp219–220
91 *London's Dilemma: the only way out*, GCTPA, 1935, p3. See also his comments in *Transport, town development and the territorial planning of industry, op cit*, pp15–18
92 Discussed in A. Sutcliffe *Multi-Storey Living: The British working class experience*, Croom Helm, London, 1974
93 Take for example Helen Rosenau's commendation of the ridiculous 'High Paddington' proposal (8,000 people to be housed above the

Paddington goods yard) at the close of *The Ideal City in its Architectural Evolution*, 1959

94   *TCP*, XXIV, 1956, p148
95   See Sutcliffe's discussion in the introduction to *Multi-Storey Living*, Routledge, London, 1959, 1974
96   eg, DOE, (Lambeth Inner Area Study), *People Housing and District*, 1974; *Housing Stress*, 1975; among many similar studies
97   Hughes (ed), *op cit*, p126
98   Osborn would respond to academic calls for more research with Mrs Hitchens' remark on the Barlow Royal Commission: 'but surely we know *something* already!'
99   *Green Belt Cities*, *op cit*, p5
100   P. Self, *Econocrats and the Policy Process*, Macmillan, London, 1975; D. Eversley, *The Planner in Society*, Faber, London, 1973
101   Peter Self in *TCP*, XLVII, 1979, p96

9

COLIN BUCHANAN
1907–

Michael Bruton

His life and times

Colin Buchanan would without doubt be described by those who are not British as being characteristically British. He is authoritative, and traditional; a man who neither wastes words nor presents a façade of affability. Yet he possesses a sense of humour which is both cutting and quirky as those who were present at the opening address he gave to the York Town and Country Planning Summer School in 1973 will confirm.[1]

He comes from an engineering family with an Indian background, having been born in Simla in 1907. Following a public school education at Berkhamsted School and an engineering training at Imperial College London, he was awarded his B.Sc. in Civil Engineering in 1929–30. *Who's Who* 1979 indicates that his professional career commenced with the Public Works Department of the Sudan Government where he worked on bridge and road building (1930–32). Axed from the Sudan in the recession he was unemployed for a year until a chance invitation led him to a post in the offices of Frances Longstreth Thompson (a former President of the Town Planning Institute) working on regional planning studies. During this time he was elected an Associate Member of the Town Planning Institute (1934). In 1935 he joined the Ministry of Transport as an Assistant Engineer until war service intervened, when he served in the Royal Engineers (1939–46) and attained the rank of Lieut. Colonel.

In the context of the times (1930–46) this must have appeared to have been a not unsuccessful career. It certainly conformed to the general pattern of career development expected of any able individual of middle-class background, and held out promise of further advancement in his chosen field. Why then did Buchanan, on his return from war service, apply himself to securing a transfer from the Ministry of Transport to the new Ministry of Town and Country Planning, 'a department crammed with youngish, brilliant people

203

apparently operating on a remarkably informal basis . . . Nothing would satisfy me but to get in with that lot'.[2] The answer perhaps lies in the socio-economic development of that period (1930–46) including a major economic recession (which had highlighted the social injustices associated with the western way of life); the Second World War (which gave rise to massive technological development and sweeping social change); and the most formative years in the development of a British statutory planning system culminating in the reports of Barlow, Scott and Uthwatt, and the post-war package of planning legislation. In this brave new world atmosphere where planning was seen as being central to the creation of a new and better way of life, it was inevitable that an able professional would be influenced by these experiences and the social welfare origins of planning, and it would seem that Buchanan's thinking and values were much conditioned by this period, as the following quotation illustrates:

To explain my standpoint I must briefly outline the broad land use planning context within which I have constantly endeavoured to view the problem . . . set. This context has been a long time in the making. It started more than a century ago with the work of the housing reformers. It was born out of back to back houses, out of overcrowding, out of privies in back yards, out of children with nowhere to play, out of ribbon development and urban sprawl. It was born out of painfully gathered experience over a century of industrialisation which made it abundantly clear that market forces in land, left to their own devices, fail utterly to produce a humane environment. The Town and Country Planning Act of 1947 (and all the other legislation flowing from the Barlow, Scott, and Uthwatt Reports) marked the great turning point. It rejected the market approach. It removed once and for all an owner's right to do what he liked with his land, and put in its place the concept of the community managing and regulating the national estate for its own convenience and delight. In particular, the community accepted . . . the need for certain essentially uneconomic (in the short term at any rate) policies such as the direction of industry to depressed localities where industrialists would not willingly go of their own accord, the maintenance of green belts which lengthened commuting journeys, and the reduction of housing densities in order to permit the insertion of open space.[3]

It is apparent from this statement that Buchanan enthusiastically supported the grand social and economic objectives implicit in the five major pieces of post-war planning legislation, viz: Distribution of Industry Act 1945, New Towns Act 1946, Town and Country Planning Act 1947, National Parks and Access to the Countryside Act 1949, and Town Development Act 1952. It is also apparent that he believes 'that the land of the country, after its people, is its most precious asset, not to be squandered, not to be exploited, not to be sacrificed for short term gains, but to be zealously guarded and enriched for passing on to succeeding generations'.[4] This commitment to (i) the need to plan comprehensively to provide a satisfactory economic, social and physical environment which is acceptable to a growing population gradually acquiring more wealth, and more leisure time, and (ii) the conservation of the nation's heritage and natural resources, which was forged during the first 16 years of his career can be clearly identified in much of his later work, and almost certainly explained his enthusiasm to join the Ministry of Town and Country Planning.

The period 1946–54 was spent 'not unhappily . . . jogging along',[5] initially in the Ministry of Town and Country Planning and latterly in the Ministry of Housing and Local Government which took on the responsibility for planning when the Ministry of Town and Country Planning was disbanded. During this period work on the New Towns programme progressed; the plans for re-building the blitzed cities began to be implemented and a concern for the environmental implications associated with the housing programme were amongst the main concerns of central government planners. At this time he claims to have become clearly aware of the 'one especially dangerous borderline for professional men acting in advisory capacities: it is the line between being well regarded as a man of sturdy independent views, not easily budged when he has thought something out, and being dismissed as altogether too opinionated and obstinate'.[6] Despite this awareness, it is apparent from his later work that it was not allowed to deflect him from his main objectives.

Important as the work during this period was, developments in the 'outside world' were perhaps more significant. The strong system of regional planning established under the Ministry of Town and Country Planning was broken up; the financial provisions of the Town and County Planning Act 1947 were repealed with the return of a Conservative government in 1951 and town planning for the next ten years 'was widely denigrated as an undesirable political activity, and accordingly described as a dirty word'.[7]

Within this general climate of opinion Buchanan was involved 'in a serious clash with the Permanent Secretary over a matter concerning the rights and obligations of professional staff in the Department'. This clash resulted from an attempt on his part to establish rational relations between civil service town planners and the Town Planning Institute. His part in the clash led to his being removed 'from normal planning work to becoming an Inspector holding public inquiries which was a very lonely kind of life where you worked by yourself' and gave first public warning that he was perhaps 'a man of sturdy independent views' although within the Ministry he was probably seen as being 'too opinionated and obstinate'.[8]

From 1954 until 1960 Buchanan was Principal Inspector for Special Inquiries and it is his involvement in inquiries of exceptional interest for which he is best remembered during this time – the Piccadilly Inquiry, the Milford Haven Inquiries and the Nuclear Power Station Inquiry at Trawsfynydd. Buchanan himself, however, recalls from this period the salutary experiences he gained on slum clearance inquiries – experiences which provided a 'grounding in slums, with its insight into poverty and the loneliness among old people, and the strange mixture of hopelessness and fortitude'; experiences that he 'would want to put every planner through until there are no more slums at all';[9] experiences which must surely have confirmed his commitment to the social purpose underlying land use planning.

On his own admission during this period Buchanan contemplated retiring mentally from his central government activities – discharging his duties to the required standard but applying his energies elsewhere. It is interesting to note that *Mixed Blessing* was written at this time. However, with his appointment as Inspector on planning cases from 1957 onwards, he began to use his Inspector's report as a method of self expression; 'to test out by discussion the planning dogmas involved – green belts; density; urban sprawl; access to highways; the real purpose of the countryside and so on'.[10] Through this medium he began to become known to limited sections of the public, and more widely known in the profession. Indeed his reports made such good reading that an edited version of the report of the public inquiry concerning development on the Monico site at Piccadilly Circus was published in *Town Planning Review* 1960–61.[11]

In 1960 he was appointed Adviser on Urban Road Planning to Ernest Marples, then Minister of Transport, and so began what he claims to be the happiest two and a half years of his life working on the Traffic in Towns Project. The resultant publication – popularly known as the Buchanan Report – became a Stationery Office best seller; was published in edited form by Penguin and made Buchanan a household name overnight. During this time he served as President of the (Royal) Town Planning Institute, and actively campaigned to broaden the Institute's membership. In 1964 he was appointed to the newly created Chair of Transport Planning at Imperial College London, and his consultancy work expanded with the establishment of Colin Buchanan and Partners. This stage in his career was paralleled by an upsurge of interest in planning, with many new planning initiatives being taken by the newly returned Labour government after 1964. The mood of the country was one of optimism for the future; with a widely held belief that the standard of living would increase; that resources would be available to shape our environment to our liking. George Brown's National Plan came and went; technology was seen to be the answer to many of our problems; sub-regional planning studies with explicit social and economic objectives were established; extensive city centre redevelopments were undertaken; massive investment in highway infrastructure took place; Concorde was developed and man walked on the moon. It is understandable that the attitudes and values of the time (1960–74) influenced the type of solutions that Buchanan suggested for planning problems in our towns and cities. With the advantage of hindsight it is possible to see many of his ideas as over ambitious and unrealistic. Yet throughout this period his concern with comprehensive planning for a social purpose, and his concern to protect the nation's heritage were clearly evident.

In 1969 Buchanan was awarded the Gold Medal of the (Royal) Town Planning Institute; he was knighted in 1972, and for the period 1973–75 he was the first Director of the School of Advanced Urban Studies at the University of Bristol – a post-graduate centre for the study of practical issues associated with urban policy and planning. These last years of his professional career were marked by a changing attitude in the country towards public expenditure and planning. The schemes and ideas which had appeared so imaginative and feasible were now seen as being unrealistic and irrelevant. The value of planning was repeatedly questioned and the attitudes and values inculcated in professional planners through their education were heavily criticised. Following the election of the new (Conservative) government in May 1979, the potential of planning to improve social welfare conditions and protect the nation's heritage has been further modified in line with the monetarist policies of the government.

His contribution to planning

Buchanan's contribution to the development of planning can best be considered under four main headings – his contribution through (a) public service and publications, (b) consultancy work, (c) the RTPI and (d) the academic world. In all these areas of his work it is possible to discern three over-riding concerns – a belief in the need for and benefits of a comprehensive planning system although this is never clearly defined; a commitment to protect the physical environment and the nation's heritage against the attempts of the market to exploit these resources for short term gain; and a commitment to pursue wider social objectives through land use planning.

Public service and publications

Buchanan's most significant contribution to the development of planning came through his public service and the publications associated with this work, for it was through these activities that he influenced both the philosophy of the profession and the attitude of the public towards planning. His two major contributions – the *Traffic in Towns* Report[12] and the Note of dissent in the Report of the Roskill Commission[13] – marked watersheds in planning thinking. Both exhibited a common sense approach towards major planning issues; both were popularised and in parts misinterpreted by planners and public.

Other publications, especially the Report of the Working Party on Car Parking in the Inner Area of London (1953); *Mixed Blessing* (1958); *The State of Britain* (1972), and his reports as a Senior Inspector although less well known, are equally significant and reinforce the three main themes which underly his work.

The Report on Car Parking in the Inner Area of London provided what is probably the first opportunity for Buchanan 'to go public' with his views on the problems of traffic in towns. In a note of reservation he (i) expressed concern at the environmental damage likely to result from the construction of car parks under central London squares such as Berkeley Square; (ii) expressed doubts as to the wisdom of subsiding long-term parkers, and (iii) advocated the development of a policy towards traffic and car parking which 'would be fair to all sections of the community, would be applicable generally without involving special treatment for London, and would be in line with the present need for economy in public expenditure'.[14] This early work as well as drawing attention to the fact that he is a man of 'sturdy independent views' with a concern for social justice, can also be seen as a precursor of the *Traffic in Towns* Report – which forever more will be known as the Buchanan Report. This work was produced by a small multi-disciplinary team of architects, engineers, planners and economists. It was concerned 'to study the long term development of roads and traffic in urban areas and their influence on the urban environment'[15] and established the intellectual foundations for the development of policy to cope with the problem of urban traffic. The report, which was set out so that the ordinary reader would find it attractive and easy to read, made the assumption that the motor vehicle was indispensable in a civilised society and would continue as a means of transport. It advanced eight main propositions:

1. Traffic is a function of activities; activities take place in buildings; the location and disposition of these buildings directly affects the type, volume and direction of traffic.

2. The 'traffic problem' consists of two elements – accessibility (ie, freedom for vehicles to penetrate to destinations and stop there) and environment (ie, the maintenance of acceptable standards of environment in relation to danger, noise, fumes).

3. Traffic can only be accommodated in towns by developing distributory highway networks serving areas which will be protected from the adverse environmental effects of traffic.

4. A rough and ready law concerning the relationship between accessibility, environmental standards and cost can be established, viz, if environmental standards are fixed for any area then a limit is automatically set to the amount of traffic it can accommodate. However, the traffic capacity can be increased without detracting from the environment by carrying out physical alterations, but at a price. Thus the amount of traffic an area can accommodate is determined by the environmental standards adopted and the amount of money which can be spent on physically altering the area.

5. In densely developed areas there is an absolute limit to the amount of traffic that can be accommodated, no matter how much money is spent on physical alterations.

6. New architectural forms are needed to accommodate the motor vehicle and protect the standard of environment.

7. The policy of spreading the traffic load across the existing street network is questionable on environmental grounds.

8. Environmental management techniques can be applied to protect the environmental standards of whole areas of towns and encourage the development of an embryonic network.

The report was not intended to be a plan for positive action. It contained no recommendations for the reconstruction of our towns and cities; it contained no recommendations for levels of investment. Rather its main message is contained in (i) the 'law' relating environmental standards to accessibility and cost, ie, 'Within any area as it stands the establishment of environmental standards automatically determines the accessibility, but the latter can be increased according to the amount of money that can be spent on physical alterations',[16] and (ii) the clarifying of the inter-relationship between land use and transport planning. Despite this, criticisms were levelled at the report on the grounds that it only examined the way in which concentrated building in existing towns could be adapted to accommodate the motor vehicle. In other words, it did not examine Green Belt developments, or new town forms; it provided no criteria for decision taking and the allocation of resources; and it ignored the economics of the scale of construction costs implied by the case studies.[17] It was also criticised by Wyndham

Thomas[18] on the grounds that the traffic architecture for the future was impossible (although to judge from the current proposals for Peterborough, especially the Queensgate Shopping Centre, he has shifted his ground somewhat in the last 16 years). Generally, however, the report was received enthusiastically by planners and public. Indeed, it was described as 'one of the important books, not only for town planning but for society as a whole. It represents a milestone in thinking equal, in my view, to the milestone represented by Ebenezer Howard and the new towns movement'.[19] It effectively synthesised the then current ideas on the inter-relationship between land use and transport drawing on North American and British (Cumbernauld) experience; it reflected the concern of the general public for the traffic problem (which in part helps explain the popularity of the report); while the suggested traffic architecture reflected the attitudes of society at the time whereby technology was expected to find the answer and resources were not seen as a problem.

The report also gives expression to the three general themes evident in Buchanan's outlook towards planning. Throughout an integrated and comprehensive approach to the problem of land use and transport is advocated; while the conclusions indicate 'the ability to command the comprehensive development or redevelopment of large areas is extremely important to the successful handling of motor traffic'.[20] The emphasis on fixing environmental standards reflects his concern to maintain a quality of life which can pass for being civilised while the development of an approach to transport policy which can accommodate the advantages of the motor vehicle and allow for the provision of an adequate public transport system is perhaps an indication of his concern with social welfare of the community at large and the individual well-being.

As a result of *Traffic in Towns*, planning thinking and planning practice have been much modified. The advantages of introducing a systematic and quantifiable approach to planning were realised and developed in sub-regional and transportation studies; the inter-relationship between land use and transport planning became accepted as a matter of course whilst the dynamic nature of this relationship is gradually being understood. Transport planning is now better integrated with land use planning through the Structure Plan system introduced in the 1968 Town and Country Planning Act. This in conjunction with the Transport Policy and Programmes (TPPs) and the Passenger Transport Plans (PTPs) goes some of the way to meeting Buchanan's recommended transport co-ordination plan. At the same time the planning profession and the public have been made forcibly aware of the erosion of the quality of the built and physical environment taking place as a result of modern technological developments. Also they have been made aware of the methods and costs likely to be involved to protect those standards against the motor vehicle. Indeed, the environmental improvements which have been implemented in many small market towns in the UK, eg, Abingdon and Hereford, owe a great deal to the ideas contained in the Report, especially the Newbury case study. Pedestrianisation has been introduced in town centres such as these through the implementation of traffic management schemes. However, the conditions in the surrounding streets which are now required to carry the additional diverted traffic leaves much to be desired – largely through a failure to undertake the construction of new diversionary works.

With the advantage of hindsight the Report can be criticised on several counts, eg, by concentrating on developing possible plans for 2001 the dynamics associated with change over approximately a 40-year period were ignored. Similarly by examining only one model of future society based on the society then in existence no thought was given to alternative futures. The technological optimism of the 1960s stands out: 'If we believe in a great future then we must believe that the standard of living will go steadily up . . . that we shall have the resources to remould our environment to our liking.[21] These criticisms would be fundamental had the report been concerned to put forward positive recommendations about the restructuring of our towns and cities. Given that it was primarily concerned to propound the inter-relationship between accessibility, environment and cost, they do not detract from the general thesis.

One major criticism has, however, been levelled at the Report in relation to the way in which it appears to advocate the use of traffic architecture to cope with traffic in high density development or redevelopment. At the time it was produced, such ideas were described as 'Fanciful, imaginative – but impossible',[22] and experience and hindsight have shown that where such comprehensive development or redevelopment schemes have been implemented on a grand scale, as at Glasgow and Cumbernauld town centre, they are alien to our urban environment; unwanted and disliked by the majority. Such criticisms are perhaps justified of the report of the Steering Group of which Buchanan was not a member. This report positively encouraged the view that large scale redevelopment was both desirable and feasible, 'It is clear that any attempt to implement these ideas would result in a gigantic programme of urban reconstruction. We see no reason to be frightened of this . . . and the rebuilding necessary to implement the ideas of the Buchanan Report . . . should not be beyond the powers of a few decades of our

212 PIONEERS IN BRITISH PLANNING

century'.[23] It is less certain that the traffic architecture criticisms are justified in relation to the main body of the Report – although traffic architecture features strongly in illustrations as a possible and ideal solution to our traffic problems, it is only offered as one amongst a range of alternative solutions. Nevertheless, the overall impression gained is that in accord with the beliefs of the times, the Traffic in Towns team favoured the adoption of a high technology, traffic architecture solution.

For the period 1968–70 Buchanan was a member of the Roskill Commission of Inquiry into the possible location for a third airport for London. After an extensive review and cost benefit analysis of alternative locations, the majority of the Commission recommended that the airport should be located at Cublington in Buckinghamshire. Buchanan produced a note of dissent objecting to all three inland sites that had been considered and recommended that the airport be located at Foulness.[24]

His short note of dissent (12 pages) is the most powerful case that he or any other planner has made for a comprehensive land use planning system. It also gives a very clear outline of his philosophy towards planning and suggests that he is a man of 'sturdy independent views not easily budged when he has thought something out',[25] who judges the evidence as he sees it. In judging the evidence he surveyed the alternative sites on foot in an attempt to assess the likely physical impact of an airport for an area of $12\frac{1}{2}$ square miles.

Four main themes are developed in his dissenting note – the need for a comprehensive approach to planning; the need to protect the environment for posterity, to ensure that short term advantages are not gained at the expense of longer term needs; the need to use major locational decisions as an instrument of social policy; and the need for careful judgement when using sophisticated methods of analysis.

The importance of a comprehensive approach to planning is emphasised throughout. The point is made that the third London airport cannot be viewed in isolation; that account must be taken of the social and economic objectives implicit in the statutory planning system; that account must be taken of the policies applied in the south-east since the 1940s, especially the policy to provide London with 'an open background' introduced by Abercrombie and upheld by successive governments since then;[26] that the social and economic needs of the area as a whole must provide the framework within which such a major locational decision is taken, and that without a national airports policy the work of the Commission had been very seriously handicapped.

Buchanan's concern to protect the environment and our natural heritage against the unnecessary intrusion of large scale developments underpins his whole statement. His description of the 'open background' is vivid and could only have been written by someone who cares deeply about its qualities.[27]

London as it happens has a particularly delectable open background. There are some bad patches where man has done his worst, but for the most part . . . it is an area of peculiar charm. The topography is nowhere extreme or violent yet it provides remarkable contrasts of a subtle kind as between the North and South Downs and the intervening Weald, or between the chalk escarpment at Ivinghoe and the Vale of Aylesbury or between the barely perceptible hills of Dengie and the dead flatness of the marshes. It is a snug, homely and very livable part of the world.

His description of the Cublington and Foulness sites, and his feel for the implications of constructing the airport at either site is equally vivid and caring.

To locate the airport squarely athwart the break between the country's two largest conurbations with the noise area extending from the south-west to north-east for forty miles and with the consequent constraint on all the modest activities that the area so conveniently accommodates at present and all those that it would accommodate in future, would seem to me to constitute nothing less than an environmental disaster.

The case for utilising the location of the third airport for social policy purposes is clearly put.

. . . the location of the airport at Foulness could, in my view, make a powerful contribution to one of the biggest social problems in the country, namely that of east London. . . . the third London airport . . . seems to me to provide a unique opportunity to introduce a new type of activity into the area . . . which will initiate a regenerative process reaching right back to the heart of London where the East End butts against the City.

The attitudes reflected in this stance relate quite clearly to the social origins of planning and Buchanan's concern to see a comprehensive planning system.
The fourth theme running through the note of dissent is the reservation Buchanan expresses about the use of the cost benefit analysis. The difficulties he encountered included uncertainty about the basis of figures used, such as user travel costs, and doubts about the validity of aggregating for each site the 'costs' to achieve a rank order.

I became more and more anxious lest I be trapped in a process which I did not fully understand and ultimately led without choice to a conclusion

214 PIONEERS IN BRITISH PLANNING

which I would know in my heart of hearts I did not agree with . . . I have the feeling that the whole cost/benefit approach has been pushed too far and too fast beyond the fairly easily quantified problems that are its usual domain.[28]

In addition he felt that cost benefit analysis should have been used to review the alternative airport sites within a land use planning framework rather than focus on a narrow comparison of the alternative sites.

Following publication of the note of dissent, it quickly became apparent that a significant body of public opinion, in addition to the local protesters, shared Buchanan's view that to locate the third airport at Cublington would be environmentally undesirable. It is difficult to know to what extent Buchanan's view moulded public opinion and to what extent it was subconsciously influenced by public opinion. Whatever the situation, it is certain that the stand Buchanan took on environmental issues; his questioning of the use of sophisticated methodology and the obvious use of common sense and professional judgement he exercised in reaching his view, encouraged other groups and individuals to question the need for other major developments which have severe environmental side effects and are propounded on the basis of complex methodology. The combination of this attitude with the formal introduction of public participation in town planning has ensured that the way in which planning decisions are reached on major developments has changed significantly. The Windscale Inquiry, the Vale of Belvoir Inquiry, the various inquiries into proposed motorways would perhaps not have evolved without the encouragement Buchanan subconsciously gave to the environmental movement.

Mixed Blessing (1959) and *State of Britain* (1972) both reflect Buchanan's over-riding commitment to a comprehensive planning system and the need to preserve and safeguard the natural environment. *Mixed Blessing* provides an introductory history of the development of the motor vehicle and reviews the social and economic effects associated with its increasing use. It also gives emphasis to the need to integrate town planning and traffic planning and the need to protect the standard of environment in our towns and cities in a comprehensive way. The book is extremely readable and although 'much of it does not appear to be aimed at any particular professional group'[29] it paved the way for Buchanan's later work on *Traffic in Towns*.

State of Britain (1972) is again an eminently readable work dealing with the state of the environment and the success of the British planning machinery. The transcript of three Chichelte lectures delivered at Oxford University in 1971 shortly after the publication of his note of dissent in the Roskill Report, the book not surprisingly reflects many of the views expressed in that note of dissent. While it is perhaps unfair to criticise lectures to a lay audience there are indications that the objectivity which appeared to underpin the note of dissent is less in evidence. White collar, middle-class prejudices and biases are on the other hand readily discernible; for example, 'Planning is not for people, it is for all life'; he 'trembles for loneliness and isolation in this crowded isle' and argues that the function of planning is 'to secure the basic decencies of civilised life'. Unlike the note of dissent, the lectures make no attempt to assess the influence of his own values and standards in reaching these views. Indeed, his stance at this stage in his career suggests that he might be 'altogether too opinionated' rather than 'the man of sturdy independent views' that his earlier works suggest.[30] Overall, however, these two books reinforce the main themes running through Buchanan's public works and publications.

Consultancy – Colin Buchanan and Partners
Colin Buchanan and Partners 'is a consultancy offering specialist services and advice in the fields of land use, transportation, social and economic planning'.[31] Formed in 1964, the partnership consisted originally of senior members of the *Traffic in Towns* team and two senior architect planners from local government. Today, Colin Buchanan is the only member of the original *Traffic in Towns* team to maintain formal connections with the consultancy as its consultant. In the period 1964–79 the firm undertook a wide variety of commissions including national, regional, metropolitan, urban, conservation and specialist research studies. Many of these commissions were based overseas, for example Kuwait, Nairobi, Salvador. Amongst the best known of the firms UK based work are the studies for South Hampshire, Cardiff, Edinburgh, Bath and West Central Scotland. The approach which the consultancy claim to use in their work 'is to unite the skills of individual specialists and the techniques of several disciplines within the framework of multi-professional teams. We always aim to produce comprehensive solutions in which all aspects of a problem are considered and to express recommendations in clear and straightforward language'.[32] This attitude is borne out by the nature of the multi-disciplinary teams appointed to work on the various commissions. It also reflects Buchanan's personal concern to see a comprehensive approach adopted towards planning.
Analysis of the reports produced by the consultancy tends to confirm that this approach has been consistently adopted in their UK based work. It also shows quite clearly that some of the ideas expounded in *Traffic in Towns* have been applied in practice. All the land use planning studies give emphasis to the inter-relationships between

land use and transport whilst the Cardiff study (1969) pays particular attention to the problems of defining environmental areas and identifying possible routes for the highway network. The Edinburgh study (1971) further develops this approach and shows that land use density and level of car useage are closely related to size of environmental areas and network spacing. It also shows that environmental areas based on these considerations may conflict with areas of functional, architectural or layout cohesion.

Yet despite the way in which much of this work followed the popularly received ideas of *Traffic in Towns*, the consultancy has come in for criticism on the grounds that the proposals they put forward invariably favour the private motor vehicle at the expense of public transport; involve a level of demolition and reconstruction which is unnecessary, unwanted, and prohibitively expensive, and take a static master plan approach to deal with problems which were expected to exist in 30 years time. The opposition from the public and the press to the proposals that the firm put forward for Cardiff, Bath and Edinburgh for example, are indicative of the way in which much of the work was received.

The implications behind these criticisms were that Buchanan was pursuing a line in practice which was at variance with the ideas in *Traffic in Towns*. Yet such views are unfair – the proposals put forward in these works are entirely consistent with the principles set out in *Traffic in Towns*. Environment and accessibility: the interrelationship between land use and movement dominate. What does emerge from the practical application of these ideas is that the massive redevelopment necessary to maintain a reasonable standard of environment whilst at the same time accommodating the level of use of the private motor vehicle which the man in the street demands, is unacceptable to the public at large. Such findings are entirely consistent with the 'law' established in *Traffic in Towns* which relates environmental standards to accessibility and cost. Yet within the profession there was a feeling that somehow the Consultancy was prepared to ignore the high ideals which were expressed in that report when it came to matters of business.

Why should this be the case? There are perhaps two main reasons. The first is that the main message of the *Traffic in Towns* report – the rough and ready law – was not fully understood either by the public or the profession. Given the optimism for the future expressed in the report; given the rather low key way in which this law was presented in the report; given the apparent emphasis in the report on the potential of traffic architecture, it is understandable that it was interpreted as an indication that the conflicting demands of different groups in society could all be satisfied through the application of

Traffic in Towns principles. Thus the environment could be enhanced; the motor vehicle could be accommodated; towns worthy of preservation could be preserved; employment and central area functions could be enhanced . . . there was something in it for everybody. It was only when these principles were translated into proposals for specific towns and cities that the implications of what was involved were fully appreciated by the residents of those towns and cities. The second reason is that the proposals put forward by the consultancy almost invariably advocated an advanced technology solution while at the same time under-estimating the role of political decision making in planning at local government level. Traffic architecture, the extensive redevelopment of central areas (Cardiff) and the construction of massive highway networks (Cardiff, Edinburgh and Bath) were consistently advanced as solutions to the problems of towns and traffic. Equally consistently these solutions were rejected by the public and their elected representatives as unnecessary and unwanted, although it should be pointed out that in the majority of situations where the advice of the consultants was rejected the local population are sweating it out in traffic and environmental conditions as bad as ever.

Similarly the implication that because the solutions advocated by the consultancy were generally rejected by the client groups, the work of the firm was inconsequential, is unfair and incorrect. For example, the proposals for Cardiff were presented by the consultancy to the City Council in 1968 'as no more than a first but major clarification of the City's traffic and development problems [with] much further study . . . required'.[33] Since that date many of the concepts integral to the consultants' report have been implemented; for example Queen Street has been pedestrianised very successfully following the construction of a short length of new highway to accommodate diverted traffic, new office employment has been concentrated on the Queen Street and the Central Stations; a comprehensive scheme for the redevelopment of part of the central area to the south of Queen Street is currently under construction. The one notable aspect of the consultants' proposals which has not been implemented is the extensive highway construction needed to improve traffic and environmental conditions throughout the City generally – and this omission can be explained by the public's dislike of the implications associated with the application of high technology solutions. Indeed, Buchanan in a paper delivered in the Department of Town and Country Planning at the University of Manchester in November 1978 summarised quite succinctly what he regards as the attitude of the man in the street to environment and accessibility, and implies that the team in rating the environment as sacrosanct put a much higher value on it than the public; 'I think the *general public* has shown that it is more interested in mobility than in the quality of the surroundings for living. People seem quite happy to trade off some depreciation of their environment for a fair degree of mobility, whereas in the *Traffic in Towns* report we tended to treat the environment as an absolute not to be allowed to fall below defined standards any more than drainage should be permitted to be deficient'.[34]

The Royal Town Planning Institute

Colin Buchanan, having been active in the Town Planning Institute for some years, presided over the Institute in its jubilee year in 1964 'by an accident of seniority'.[35] During his period of office he set in motion the debate on the findings of the Special Committee on Membership about the role of the Institute and its membership policy. This 'debate' which was completed under the presidency of Leslie Lane in 1965 split the membership of the Institute.

The issues to which the debate was addressed were the areas of concern of planning, and the type of people required to work in planning. In discussing these points, Buchanan's own position was made abundantly clear. Thus planning 'is concerned with those aspects of the processes of government, including the management and planning of the country's economic fortunes, which impinge on the use and development of land' while 'Having regard to the nature of planning, to the breadth of matters it covers, to the vast ramifications of some of the problems with which it deals and to the varied nature of the professional contributions that are involved I would expect to find an Institute with a large and varied membership . . . [of] . . . persons admitted on equal terms but on the basis of their individual professional skills. The pre-requisites for entry would be a broad understanding of the aims and objectives of planning and a particular contribution to the practice of planning of the particular skill the candidate professes'.[36]

These two quotations taken from his Presidential Address in 1963 give a firm indication of his commitment to a comprehensive approach to planning whereby physical land use planning is seen as part of a wider spectrum of social and economic planning. However, the membership of the Institute opposed these ideas at an Extraordinary General Meeting called by Thomas Sharp and 28 other corporate members in January 1965. The results of a questionnaire survey on proposed changes in membership policy received in February 1965 showed a majority against any change, whilst the Council election results later in the year saw the membership unseat many long-standing Council members who had led the move for change.

The stand taken by Buchanan over this issue resulted in his being heavily criticised by other professionals in the Institute who felt that the standing of the profession would be down-graded if the 'team-work' approach advocated were to form the basis of admission to the Institute. Indeed Lewis Keeble went so far as to imply that some members of Council were disloyal when he stated that he did 'not think the first allegiance of all members is to the Institute'[37] while many 'grass roots' members saw the proposals as a prelude to the Institute being taken over by the RIBA. During the next two to three years Buchanan quietly withdrew from the affairs of the Institute, although it is ironic to note that by 1972 the same issues had been resurrected and debated with the membership this time favouring a role which was similar to that advocated in 1964 by Buchanan; 'an Institute of environmental planning maintaining and re-inforcing its pre-occupation with the total physical environment of town and country, but adapting the profession to include all those directly involved in the physical planning process; also to relate the process of physical planning to corporate planning'.[38]

Buchanan and the academic world
During the last twelve years of his career Buchanan held two unique and potentially significant academic posts: as the first holder of the Chair in Transport Planning at Imperial College London (1963–73), and latterly as the first Director of the School for Advanced Urban Studies at the University of Bristol (1973–75). Both posts were created in response to changing perceptions of the nature of planning and offered great potential for influencing the educational philosophy adopted in planning.
The Chair in Transport Planning at Imperial College was offered at the culmination of the work of the *Traffic in Towns* team. In addition to Buchanan, the college appointed four other members of the team – Geoff Crow, Bill Crompton, Anne MacEwan and Peter Hills – and a post-graduate course in Transport Planning was established, which took its first main intake in September 1964. This course reflected much of the basic thinking of Buchanan and the *Traffic in Towns* team: it adopted a multi-disciplinary approach, and was concerned to inter-relate land use and transport planning within a wider socio-economic framework. Students from a wide range of disciplines were attracted from practice and overseas, and in an atmosphere of excitement and commitment the ideas which had emerged in *Traffic in Towns* were debated, dissected, developed and assimilated; the values inherent in the philosophy of Buchanan and his team towards planning were absorbed (albeit with reluctance on the part of some) and the careers of many of the students from the early years of that

course took on dramatic new directions, and spread the *Traffic in Towns* philosophy to other countries.

Research into some of the basic concepts outlined in *Traffic in Towns* was set in motion and the work of Bill Crompton and Dennis Gilbert on the measurement of environmental intrusion in particular held out much promise for the future. And yet 16 years after the establishment of this course the excitement and promise which this new multi-disciplinary approach offered appears to have evaporated. The educational lead offered at Imperial College in 1964 does not appear to have had the impact it promised, either in the world of practice or education. Rather this promise now appears to be more in evidence at the School for Advanced Urban Studies (SAUS) where Buchanan became the first Director in 1973.

The establishment of SAUS at the University of Bristol arose out of a proposal by Baroness Sharp in 1970 that a post-graduate centre be established for the study of transport policy. This proposal was eventually extended to incorporate a consideration of urban policy and governance with an emphasis being placed on the practical implications of economic, environmental, housing, social and transport policy, rather than a more generalised theoretical study of these issues. Given Buchanan's commitment to a wide-ranging and comprehensive approach to planning, and his extensive practical experience, it is not surprising that he was appointed the first Director of the School.

His contribution to the development of the School is difficult to judge given that he only held office for three years. However, examination of the brochure outlining the programme of short courses for the School in 1980 would seem to indicate that he was successful in directing it towards adopting a philosophy which reflected his own outlook, as the following quotation from that brochure indicates:

[The School's] broad aim is to contribute to the development of the theory and practice of public policy and its activities are directed at those who are involved with the formulation, development and implementation of urban policies . . . it is the interrelatedness of policy areas that is of most concern and most of the School work bridges the gaps between subject areas, professional boundaries and academic disciplines . . .[39]

Certainly the appointment of Tony Eddison (the current Director of the School) as his deputy made it clear that such a development was likely and subsequent events have shown that to be the case.

Conclusions
Colin Douglas Buchanan, professionally qualified as an engineer, an architect and a town planner, is probably the most popularly known

planner of this or any other generation; a man of independent views who attracts loyalties from those who work closely with him; a man of charisma who possesses the ability to put over professional views simply and clearly and in a way which, in general terms, finds sympathy with the man in the street. Yet at the same time a difficult man to know; a man who appears aloof and insensitive and who attracts on occasion the ire of professionals and academics working in the same fields.

Born in 1907 he has lived through a period of great social, economic and political change. In his lifetime the motor vehicle and the aircraft have developed from obscurity to prominence; in his lifetime two world wars and the associated social, economic and political change have taken place; in his lifetime the major influences on the development of planning thought have been fashioned into the statutory planning system we possess today. Inevitably he has been influenced by these developments, just as in the last 25 years he himself has influenced them. His major contributions in public service; his publications – such as *Mixed Blessing*, *Traffic in Towns*, the note of dissent in the Report of the Roskill Commission on the Third London Airport – have anticipated and guided changes in attitude towards planning among the professionals. At the same time they have in part reflected the attitude of the man in the street towards major planning issues. *Mixed Blessing* (1958), which was the first authoritative review of the impact of the motor vehicle on our society, attempted to 'reveal and perhaps clarify some of the problems arising from this ingenious invention'.[40] As Urban Road Planning Adviser in the Ministry of Transport in the period 1961–63 Buchanan led the *Traffic in Towns* team whose final report advocated the introduction of a systematic methodology and approach to policy making in urban areas which would utilise to the full the advantages associated with the use of the motor vehicle, without detracting from other aspects of our way of life which society values.

The early work of the consultancy which he established reflected this thinking. In particular the South Hampshire Study 1966 was well received professionally and showed evidence of the systematic application of planning ideas and procedure in a way which respected the values held by society in relation particularly to low density living and ready accessibility. His note of dissent in the Report of the Roskill Commission on the Third London Airport marked a reaction against the unthinking systematising of methodology and was at the same time a re-affirmation of his concern to maintain civilised values and standards.

In all his personal works it is possible to identify three over-riding concerns – a belief in the need for and benefits of a system of comprehensive land use planning; a passionate commitment to protect the physical environment and the nation's heritage against the attempts of the market to exploit these resources for short term gain; a commitment to using land use planning to secure wider social objectives such as the improvement of living standards, and the redistribution of economic opportunity. The attitude and approach he adopted toward these concerns has found much sympathy with the general public. Although the same attitude and approach has permeated his work with the RTPI and in the academic world, in these areas his ideas were not always sympathetically received or implemented, whilst much of the work produced by his consultancy has been criticised unfairly for failing to measure up to the values and standards set in his more general work. Although not strictly speaking a pioneer in British planning, he has had a most profound influence on planning thinking and planning practice.

Acknowledgements

In the preparation of this chapter I was considerably assisted by Mrs Janice Sims (Librarian, Department of Town Planning, UWIST) and Maurice Hanson (Librarian, Transport Section, Imperial College, London) in their compilation of a select list of books, articles, and reports with which Buchanan was involved, and reviews of those works. Space precludes the reproduction of that list in this volume, but grateful acknowledgement should be made.

Notes

1 Town and Country Planning School, *Proceedings* of the Town and Country Planning Summer School, York, 1973, RTPI, London, 1973
2 C. D. Buchanan, Presidential Address 1963, JTPI, December 1963, Vol 49, pp334–343
3 C. D. Buchanan, Note of Dissent in Roskill Lord Justice. Report of Commission of Inquiry Third London Airport, HMSO, London, 1971
4 *Ibid*
5 C. D. Buchanan, 'If the day be clear', JTPI, February 1968, Vol 54, pp51–55
6 *Ibid*
7 Percy Johnson Marshall, Review of State of Britain, JRTPI, May 1972, Vol 59, p249
8 C. D. Buchanan, 'If the day be clear', *op cit*
9 *Ibid*

10 *Ibid*
11 C. D. Buchanan, Report of the Public Inquiry concerning development on the Monico site at Piccadilly Circus, *Town Planning Review*, Vol 31, (1960–61), pp241–289
12 Ministry of Transport, *Traffic in Towns* Report, HMSO, London, 1963. (The Buchanan Report)
13 C. D. Buchanan, Note of Dissent, *op cit*
14 MoT, Report of the Working Party on Car Parking in the Inner Area of London, HMSO, London, 1953
15 MoT, *Traffic in Towns, op cit*
16 *Ibid*
17 M. E. Beesley, and J. F. Kain, 'Urban Form, car ownership and public policy: an appraisal of Traffic in Towns', *Urban Studies*, Vol 1, November 1964, pp174–203
18 Wyndham Thomas, Buchanan Report: a comment on traffic in towns, *Town and Country Planning*, January 1964, Vol 32, pp10–12
19 W. Burns, 'Review of Traffic in Towns', JTPI, Vol 50, 1964, pp35–36
20 MoT, *Traffic in Towns, op cit*
21 MoT, *Traffic in Towns, op cit*
22 Wyndham Thomas, *op cit*
23 MoT, *Traffic in Towns, op cit*
24 C. D. Buchanan, Note of Dissent, *op cit*
25 C. D. Buchanan, 'If the day be clear', *op cit*
26 P. Abercrombie, *Greater London Plan*, Ministry of Town and Country Planning, London, 1944
27 C. D. Buchanan, Note of Dissent, *op cit*
28 *Ibid*
29 J. A. Proudlove, Mixed Blessing: a review, *Town Planning Review*, Vol 29, (1958–59), pp129–131
30 C. D. Buchanan, 'If the day be clear', *op cit*
31 Colin Buchanan and Partners, *Colin Buchanan and Partners, Planning and Transportation Consultants, Architects, and Economists, London*, undated
32 *Ibid*
33 C. D. Buchanan, Unpublished personal correspondence, 1980
34 C. D. Buchanan, 'Whose Side are the Angels on?' Unpublished paper delivered to the Department of Town and Country Planning, University of Manchester, 1978
35 C. D. Buchanan, Presidential Address, *op cit*
36 *Ibid*
37 Lewis Keeble, Statement at Extraordinary General Meeting of the Town Planning Institute, January, 1965, quoted in G. E. Cherry, *The Evolution of British Town Planning*, Leonard Hill, London, 1974
38 Gordon E. Cherry, *The Evolution of British Town Planning*, Leonard Hill, London, 1974
39 SAUS, Prospectus: School for Advanced Urban Studies, University of Bristol, Bristol, 1980
40 C. D. Buchanan, *Mixed Blessing*: the motor in Britain, Leonard Hill, London, 1958

INDEX

Roman numerals refer to the illustrated section in the middle of the book

225

232 INDEX

Thomas, Wyndham 190, 196, 210, 223
Thompson, Francis Longstreth 31, 36–7, 131, 151, 203
Thomspon, Maxwell and Fry 15
Thomson, J. Arthur 50, 54, 67
Todmorden 171
Toronto 24–5
Tow Law 139
Town and Country Planning Act 1932 94, 112–13, 133, 135, 149
Town and Country Planning Act 1947 13, 93, 122, 138, 171, 204
Town and Country Planning Association 10, 123, 144, 185–93, 199, 201, (xxv), (xxix)
Town and Country Planning, Ministry/Minister of 13, 15, 114, 115, 119, 122, 137–8, 139, 144, 203, 205
Town and Country Planning Summer School 36, 131, 142, 182, 203, 222
Town Development Act 1952 204
Town extension plan 92
Town Planning Act 1925 133
Town Planning Congress/Conference 1910 91, 107, 126, 133
Town Planning Conference, Transactions of 149
Town planning education, courses 28–30, 31–2, 56, 141–2, 149, 172
Town Planning Institute, see Royal Town Planning Institute
Town Planning Institute of Canada 28–9
Town Planning Review 16, 104, 110, 112, 122, 165, 206
Towndrow, F. E. 199
Townscape 156–7
Toynbee Hall 52, 73
Toynbee, Arnold 72
Tracy, M. 71
Traffic 133, 208–10, 216–17
Traffic in Towns 11, 115, 128, 206, 208–12, 214–16, 219–21, 223, (xxxi), (xxxii)
Traffic planning 214
Transport 193, 198, 206
Transport, Ministry, Minister of 11, 112–3, 122, 159, 203, 206, 221, 223
Transport Policy and Programmes 210
Trawsfynydd 206
Tredegar 13
Tremadoc, Caernarvonshire 156
Tripp, Alker 3, 114–15, 121
Trunk Roads Act 1936 113
Tudor Walters (Sir John) Committee, Report 6, 83, 90–1, 95–7, 100, 182
Tyerman, D. 199, 201
Tyrwhitt, Jacqueline 142, 184

Unhealthy Areas Committee 134, 149, 184
United States, USA 33–36, 87, 95, 189

Unwin, Edward 93
Unwin, Raymond 1, 9, 15, 20, 23, 39, 43, 72–102, 133–34, 183, (vii), (viii), (ix), (xi), (xiii)
Uthwatt Committee, Report 116, 128, 199, 204

Valendas, H. E. von Berlepsch 85, 100
Vienna 104
Villages 26, 155–6, 174, (xvi)
Vincent, H. D. 16
Vivian, Henry 14, 82, 84

Wade, C. P. 87
Wales, South Wales Regional Survey Report 126, 134
Ward, J. T. 192, 201
Ward, Stephen 149
Warren, H. 198
Warwick 119, 122
Watson, J. Paton 120, 129
Weaver, J. C. 43
Webb, Sir Aston 89, 92
Webbs (Beatrice and Sydney) 178
Wells, H. G. 177
Welwyn Garden City 3, 10, 14, 152, 180–1, 182–3, 190, 198–9, (xxviii)
West Midlands 10, 107, 119, 121–2
West Midlands Group 119, 129
West Midlands Plan 129
Weston and Stone 201
Whitten, R. 45
Whittick, Arnold 192, 199
Wibberley, Gerald P. 192, 201
Williams-Ellis, Clough 110, 123–5, 127, 130, 159, 175
Wilson, Hugh 166
Wiltshire 147
Winchester 124
Windscale 214
Wirral 103, 110
Wolverhampton 22
Women's National Health Association of Ireland 59, 70
Womersley, Lewis 166
Works, Minister of 120
Works and Buildings, Ministry of 137, 155, 186–7
Works, Office of 137
Wright, Henry 32, 35, 44
Wright, Henry and Stein, Clarence 101
Wright, Myles 16
Wythenshawe 13, 90 101

York 78
Young, Hilton 136

Zueblin, Charles 70

L. I. H. E.
THE MARKLAND LIBRARY
STAND PARK RD., LIVERPOOL, L16 9JD